# SOCIAL INFLUENCE

(Tur)

0335153402

# MAPPING SOCIAL PSYCHOLOGY

Series Editor: Tony Manstead

*Current titles:*

**Icek Ajzen:** Attitudes, Personality and Behavior
**Robert S. Baron, Norbert L. Kerr and Norman Miller:** Group Process, Group Decision, Group Action
**Steve Duck:** Relating to Others
**J. Richard Eiser:** Social Judgment
**Russell G. Geen:** Human Aggression
**Howard Giles and Nikolas Coupland:** Language: Contexts and Consequences
**John Turner:** Social Influence
**Leslie A. Zebrowitz:** Social Perception

*Forthcoming titles include:*

**Marilyn B. Brewer and Norman Miller:** Intergroup Relations
**Richard Petty and John Cacioppo:** Attitude Change
**Dean G. Pruitt and Peter J. Carnevale:** Bargaining and Third Party Intervention
**Wolfgang Stroebe and Margaret Stroebe:** Social Psychology and Health

# SOCIAL
# INFLUENCE

## John C. Turner

OPEN UNIVERSITY PRESS
MILTON KEYNES

Open University Press
Celtic Court
22 Ballmoor
Buckingham
MK18 1XW

and
1900 Frost Road, Suite 101
Bristol, PA 19007, USA

First published 1991
Reprinted 1993

**British Library Cataloguing in Publication Data**

Turner, John C., *1947–*
    Social influence.—(Mapping social psychology)
    1. Social Influence
    I. Title II. Series
    302

    ISBN 0-335-15340-2 (pbk)
    ISBN 0-335-15341-0

Typeset by Rowland Phototypesetting Ltd,
Bury St. Edmunds, Suffolk
Printed and bound in Great Britain by
Woolnough Bookbinding Ltd, Irthlingborough

To Penelope, Jane Imogen
and Isobel Rose

# CONTENTS

# FOREWORD

There has been a need for a carefully tailored series of reasonably short and inexpensive books on major topics in social psychology, written primarily for students by authors who enjoy a reputation for the excellence of their research and their ability to communicate clearly and comprehensibly their knowledge of, and enthusiasm for, the discipline. My hope is that the *Mapping Social Psychology* series will meet that need.

The rationale for this series is twofold. First, conventional text-books are too low-level and uninformative for use with senior undergraduates or graduate students. Books in this series address this problem partly by dealing with topics at book length, rather than chapter length, and partly by the excellence of the scholarship and clarity of the writing. Each volume is written by an acknowledged authority on the topic in question, and offers the reader a concise and up-to-date overview of the principal concepts, theories, methods and findings relating to that topic. Although the intention has been to produce books that will be used by senior level undergraduates and graduate students, the fact that the books are written in a straight-forward style should make them accessible to students with relatively little previous experience of social psychology. At the same time, the books are sufficiently informative to earn the respect of researchers and instructors.

A second problem with traditional textbooks is that they are too dependent on research conducted in or examples drawn from North American society. This fosters the mistaken impression that social psychology is a uniquely North American discipline and can also be baffling for readers unfamiliar with North American culture. To combat this problem, authors of books in this series have been encouraged to adopt a broader perspective, giving examples or citing research from outside North America wherever this helps to make a point. Our aim has been to produce books for a world market, introducing readers to an international discipline.

In this volume, John Turner has accomplished the difficult task of writing a book that is both an introduction to the topic of social influence and a sophisticated theoretical analysis of social influence processes. Social influence is a topic that is absolutely central to social psychology, embracing research domains such as the formation of social norms; social conformity; group polarization; minority influence; and power and authority. Everyday life is replete with argument, controversy and conflict, and these are phenomena that involve social influence processes. Conflicts arise at least in part because social groups share beliefs or act in similar ways, and then reject persons who deviate from these norms or enter into disputes with groups that are characterized by different patterns of shared beliefs or behaviours. Professor Turner shows how the key to understanding social influence phenomena is the concept of social norm. A norm is both descriptive, reflecting real similarities between people, and prescriptive, reflecting shared beliefs about appropriate opinions or behaviours. These shared norms emerge from social interaction between people who are related to each other psychologically as members of a social group, and who feel a certain pressure to conform to these norms. However, conformity is not simply a matter of group members converging towards the average of their individual opinions or behaviours, for under certain conditions members of a social group converge on a position that is more extreme than the average of their individual positions. Moreover, conformity does not always take the form of minorities within social groups moving towards the position adopted by the majority, for under certain conditions minorities can wield sufficient influence to induce the majority to move towards them.

Professor Turner addresses these and many other issues in the course of this book. The scope of the task he has undertaken should not be underestimated, for the literature on social influence is vast and involves many disparate paradigms. A strength of this book is the way in which the author not only carefully describes the procedures and findings of key studies but also exposes the problems posed by these findings for established theoretical accounts of social influence, which emphasize the dependency of the individual on others for information or for social acceptance. The author has succeeded in fitting together the confusing fragments of this jigsaw in a way that creates a coherent and meaningful pattern, while at the same time doing proper justice to the original studies. Moreover, he has set about the business of re-evaluating and reinterpreting the findings of many classic studies, the end-product being an integrative theory, namely 'self-categorization theory', which has the potential to resolve many inconsistencies in the literature and to account for a diverse set of social influence phenomena. Traditional explanations of influence in terms of the dependency of the individual on others for information or acceptance are replaced by a unified view in which the categorization of others as similar to self produces shared expectations of agreement, and thereby provides the basis for social influence. In short, this book introduces the student to social influence processes without unduly simplifying the subject-matter, and at the same time confronts the more knowledgeable reader with both a critique of conventional wisdom and a fresh theoretical perspective on social influence.

Tony Manstead
*Series Editor*

# PREFACE

This book is about the social psychology of social influence. It aims
to do several things: provide an advanced level textbook and detailed
review of the literature, develop an argument for the theoretical unity
of the field and introduce a new theory. Essentially, I have tried to
sum up what social psychologists have found out about influence
since the 1920s, to assess critically the current major theories and to
identify the key theoretical issues that should direct future research.
The fact that I have tried to be (constructively) critical, rather than
merely repeat received wisdom, is not an indication of pessimism. On
the contrary, I think researchers in this field can take great pride in
what they have achieved. It has produced fascinating, important and
unexpected empirical discoveries, profound ideas and theorists of
real stature. The arguments going on are a sign and a part of the real
progress that has been and is being made.

I am tempted here to begin replying to some of the reactions I
expect this book to provoke, but I won't. What matters for the
moment is that I should make the simple point that the fact that I
might disagree with some of my colleagues' conclusions does not
mean that I do not admire their work or judge it important. In fact, I
am perfectly aware that where I disagree I have also been influenced.

There is one omission that should be explained. Originally, I
intended to include a chapter on persuasion. Then I discovered that
another book in the series would be covering this topic in more detail
than I would have space for. I also found that discussing the other
areas in the field in the way I thought necessary used up all the space
allotted to the book. The choice was between leaving persuasion out
(of the book but not the series) or a too short chapter at the expense

of the others. So I left it out. However, I very much hope that the relevance of what I am saying about influence in general (especially in Chapter 6) to persuasion will not be too difficult to see. To this end I have taken the liberty of briefly alluding to work on persuasion in Chapter 6.

I wish to acknowledge the contribution to the book of all the colleagues with whom I have done research on influence or directly related matters: John Colvin, Barbara Davidson, Alex Haslam, Mike Hogg, Craig McGarty, Penny Oakes, Phil Smith, Steve Reicher and Margaret Wetherell. I am also grateful to other friends in the field who have made discussion of relevant issues so consistently interesting and enjoyable. This book took a long time to complete. It would have taken even longer but for my sabbatical visit to the Department of Psychology at the University of Exeter, UK, from September 1988 to February 1989. I wish to express my thanks to the members of the department, in particular Dick Eiser and Steve Reicher, for the hospitality and intellectual environment – it was very much appreciated and enjoyed. I am also grateful to Tony Manstead for giving me the opportunity to write the book and for his patience while it was being completed.

*John C. Turner*

# INTRODUCTION: BASIC CONCEPTS AND CLASSIC STUDIES

## What is social influence?

This book is about the social psychology of social influence. What is social influence? The most obvious definition is that it comprises the processes whereby people directly or indirectly influence the thoughts, feelings and actions of others. Unfortunately, this is too broad. It would make the study of influence (for the rest of this book, unless specified otherwise, influence is to be read as *social* influence) coincide with the whole of social psychology. G. W. Allport (1985, p. 3), for example, defines social psychology as 'an attempt to understand and explain how the thoughts, feeling, and behaviour of individuals are influenced by the actual, imagined, or implied presence of others'. He goes on to say that 'implied presence' of others refers to the position of the person being influenced in a complex social structure and their membership of a cultural group. This may be a reasonable definition of social psychology, but influence researchers have something much more specific and limited in mind.

In everyday terms, influence researchers are concerned with some very challenging and fascinating puzzles. How can one persuade another individual or group to change their beliefs, opinions and attitudes? How can one convince somebody that views they believe are right are wrong, and that views they had previously considered wrong are right? Why do the members of a social group, a subculture, a society, tend to hold similar beliefs and act in similar ways? Why are people who are different from the norm so often disliked and rejected? When do we want people to agree with us and when

don't we care? Why do social groups have different social values and
see the world differently? When do people change their values and
when do they become more committed and fanatical about them?
Social life is full of argument, controversy and conflict about what is
socially and morally right and wrong. It's the stuff of politics, but
also of daily conversation and gossip. What determines one's beliefs
in the appropriateness of one's conduct, what creates self-doubt and
uncertainty?

These are all issues of social influence. They are issues basic to
social life. In social psychology, they are studied in research areas
such as social conformity, persuasion and attitude change, power
and authority, group polarization, minority influence and the formation of social norms. What they have in common is the problem of
*normative social similarities and differences* between people in their
perceptions, cognitions, feelings and actions. The key idea in understanding what researchers mean by social influence is the concept of a
*social norm*. Influence relates to the processes whereby people agree
or disagree about appropriate behaviour, form, maintain or change
social norms and the social conditions that give rise to, and the effects
of, such norms. There is as yet no definitive scientific theory of social
norms. Our understanding of what a social norm is changes with our
understanding of the influence process. There is nevertheless a good
working idea of what the concept of social norm implies.

## Social norms and subjective validity

Not all similarities and differences between people are normative.
Influence research began as an attempt to explain the psychology of
the group. Group behaviour, the actions of a crowd, a society, a
culture, is characterized by striking and pervasive uniformities of
individual belief and action. For example, members of a political
party will share the same ideology, members of a culture will have the
same incest taboos, and a crowd of soccer hooligans will agree about
who is the enemy. Around the beginning of this century, these kinds
of social uniformities were explained as arising from processes of
mutual influence between group members. This is still one important
meaning of the concept of social norm: the idea of social uniformities
among the members of a social group that arise more or less directly
from their social interaction and relationships. Researchers are
interested in specifying similarities and differences that arise from

social relationships, rather than 'accidental' similarities and differences that reflect causally isolated individual reactions to common stimulus conditions. How do psychological forces for agreement and consensus arise from social interaction itself?

A second basic idea is that such similarities express a prescriptive rule or social value. A social norm is a generally accepted way of thinking, feeling or behaving that it is endorsed and expected because it is perceived as the right and proper thing to do. It is a rule, value or standard shared by the members of a social group that prescribes appropriate, expected or desirable attitudes and conduct in matters relevant to the group. The Catholic Church believes that it is morally wrong for people to practise birth control: it sees this as a religious issue and insists that Catholics follow its teachings in this respect. Orthodox Catholics accept that they should not practise birth control: it is wrong, improper and undesirable, not only for them, but also, they believe, in some absolute moral sense.

Social norms vary in how important they are to the group and in the intensity of social approval and rejection that conformity and non-conformity attract. Group members who conform to norms tend to be socially approved of, whereas those who deviate tend to be disapproved of and in the extreme may be punished and excluded from the group.

It is important to understand that there is more to social norms than the idea of liking or preferring some form of behaviour. It is not just that people have shared preferences about what they like doing. The idea of a norm conveys a feeling of 'oughtness' about certain behaviours: there are things that we *ought* to see, believe, feel and do (whether we want to or not); there is an element of moral obligation, duty, right, justice. Mothers are not just expected to love and care for their children as a preference – we feel that they ought to and, if they don't, they are failing in their duty as mothers and indeed as human beings. Social norms express social values and normative judgements are value judgements. In this sense, they are external to the individual, being the property of a culture, and constrain the actions of individuals. Social values are experienced as if they have an independent, external reality. One can hardly doubt the importance of social values in human life, that we have them, that they matter, that society depends upon them.

In sum, social norms are apparent in similarities and differences between people's behaviour that reflect shared and conflicting social values. They are descriptive, reflecting actual similarities, and prescriptive, reflecting shared beliefs about appropriate, valued conduct. In ordinary language, we speak of traditions, customs morals, the law, the fashionable and unfashionable, 'well-known facts' and 'public opinion', and so on.

A fundamental theoretical concept that describes the subjective aspect of holding a social norm is 'subjective validity' (Festinger, 1950). When one engages in some action with a feeling of confidence in its appropriateness, correctness and social desirability – when one is following a firmly established norm – one is said to have subjective validity. It is one's subjective conviction that some idea, judgement or action is right (correct, proper, and so on). If a social norm is a shared belief that a certain course of action is appropriate in a given situation, then, when individuals act in line with the norm, they experience their behaviour as subjectively valid. It is easy to see the close connection between the concept of subjective validity and the problem of persuasion, for example: persuasion is the art of getting people to see that their existing ideas are wrong (subjectively invalid) and that new ideas are right (subjectively valid). In many ways, the central theoretical problem of social influence is to uncover the bases of subjective validity and invalidity. In the rest of this book, just as in everyday language, many terms will be used relatively interchangeably for subjective validity, of which probably the most important are (subjective) certainty, competence, correctness and just being 'right'.

## Private acceptance and public compliance

Sometimes we have to conform to the norms of other people, even though we do not share them. We are forced, like it or not, to do things, whether trivial or important, that we do not think are right. This distinction between conforming to one's own norms (pro-normative behaviour) and conforming to those of others that one does not privately accept (counter-normative behaviour) makes necessary a distinction between the private acceptance of influence and public compliance with others' expectations. Influence that leads to private attitude change (but may or may not be directly expressed in overt words and deeds) is termed private acceptance. Influence that changes overt behaviour in the intended direction (but may or may not lead to private attitude change) is termed public compliance. Although, in fact, private acceptance and public compliance can often go together, the terms tend to be used as conceptual opposites.

Theorists assume that in the absence of opposing forces, private acceptance of a new belief will naturally tend to change public behaviour, and so tend to reserve the term 'compliance' for counter-normative behaviour that would not take place but for some kind of coercive social pressure, i.e. for compliance *without* acceptance.

Because we cannot see into people's minds, it is by no means easy to tell whether acceptance has taken place or whether compliance represents acceptance (Allen, 1965). By and large, researchers have assumed that, if behaviour persists in the absence of surveillance by the influencing agent, it has probably been internalized (accepted), but that, if it is only displayed in face of definite social pressure, it is probably only compliance. An example of acceptance is provided by Newcomb's (1943) research on women students who changed their political attitudes during their time at Bennington College in the 1930s from a conservative to a liberal ideology. They were found to have maintained their liberalism long after they had left college and their college friends. An example of compliance without acceptance is provided by Coch and French's (1948) observation in an industrial setting of a woman worker whose productivity increased dramatically once she was removed from the presence of a group of fellow workers. The group had a strictly enforced norm about the appropriate rate of work. The observation of behaviour in private and public settings to distinguish acceptance and compliance is not without theoretical problems (see Chapter 6).

## Reference and membership groups

These examples illustrate a closely related distinction between reference groups and membership groups. A reference group is one that is psychologically significant for one's attitudes and behaviour. Kelley (1952) and others define reference groups in terms of two functions of self-reference: they are groups with which one compares oneself to evaluate one's own situation and attributes (the comparative function) and from which one takes one's norms and values (the normative function). A membership group is one that a person is *in* by some objective criterion, but which that person may not refer to psychologically for self-evaluation and social values.

A distinction is also made between positive and negative reference groups. A positive reference group is one that one privately accepts or aspires to belong to, that one identifies with, is attracted to and feels psychologically involved with. A negative reference group is one that one privately rejects or 'dis-identifies' with, i.e. that one uses to define who one is *not* and what one does *not* want to be. One compares oneself to a positive reference group to define what one should feel and how one should act; with a negative reference group, one compares to define what one should *not* feel and how *not* to act. In this book, as in the research literature, the term 'reference group' will be used to mean 'positive reference group' unless otherwise indicated.

If a person who is unemployed and poor feels very dissatisfied because she compares herself to the rich and at the same time endorses the values and attitudes of the rich, perhaps tries to speak, dress and act like them, then the rich are a (positive) reference group for her. The unemployed person, however, is not rich; she may aspire to be a member of the rich, but what she is, in fact, is a member of the unemployed. In this case, the unemployed are her membership but not reference group, and the rich are her reference but not membership group. If she hates being a member of the unemployed and not only copies the rich but tries to act differently from what she defines as being unemployed, then the latter is not only a membership group but also a negative reference group.

Positive reference groups exert influence upon their actual or aspiring members which, by definition, usually leads to private acceptance. Compliance, on the other hand, tends to be induced by negative reference groups that have power derived from being membership groups. If one is in a group and cannot escape it, then one tends to be at the mercy of its approval and disapproval and the sanctions they imply. A good example is provided by the position of an unwilling conscript in the army. For so long as she is in the army, she must comply with its rules and regulations, however much she privately rejects them, as her membership grants the group massive powers of coercion. Interestingly, researchers have taken the typical instance of compliance to be where a person seeks to preserve membership in a positive reference group. We shall discuss some of the issues later, but I believe the above example of the unwilling conscript is more faithful to reality.

## Influence and power

Moscovici (1976) takes things a step further by distinguishing between influence and power, influence being that which produces subjective acceptance and conversion and power being the basis of coercive compulsion and compliance. These correlated distinctions between acceptance and compliance, reference and membership groups, and influence and power, are a recurring theme in the social psychology of influence. We shall see presently that they are aspects of a dual-process conception of influence that appears in many forms throughout the history of research in this area. Essentially, reference groups exert persuasive influence leading to the private acceptance of their norms, pro-normative behaviour and subjective validity. Membership groups (if they are not positive reference groups) exercise coercive power, enforcing public compliance with their norms and leading to counter-normative behaviour and a false presentation of self. A further aspect of this dual-process model lies in the very conceptualization of social norms, either as 'shared frames of reference' that introduce stability and cognitive coherence into reality (Sherif, 1936), or as a set of 'shared expectations' held by others that exert implicit group pressure to conform (Deutsch and Gerard, 1955).

The current distinction between influence and power is relatively new in the field. It was normal from the 1940s until Moscovici's work in the 1970s to treat power as the basis of influence and influence as the exercise of power. In this field theory tradition initiated by Kurt Lewin (e.g. Cartwright and Zander, 1968), private acceptance and public compliance were both seen as forms of influence and the difference between them lay in the *type of power* on which influence was based (e.g. power based on information versus power based on the control of rewards and costs). The more recent conceptualization sees influence and power as *alternative* processes of modifying others' behaviour, equating acceptance with the exercise of influence and compliance with the use of power (Hollander, 1985). Moscovici's arguments will be discussed presently, but, in the meantime, the important thing to keep in mind is the distinction between persuasive influence and coercive compliance that all theorists have found it useful to make.

## Modalities of influence

Moscovici (1976, 1985) also usefully suggests that there are three basic modalities of influence (which define how people react to conflict): normalization, conformity (or majority influence) and

innovation (or minority influence). These embody influence processes relating to the formation, maintenance and change of social
norms. Normalization is the process of avoiding conflict within the
group by making mutual compromises and gradually converging on
each other's point of view. Conformity is the resolution of conflict
through the movement of deviates to the position of the majority.
Innovation reflects the creation of conflict within the group by a
minority of members and its resolution through the movement of the
majority towards the minority. The following chapters will discuss
research relevant to all three processes. The research, however, does
not fall neatly into these three categories. The remainder of this
chapter will outline some classic early studies on normalization and
conformity. Then, Chapters 2, 3 and 4 will present work on social
conformity, group polarization and minority influence, respectively;
the latter two chapters being particularly relevant to normalization
and innovation. We shall then discuss power and compliance as
processes distinct from influence in Chapter 5 and finally look in
detail at the relationship between self-categorization, group membership and influence in Chapter 6. In this concluding chapter, I shall
try to integrate influence phenomena within a unified theoretical
scheme consistent with both classic and contemporary trends.

## Classic studies of social influence

The concept of 'suggestion' was a precursor of modern theories of
influence. Suggestion referred to the irrational acceptance of influence from others on the basis of social and emotional ties.
Hypnosis was taken as a model of the suggestion process. In fact,
hypnosis was assumed to be an extreme form of suggestion. Suggestion explained how the psychology of people *en masse* seemed to
differ from the psychology of the individual in isolation. It explained
the development of shared uniformities in crowd behaviour on the
basis of this process of irrational mutual imitation (LeBon, 1896).

Modern experimental research began by looking at what seemed to
be unconscious processes of mutual suggestion and imitation within
groups. One can date the start of experimental research on influence
from F. H. Allport's (1924) findings that individuals gave less
extreme and more conservative judgements of odours and weights in
the presence of others than in isolation. This tendency of individuals
in groups to moderate their judgements was described as 'conform-

ity'. He explained it as based on an instinct of submission to the group. In 1921, Moore exposed his subjects to majority and expert opinions on matters of ethical, linguistic and musical judgement. He found that individual judgements were much affected by such opinions. Allport's work on 'social facilitation' is also relevant, being an attempt to explain suggestion in the group in the language of conditioned responses. He found that the presence of others enhanced individuals' performance on simple tasks but reduced performance on more complex tasks.

These studies suggested processes of convergence in the group (i.e. people seemed to move towards and become more similar to each other). The major step forward in this respect was taken by Sherif (1936). His research linked the formation of social norms with the development of consensus within groups. He defined social norms as 'customs, traditions, standards, rules, values, fashions, and all other criteria of conduct which are standardized as a consequence of the contact of individuals' (1936, p. 3). He argued that just as all perceptual and cognitive experience of the physical world reflects 'frames of reference', i.e. comparative contexts, standards or anchors against which stimuli are judged, so social judgements of what is appropriate or inappropriate, correct or incorrect, reflect shared, internalized, socially derived frames of reference or social norms. Where reality is ambiguous and fluid we develop and internalize shared frames of reference to introduce order, stability and coherence into our relations with the stimulus world and each other.

In his experimental paradigm, Sherif showed the development of perceptual norms. The (male) subjects were placed in a completely darkened room and over a series of trials observed short displays of a pin-point of light (displayed for two seconds after the light is first reported moving by subjects). The task was to state out aloud the distance the point of light appeared to move on each trial. In fact the light did not move. That it appeared to do so reflects on optical illusion known as the autokinetic ('self-moving') effect, of which subjects were unaware. The distance the light appears to move under such conditions is erratic, varying across trials and perceivers.

In one set of conditions, the subjects initially performed the task in isolation and were then brought together in groups of two or three. When in isolation, the subjects gradually developed a characteristic individual range of distance within which their judgements fell and a modal, most frequent judgement. These personal 'norms' differed

between individuals and seemed to be based on the subjects' tendency to compare later 'movements' with their earlier estimates. Over
time, an internal frame of reference developed based on the
individual's experience of his own earlier judgements, thus stabiliz-
ing subsequent estimates. When individuals with differing personal
norms were brought together to make successive public estimates on
each trial, there was a gradual mutual convergence in their estimates
reflecting the development of a shared frame of reference. After a
number of collective sessions, the differences between group members' estimates tended to be negligible; they consistently made
judgements at about the average of their initial individual responses.
The impact of this social norm persisted even when individuals again
made judgements in isolation. That is, the collective norm did not
represent a compliance effect but was internalized: individuals did
not revert to their earlier personal norm when given the opportunity.
It seems that subjects made use of each others' judgements to develop
a shared frame of reference in the same way that they had earlier used
their own judgements. It appears, too, that subjects were relatively
unaware of being influenced by the other judges. They appear to be
largely unconsciously adjusting their judgements in the light of
others' reports to arrive at a stable, agreed picture of a shared but
initially unstructured world.

In another set of conditions, the subjects initially made judgements
in groups of two or three and only then made isolated individual
estimates. It was found that progress towards a shared social norm
was even more rapid and complete under these conditions.

In some later interesting variations of the basic experiment, it was
found that the effect of the collective norm on individual judgement
persists for as long as a year after its formation (Rohrer *et al.*, 1954),
that even arbitrary norms established with the help of confederates
will tend to persist across a number of 'generations' of naive group
members (Jacobs and Campbell, 1961), but that such arbitrary,
artificially contrived norms will tend to decay more rapidly across
generations the more unnatural they are (MacNeil and Sherif, 1976).

Sherif (1936) showed how social norms can arise in groups as a
collective response to new, unstructured, ambiguous situations,
introducing stable and coherent knowledge of the situation. He
conceptualized them as shared frames of reference arising from
social interaction and functioning as internalized cognitive structures. They constrained but did not coerce individual judgement.
Empirically, they arose from a process of mutual and gradual

convergence of the responses or personal norms of individual group members. Subsequent research quickly demonstrated the importance of reference groups in the acquisition of social norms and the power of group norms to modify individual attitudes and behaviour.

Newcomb's (1943) study illustrated in a real social setting how people gradually internalize the norms of the groups they join and how such norms can persist for many years. The study was carried out in the 1930s at Bennington College, a small, private American university college for women. The students came from wealthy, privileged backgrounds and mostly arrived at the college with conservative political and economic values. The staff and senior students, however, held more liberal, radical attitudes. They tended to support progressive taxation, trades unions, the right to strike and economic planning, but were against fascism and unbridled capitalism.

For several years, Newcomb measured students' political and economic attitudes as they progressed through college. He found that most of the students gradually discarded the reactionary values with which they arrived in favour of the more left-wing attitudes that were normative at the college. There was a general and lasting change in students' political philosophy as a result of participating in the college community. Later research (Newcomb et al., 1967) followed up the same Bennington students 25 or more years later and found that they had not reverted to their earlier views once they had left the college. They were still more liberal in 1960 than a comparable group of women of the same social and economic status, and so were their husbands. The more left-wing they had been in the 1930s, the more likely they were to vote for Kennedy (the more liberal candidate) than Nixon, for example, in the 1960 American presidential election.

How and why did the students change at college? They quickly learned that radical attitudes and values were popular and admired in the college. Such views were espoused by staff and older students, people who were high in prestige. In classes, in informal discussions (which were encouraged) and in social encounters, the students were exposed to radical opinions, heard them argued for and the opposing views attacked. There were many attractive things about their new college life and the most active, popular students, the leaders, those that identified with the college, strongly promoted liberal attitudes. Liberal attitudes were part of belonging to a highly cohesive community and being involved in an attractive new life. Not all of the students, however, changed. A minority of conservative girls tended to resist immersion in community life. They were the least popular, were little involved, made few contacts and generally kept to a small group of like-minded friends. Staff perceived them as overly dependent on their parents. Being at Bennington College, having it as a membership group, did not inevitably lead to the adoption of its norms and values. What mattered was whether or not the college became a positive reference group. The girls who became more liberal were the ones who became psychologically involved in being at the college, who identified with the older, active students and the staff. The girls who remained conservative tended to keep aloof from college life, maintaining as reference groups their family and friends from home and relating at college to only a small clique of conservative friends.

Lewin's (1947) group decision studies showed how difficult it is to change individuals' behaviour in isolation from the norms they share as group members. He believed that when a person's attitude was anchored in a group it was necessary to change the group as a whole before one could change the attitude. The experiments tested alternative procedures for encouraging American housewives to buy foodstuffs, such as kidneys and hearts, that they would not normally buy. In one study, three groups of from 13 to 17 housewives attended interesting lectures that linked the importance of good nutrition to the war effort (this is 1943), emphasized the valuable nutritional aspects of intestinal meats and discussed health and the economy. The lectures were designed to promote the buying and serving of intestinal meats. In three other groups, a nutrition expert introduced the same topic, provided factual information and encouraged the group members to discuss the issues among themselves. The group members were asked to come to a consensus about buying the food and at the end of the discussion to indicate whether they would serve the meats. A follow-up survey showed that only about 3 per cent of the lecture groups but 32 per cent of the discussion groups had actually been influenced to change their food habits to some degree. Similar results were obtained in experiments on feeding cod liver oil and orange juice to babies.

Later studies (Bennett, 1955; Pelz, 1958) showed that what was important in group discussion conditions was not so much the discussion *per se*, but the process of reaching a definite decision that could be perceived as being in line with the consensual position of the group. It was important that group members became aware of a new shared norm in the group favouring the advocated course of action and that they made a commitment to carrying it out.

Asch (1951, 1952, 1956) disagreed with the idea embodied in the concept of suggestion that influence in groups was an irrational, unconscious process, implying an arbitrary submission to social pressure. He argued that convergence in the Sherif paradigm was a rational attempt to make sense of an ambiguous, shared world in which the same object of judgement implied agreement among the perceivers. He hypothesized that if individuals were faced by a group consensus that was unambiguously incorrect (*contrary to fact*, as he put it), they would not conform but remain independent.

To test this hypothesis, he created a seminal experimental paradigm in which subjects assumed they were performing a visual discrimination task. Seven to nine individuals were present and in face-to-face contact in the session. They were presented with a target line and a set of three comparison lines on each trial. Their task was to state publicly and in the same fixed order (determined apparently accidentally only by the seating arrangement) which comparison line matched the target line in length. There were 18 trials. In fact, only one person present was a naive subject. This person responded next to last. The others were confederates of the experimenter who had been instructed to give a unanimously incorrect response on 12 'critical' trials, selecting a longer comparison line on six trials and a shorter line on the other six. A control condition in which the subjects carried out the task privately, without any group pressure, showed that the perceptual task was easy and unambiguous. Fewer than 1 per cent of the control subjects' judgements were errors. The question is: Did the subject go along with the unanimously incorrect response of the group on the critical trials or remain independent and give the correct response?

There were several findings from the original series of studies (Asch, 1956). About one-third of responses on critical trials showed conformity to the group. This percentage has proved highly reliable across studies. There were large individual differences between subjects. A quarter of the subjects showed no conformity and remained independent throughout, while a similar percentage moved towards the group on eight or more trials. One-third of the subjects conformed on 50 per cent or more trials. A small minority of subjects (6 out of 123 from three experimental groups) conformed on all trials. After the studies, all of the subjects were interviewed, and it is clear that the disagreement of the group created concern, uncertainty and self-doubt. The subjects found the conflict between themselves and the group puzzling and worrying and tried to explain it; as the contradiction continued, they became concerned and anxious and began to doubt their accuracy and feel tempted to join the majority; eventually, they began to feel self-conscious, lonely and conspicuous, afraid of public exposure to personal and group disapproval.

The majority of subjects experienced cognitive and emotional conflict, being unsure of who was right and who was wrong and feeling the 'conformity conflict' between sticking to what they saw and going against the group or agreeing with the incorrect group. What differentiated the 'independents' from the 'yielders' was how they coped with the conformity conflict. Among the independents, there were those who remained vigorously confident in their perceptions, those who were emotionally withdrawn but acted on the basis of explicit principles about being an individual, and those who manifested considerable doubt and tension but felt compelled to deal adequately with the task. Among the yielders, there were also different motivations: a small minority seemed to suffer a distortion of perception, claiming that they actually saw what the group reported; others (the majority of yielders) knew that they saw things differently from the group but judged that their perceptions were inaccurate and that the majority were correct; still others went along relatively cynically, not believing that the group was correct, but not wanting to stand out, appear different from or inferior to others or be subjected to ridicule for appearing defective in the eyes of the group.

Asch performed some interesting experimental variations. When the naive subject was not required to announce his judgements publicly but stated them in writing (while the majority still made public estimates), conformity dropped significantly to about 12.5 per cent of critical responses. When the magnitude of the discrepancy between the target lines and the comparison lines was reduced so that the task became perceptually more difficult and the stimulus situation more ambiguous, conformity increased. There was an inverse relationship between the magnitude of the discrepancy and the degree of social conformity. There was also a marked effect for the disruption of the unanimity of the group. When one confederate 'joined' the naive subject and began to give correct answers differing from the majority, conformity dropped to only 5.5 per cent of critical responses. This liberating effect of the partner was observed even if the partner began responding correctly half-way through the series of trials, and disappeared totally if the partner deserted the naive subject half-way through the trials after having begun by responding correctly.

The 'partner' or 'supporter' effect is all the more striking in view of apparently negligible importance of group size. Asch found that if the subject was confronted with just one incorrect confederate, there was little conformity (a mean of 0.33 errors out of 12). A majority of two produced 1.53 errors and a majority of three 4 errors (the basic finding of a third of responses), but a majority of four (4.20 errors) or more up to a group of 16 (3.75 errors) did not significantly increase this degree of conformity. Thus the unanimity of the group is much more important than the number of persons giving the incorrect response: it is consensus, not numbers, that matters. As Asch (1951, p. 186) points out: 'a unanimous majority of three is, under the given conditions, far more effective than a majority of eight containing one dissenter' and 'the effects obtained are not the result of a summation of influences proceeding from each member of the group; it is necessary to conceive the results as being relationally determined'.

Other findings suggest strongly that conformity is not, except for a minority of subjects, all or nothing. Subjects show signs of trying to compromise with the group. If the group makes a 'moderate' error, i.e. a choice that is less discrepant with reality than the alternative incorrect comparison line available on that trial, subjects' errors will all be moderate. If the group makes an 'extreme' error, however, about 20 per cent of errors are moderate, i.e. intermediate between the group and the correct response. Similarly, if a moderate or 'compromise' partner appears (who always disagrees with both a consistently extremist majority and the subject and makes moderate errors), the *frequency* of errors made by the subject is not reduced but about 76 per cent will be moderate, compared to 42 per cent in a control condition where the subject faces a unanimous extremist majority. The subject never goes beyond the group and, even when moving towards it, may seek to compromise.

Finally, in a fascinating reversal of the situation, Asch (1951) replaced the confederates with naive subjects so that there was a majority of 16 naive subjects facing one incorrect confederate. Under these conditions, the subjects behaved completely differently. Now, confident of their correctness and self-assured, they greeted the incorrect confederate with disbelief, amusement and scorn.

These studies showed the powerful pressures for conformity to the group experienced by subjects who face even a perceptually structured situation and a norm contrary to fact, and the tension, uncertainty and self-doubt involved in being an unwilling deviant. Asch had proved that, under perceptually unambiguous conditions, at least a minority of subjects would remain totally independent and that a majority of subjects would remain independent most of the time. Nevertheless, the pervasive inference drawn from these studies has been of the weakness of the individual in face of the group and the strength of spontaneous pressures for conformity inherent in the group context.

## Conclusion

Social interaction between people who are related to each other psychologically as members of positive reference groups gives rise to shared social norms in relevant areas. Social norms and values are basic to human social life in providing order, coherence and stability at both the macro-level of society, history and culture and the micro-level of interpersonal relations and individual conduct. There is good evidence that people form and conform to social norms, that there are influence processes inherent in social relationships and implicit pressures for agreement even without instructions to agree or explicit group membership. Neither Sherif nor Asch informed their subjects that they should cooperate with each other or made any effort to stress that they should act as a cohesive group. The social and emotional ties between the subjects were weak at best. The observed pressures for uniformity seem cognitively and socially motivated rather than being based on an irrational process of suggestion. They appear motivated by a desire for perceptual structure, to make sense of things, or to fit in with others. What are the origins of such pressures? In Chapter 2 we shall survey the major theories and relevant research on social conformity.

## Suggestions for further reading

Allport, G. W. (1985). The historical background of social psychology. In G. Lindzey and E. Aronson (eds), *The handbook of social psychology*, Vol. 1, 3rd ed. New York: Random House. For those interested in the historical origins of research on social influence.
Asch, S. E. (1952). *Social psychology*. Englewood Cliffs, NJ: Prentice-Hall.

An excellent book, with outstanding discussions of group behaviour and social influence.

Asch, S. E. (1956). Studies of independence and conformity: A minority of one against a unanimous majority. *Psychological Monographs: General and Applied*, 70, 1–70. Whole No. 416. A detailed summary of the most well-known studies ever conducted on social conformity.

Festinger, L. (1950). Informal social communication. *Psychological Review*, 57, 271–82. The original statement of the concept of subjective validity and the seminal theory of social influence with which it is associated.

Sherif, M. (1936). *The psychology of social norms*. New York: Harper and Brothers (Harper Torchbook edition, 1966). An important, influential and pioneering book on social norms, still relevant, enjoyable and worth reading.

# 2 / SOCIAL CONFORMITY

## Theories of conformity

The early studies showed that there are pressures for uniformity in social groups which lead individuals to form social norms and that shared norms influence perception and behaviour. What are the origins of uniformity pressures? What functions do they serve? Much research on social conformity has been guided by attempts to provide systematic theoretical answers to these questions. In this research, the major but not the only paradigm has been to look at the relationship between a deviant individual and a consensual group and to investigate variables that determine the degree to which the individual conforms to the group. Social conformity is defined as movement on the part of the discrepant person(s) towards the group norm as a function of explicit or implicit social pressure from group members (Allen, 1965; Kiesler and Kiesler, 1969). The opposite of conformity is usually taken to be independence (or sometimes anti-conformity, i.e. movement away from the group, Allen, 1965). We now move from simply illustrating the fact of influence to testing explicit theories of the influence process.

Three highly influential theories of social conformity were published in the 1950s: Festinger's (1950) theory of informal social communication and his (1954) theory of social comparison processes, and Deutsch and Gerard's (1955) distinction between informational and normative social influence. These will illustrate the direction of theoretical thinking.

## Uniformity pressures in informal social communication

Festinger's (1950) theory is a theory of pressures towards social uniformity in informal, task-oriented groups. He was interested in uniformity pressures in spontaneous communication between members of face-to-face groups engaging in some task. His theory specifies the sources of uniformity pressures, the variables determining their magnitude, the modes of achieving uniformity and their effect on communication.

Festinger hypothesized that such pressures have two sources or functions, which he termed *social reality* and *group locomotion*. The social reality function is to provide group members with subjective validity for their beliefs, opinions and attitudes. If one holds some belief that, for example, the Earth is flat, then one can be more or less confident about its validity. One may be sure that water is heavier than air, but less sure that smoking reduces stress. This feeling of subjective confidence in the validity of one's beliefs Festinger terms subjective validity. Subjective validity, he suggests, is provided by reality testing: if one wants to know whether a belief is true one can try to test the belief against reality. Festinger proposes that there is a continuum from physical to social reality testing that orders the bases of subjective validity. At one pole of the continuum is high dependence on physical reality testing and low dependence on social reality testing; at the other extreme is high dependence on social reality and low dependence on physical reality.

For example, if one believes that a sheet of glass is fragile, one can test that belief by hitting it with a hammer and seeing if it breaks. This is a belief whose subjective validity depends upon physical reality testing. However, suppose one believes that socialism is the way forward for humanity. How can one test whether this belief is true or false? There are no obvious physical tests that can be carried out. In this instance, argues Festinger, given that physical tests are impossible or difficult to carry out, the subjective validity of one's belief depends upon social reality testing, i.e. it depends upon *consensual validation*: 'where the dependence upon physical reality is low, the dependence upon social reality is correspondingly high. An opinion, a belief, an attitude is "correct", "valid", and "proper" to the extent that it is anchored in a group of people with similar beliefs, opinions, and attitudes' (1950, p. 272).

There are three points which summarize the social reality function of groups in Festinger's theory:

1 Social reality testing is a process of testing the consensual support for a belief: a belief, opinion or attitude is assumed to be correct, valid or appropriate if it is anchored in a like-minded group of people. If other people agree and share my attitude, then it has subjective validity.

2 Not everybody's agreement matters for social reality testing, only the agreement of members of appropriate reference groups. Festinger believes that people who are similar to oneself are the appropriate reference group for social reality testing. Uniformity pressures and group formation have a reciprocal influence on each other. One joins groups of people with whom one agrees (is similar) and uniformity pressures within such groups produce stronger agreement, more similarity, and hence more identification with the group.

3 Dependence on social reality testing increases as dependence on physical reality testing decreases. The less one can make physical reality tests, the more important becomes the agreement of similar others to validate one's beliefs.

The group locomotion function is the idea that pressures for uniformity may arise because such uniformity is perceived as desirable or necessary for the group to move towards some goal. Group locomotion simply means the movement of the group to a goal. Festinger hypothesizes that the magnitude of such pressures will increase to the degree that (a) members perceive that group movement would be facilitated by such uniformity and (b) members are dependent on each other to reach the goal. The group locomotion function reflects the dependence of the individual on the group for reaching some valued goal and the belief of group members that unity and agreement are necessary to reach the goal.

Festinger suggests that uniformity pressures function in the same way irrespective of their source in social reality or in group locomotion. They increase in magnitude with the degree of *discrepancy* or disagreement within the group, the degree of *relevance* of the discrepancy to the functioning of the group, and the *cohesiveness* of the group. He assumes that informal social communication in the group tends to serve uniformity pressures, being directed at the source of discrepancy, the deviant. Uniformity is achieved by changing the deviant to bring him or her back into line with the majority, changing the group to produce agreement with the deviant or rejection of the deviant from the group. Whether the deviant or the group moves towards the other is a matter of their relative power.

There is good evidence for Festinger's theory. Numerous studies confirm that both pressures towards uniformity within groups and the degree of agreement actually reached about group standards is positively related to the degree of cohesiveness of group members (Allen, 1965; Shaw, 1976). Group cohesiveness was originally defined as the sum total of forces acting on members to maintain their membership in a group (e.g. Festinger *et al.*, 1950). It is now defined more simply as the degree of attraction to the group (see Hogg, 1987).

Festinger *et al.* (1950), for example, related the pattern of sociometric choice among residents of 'courtyard' groups on a student housing project to the degree of agreement within courts about a relevant salient issue. Each tenant in the 'Westgate' courts was asked to name the three persons within the community with whom they had the most contact. These data were used to construct an index of the proportion of their social life that members of each court spent with other members of their own court. This represents an index of the cohesiveness of the courts, i.e. the attractiveness of members of one's own court compared to members of other courts. The researchers also measured attitudes to a newly formed tenants' organization. They found that attitudes to the tenants' organization within Westgate varied widely from favourable to unfavourable between courts but were relatively homogeneous within courts. They assumed that such attitudes had become normative for the courts on the basis of social contact within them. The proportion of opinion deviants within each court was calculated. The higher this proportion, then, the less the uniformity of attitude within each court. A significant negative correlation ($-0.74$) was found between the proportion of opinion deviants and the index of cohesiveness: the more cohesive the court, the greater the uniformity of attitudes among members towards the tenants' organization.

In a subsequent experimental study, Back (1951) demonstrated a causal relationship between group cohesiveness and uniformity pressures. Previously unacquainted pairs of subjects were brought together in each session. The subjects were made attractive to each other in half the pairs (high cohesive conditions) and much less attractive to each other in the other half (low cohesive conditions). Attraction within pairs was based ostensibly on the personal attractiveness of the other, or the chance of getting a prize for a good story, or the perceived competence of the other on the task. Before meeting, each person had written a story about a series of three pictures that they had been shown. The pairs of subjects then compared and discussed their interpretations of the pictures. After discussion, the subjects wrote final individual versions of the story. The subjects were unaware that they had seen slightly different pictures and had, therefore, written differing stories. By observing communication within the pairs and also assessing the degree to which a person had changed their story towards that of their discussion partner from the first to the second versions, Back was able to measure influence within the pairs.

It was found that high cohesive pairs showed a stronger tendency than low cohesive pairs both to attempt to influence each other in communication and actually to change their stories in the direction of the partner. Members of these pairs also showed more resistance to influence attempts from the partner (although, ultimately, they were induced to move). The uniformity pressures within high cohesive pairs, therefore, did not induce passive acceptance of the other's opinion, but rather were embodied in active attempts at mutual influence. The basis of cohesiveness did not affect the influence process, but it did lead to slightly different styles of social interaction.

There is also good evidence for the importance of the relevance of the discrepancy to the norms, values and goals of the group. Kiesler and Kiesler (1969, p. 31) summarize the results of several studies by suggesting that individuals will conform more to the group to the degree that (a) they accept and understand the group goal, (b) the norm is perceived as relevant to the goal, (c) the group is successful in reaching its goals and (d) cooperative interdependence is perceived as likely to enhance success.

A more recent study that demonstrates the importance of normative relevance to predicting conformity was conducted by Boyanowsky and Allen (1973). Employing the Asch paradigm, they replicated the usual finding that a social supporter (another person giving the correct response) reduces the subject's conformity to an incorrect majority (see Chapter 1). Specifically, they found on some trials that both prejudiced and unprejudiced white subjects conformed less to a white majority when they had either a black or white social supporter. This was only true, however, on physical and general opinion judgements, where ethnicity was not a relevant group membership, even for prejudiced subjects. If one is trying to judge the lengths of lines correctly, for example, the appropriate reference group is something like all human beings from the same scientific and linguistic culture with good eyesight – a group that includes both blacks and whites. When the judgements concerned matters of personal opinion, the prejudiced subjects conformed less to the white majority when they had a white supporter, but were not affected by the presence of a black supporter. The unprejudiced subjects conformed less to the majority in either case. The prejudiced subjects presumably perceived their ethnicity as relevant to how they made these more personally involving judgements and so referred themselves solely to the white people in the situation, either ignoring the supporter if the person were black or being influenced (to conform less) if the supporter were white. Thus even for people who defined being black or white as important to them (prejudiced subjects), it was *only* on relevant items that this group membership affected their conformity.

Schachter (1951) illustrated the role of discrepancy in a classic experiment on the rejection of deviants. The design of this study followed the conceptual scheme of Festinger's theory and independently manipulated the three variables of group cohesiveness, relevance and discrepancy. The subjects were students who were recruited as volunteers to join undergraduate clubs: case study, editorial, movie and radio clubs (there were eight experimental groups in all, two clubs of each type). The case study and movie clubs represented high cohesive groups, as the members had expressed a strong interest in joining them. The editorial and radio clubs were low cohesive groups, because the members had expressed little interest in joining them. Each group discussed the same topic, a fictitious case history of a juvenile delinquent called 'Johnny Rocco'. This case history discussion was made relevant to the purposes of the case study and editorial clubs, but irrelevant to the movie and radio clubs. Thus high cohesive-relevant (case study), high cohesive-irrelevant (movie), low cohesive-relevant (editorial) and low cohesive-irrelevant (radio) groups were formed.

Each group comprised five to seven naive subjects and three trained confederates of the experimenter. The case history of Johnny Rocco was constructed to elicit a sympathetic and lenient reaction from group members. During discussion, the confederates played one of three roles: the 'mode' adopted the modal position of the group, agreeing at all times with the majority view that Rocco should be treated leniently; the 'slider' initially took a deviant position recommending the harshest possible treatment, but gradually came to agree with the majority; and the 'deviate' consistently maintained an extremely deviant stand throughout the discussion, advocating the harshest possible treatment. Communication within the group was observed and measures of rejection of group members were obtained. Festinger's theory predicts that where neither the deviant nor the group can be persuaded to change their position, uniformity can be re-established and discrepancy eliminated within the group by excluding the deviant from group membership; the deviant will be socially rejected.

After the meeting, the members were asked to nominate members by secret ballot for various committee jobs that differed in desirability and importance. The assignment of the mode and the slider to the different jobs was around the chance level, but the deviate was over-nominated for the least desirable and under-nominated for the most desirable jobs in all conditions except the low cohesive-irrelevant. The tendency to restrict the deviate to the least important role in the group was stronger in the relevant than irrelevant conditions.

Members were also told that it might be necessary to reduce the size of the club and on this pretext asked to list other club members in the order of the subject's preference for having them remain in the group. This is a straightforward measure of social acceptance or attraction. In all conditions the deviate was ranked much lower than the mode and slider and this effect was stronger in the high than low cohesive conditions.

Communication in the groups tended to be directed at the deviate – and initially the slider – in an attempt to bring them back into line. Communication to the slider dropped off as he moved towards the group, whereas that to the mode stayed at a constant low level throughout. Communication to the deviate was highest in the high cohesive-relevant groups, but eventually at the end of discussion it decreased, as if the group finally opted for rejection over persuasion.

A massive study by Festinger and Thibaut (1951), employing 600 student subjects in 60 groups, also found evidence that people tend to communicate more with other members the more the other person's views differ from those of the communicator. This was particularly so where uniformity was important to group members. Uniformity pressures did lead to change on the part of members, produced greater uniformity within the groups and under certain conditions a tendency to exclude people with extreme opinions. Other studies in this tradition by Festinger and his colleagues (Festinger *et al.*, 1952; Gerard, 1953, 1954) confirm the general picture and also provide some evidence that the deviant can sometimes change the group.

The social reality hypothesis that people tend to become more dependent on the agreement of others as physical reality testing becomes less possible, implies strongly that conformity to the group will increase as the stimulus situation being judged becomes more objectively ambiguous, difficult, complex, problematic or otherwise perceptually unstructured. The less one can rely on one's own direct perceptual and behavioural contact with the physical world, the more susceptible one should be to influence from others. Once again, there is solid evidence for this idea in some form or another.

It is supported, for example, by the contrast between Sherif's and Asch's conformity paradigms. In Sherif's paradigm, in which the stimulus situation is deliberately ambiguous, the majority of subjects are influenced by the group. Influence is accepted readily with little awareness and persists in the absence of the group for long periods (Bovard, 1948; Rohrer *et al.*, 1954). In Asch's paradigm, in which the stimulus situation is perceptually unambiguous and the group norm contrary to the evidence of one's senses, about 25 per cent of subjects do not conform at all and only about 33 per cent show conformity on more than half the critical trials. Moreover, the influence is accepted only reluctantly, with much conflict, and is short-term (Allen, 1965). In general, then, the more physically ambiguous, difficult or complex the task, the more conformity to the group.

## Social comparison processes

Festinger's (1954) theory of social comparison processes is a development of his ideas about social reality testing. It is concerned with the subjective validity of opinions and the appraisal of abilities. The theory attempts to explain how the agreement of others provides subjective validity. The most important ideas of the theory are that:

1 People need to evaluate their opinions and abilities.
2 To the extent that objective, non-social means of appraisal (i.e. physical reality tests) are unavailable, people rely on social comparison processes to evaluate themselves. To the extent that reality is objectively ambiguous and unstructured, people evaluate themselves by comparing with others rather than by direct physical tests.

3 People tend to compare themselves only with similar others. Others are more 'comparable' the more similar to oneself they are in opinions and abilities. One does not compare with people very different from oneself.
4 The more similar the people with whom one compares one's opinions and abilities, the more stable, accurate and precise is the information gained from comparison, i.e. the more informative is the comparison.
5 To the extent that people need to evaluate themselves, they will tend to be attracted to similar others and to reduce differences between themselves and others (moving towards others and seeking to influence others to become more similar to themselves) in order to increase the social comparability between themselves and others. In the case of abilities, this leads to competitive tendencies to be slightly better than others.

This theory, therefore, derives attraction (to similar others), group formation, competition and pressures for uniformity from people's need to evaluate themselves through comparison with similar others. People seek out similar others, join groups of like-minded others, reject deviants with very different opinions, influence and are influenced by others so that they can make informative comparisons and gain stable, accurate and precise information about themselves. The theory explains the competitive tendency in the case of abilities by noting that different degrees of ability are more or less positively valued and that people tend to compromise between wanting to be similar and wanting to be better by seeking situations in which they can be slightly superior.

As evidence for the theory, Festinger (1954) and others (Allen and Wilder, 1977; Suls and Miller, 1977) point out that (a) being different from others induces instability and uncertainty in self-evaluation, (b) similarity to reference groups induces stability and confidence, (c) feedback about one's objective correctness or competence (i.e. about physical reality) reduces the influence of others, and (d) one moves towards similar others and chooses to compare with similar others.

There are two conceptual complications in the theory that are worth noting. First, the theory is trying to explain, among other things, what it is about the agreement of others that provides subjective validity for one's opinions. Its answer is that one can obtain more exact, accurate and stable information about where one stands by comparing with similar than different people. This, however, is rather an indirect process of validation compared to the 1950 theory. The earlier theory implies that the agreement of others *directly* confers validity. Their agreement indicates that one is right. The 1954 theory implies that validation is *indirect*, in that the motivation to conform to the majority is not *to be correct* but rather *to make possible more fine-grained comparison*. It reads as if gaining exact information about one's position were the same as gaining information that one's position is correct. In fact, of course, there is no logical requirement that a more exact appraisal of where one stands on an issue means that one must discover that one is *correct*. A more informative comparison might equally demonstrate that one is *incorrect* (resulting in a movement to a different position and away from the consensus).

There is an ambiguity in the theory here that is never properly resolved. Defining one's level of ability or an opinion more exactly through close comparison is not the same as validating an opinion as correct (cf. Goethals and Darley, 1987, p. 23). I must also say that I feel that the earlier view that one conforms in order to be right is more plausible than the later view that one conforms for better information about where one stands. Most researchers, like Festinger, seem simply to have assumed that these are the same (see Festinger, 1954, p. 120). Some (e.g. Allen and Wilder, 1977, pp. 192–3) have wrestled hard with the contradictory implications of the theory.

Secondly, it has been pointed out (Goethals and Darley, 1977; Jellison and Arkin, 1977) that the idea that one only compares with similar rather than different people contains a paradox. If one does not and cannot compare properly with different people, how can one know that they are different? Being similar and being different are both comparative relationships. Defining someone as different is a comparative judgement. Therefore, in order not to compare with different people, one must have compared with them to know that they are different! If one can and does compare with different people, then the rationale for the major predictions of the theory seems to collapse.

One solution has been suggested by Goethals and Darley (1977, 1987; Wheeler and Zuckerman, 1977). They propose 'the related attributes hypothesis', i.e. that one can compare with people who are either similar or different in terms of ability or opinion providing they are similar on background attributes related to and predictive of the opinion or ability being evaluated. For example, 'in evaluating one's opinion about disinvestment in South African businesses, an American would want to compare with others who are similar in general political orientation and dislike of apartheid, believing that these factors are related to and predictive of opinions on disinvestment' (Goethals and Darley, 1987, p. 26). In other words, one compares with people who *should* be similar (by virtue of related attributes), even if they are not. This is an important revision of the similarity hypothesis, which makes a great deal of sense.

If one can compare with different people who share related attributes, then presumably such comparison can and does provide information. *A priori* such information may be less fine-grained but is no less stable and accurate, e.g. a person can certainly know that he or she is less intelligent than Einstein or more left-wing than Hitler. Tajfel and Turner (1986) point to one instance where comparing with very different people plays an important role in self-evaluation. They argue that social comparisons are commonly made between one's own groups and members of other social groups, and that such intergroup comparisons, unlike intragroup comparisons, produce a need to enhance rather than decrease discrepancies between self and others. They suggest that social groups provide a positive social identity for their members by making themselves positively distinctive from other groups (outgroups, negative reference groups), e.g. ancient civilizations often prided themselves on being very different from the surrounding 'barbarians'. There are times, then, when it is important to compare with people who are different from self, evaluate oneself in terms of such differences, and even to maintain such differences.

If comparison with different people is possible (because they share related attributes) and informative, then Festinger's argument that we are attracted to similar others and conform to the group because similarity is the precondition of comparison seems weakly founded. We do not have to change our own or other's positions to compare, we need only find some shared related attribute. It is true that such an attribute still defines a similarity, but the point is that such attributes function as common standards or anchors within which comparison with a range of others can take place. There are some complex conceptual issues here, but the evidence and more recent theorizing do suggest that the human capacity for social comparison is much more varied than Festinger (1954) originally anticipated (see Goethals and Darley, 1977, 1987; Turner, 1985; Wheeler and Zuckerman, 1977).

Nevertheless, the fundamental idea of Festinger's theory that social reality testing is accomplished by social comparison processes is a powerful one that has proved extremely fertile in research. The hypothesis that one compares oneself with similar others to determine what is correct, appropriate and desirable (and that the more uncertain one is the more one does so) has led to several fascinating and important empirical discoveries. Three major applications of this idea will serve to illustrate its power.

## The psychology of affiliation

Schachter (1959) was interested in the conditions under which people affiliate with others. On the basis of social comparison theory, he argued that one motive for affiliation is to seek out comparative information from others to reduce uncertainty about what one is feeling and how to react. He created an experimental paradigm in which subjects experienced an intense, novel situation and were then given the opportunity to be with others. The subjects were female students who came to the session in groups of five to eight. They were met by 'Dr Gregor Zilstein of the Medical School's Department of Neurology and Psychiatry', who told them that the study was concerned with the effects of electric shock and that they were going to receive a series of such shocks.

There were two experimental conditions designed to manipulate the degree of fear experienced by subjects. In the high fear condition, Dr Zilstein described the shocks in a way that made them sound extremely frightening, painful and possibly physically dangerous. In the low fear condition, the study and the shocks were described as enjoyable and fun, e.g. the shocks were more like a 'tickle or a tingle than anything unpleasant'. The subjects in the former condition did indeed report that they expected the shocks to be much more unpleasant than did the subjects in the latter condition (about 20 per cent of the high fear subjects, but none of the low fear ones, refused to continue). Before the study proper, the subjects were informed that there would be a delay while the main laboratory room was made ready. They could choose to wait alone, together with some of the other subjects, or they could say if they didn't care. The experiment then ended and no shocks were given. A total of 63 per cent of the high fear but only 33 per cent of the low fear subjects chose to wait with others.

These results suggest that the experience of an intense emotion, high fear, created uncertainty in the subjects about what they were feeling and how they should react. They sought the company of others to compare themselves, gain information about appropriate behaviour and reduce their uncertainty. In a second study, Schachter (1959) showed that the high fear subjects would only choose to wait together with other women also waiting to undergo the same shock experience. About 60 per cent chose to wait with women in a similar situation, but not one subject chose to wait with women who were just waiting to see their professors rather than participating in the study. Just as social comparison theory would predict (although other explanations are possible), people only sought to compare with similar others – comparison with people in a different situation would not provide appropriate information to reduce uncertainty.

Gerard and Rabbie (1961; Gerard, 1963; Rabbie, 1963) performed studies showing that the tendency to affiliate with others can be influenced by increasing or decreasing the amount of prior information available to subjects about their internal state and so varying uncertainty (independently of high or low fear). Other studies show that internal states other than fear can be employed to create uncertainty and increase the need to compare with others in a similar state/situation (Cottrell and Epley, 1977). The greater a person's uncertainty about the situation they are in, what they are feeling and the appropriate way to behave, the stronger the tendency to affiliate with similar others for social comparison purposes.

## The psychology of emotions

Schachter and Singer (1962) applied social comparison theory to the psychology of emotions. They proposed that the experience of different emotions such as anger, joy, fear, misery, etc., is made up of two components: a state of undifferentiated physiological arousal common to all emotions and a cognitive label that gives different cognitive meaning to the arousal state and produces the differences in subjective experience. So, for example, two people may experience the same state of physiological arousal (indicated by increased heart and pulse rate, sweating palms, face flushes, etc.) but different emotions depending on how they label and make sense of that arousal. If one explains it in terms of getting a job promotion, he or she may feel happiness or excitement. If it is explained as a reaction to getting the sack, the person may feel angry or depressed. Schachter and Singer hypothesized that one source of cognitive labels under conditions of emotional uncertainty is comparison with others in the same situation.

To test these ideas, they designed a study that was introduced to subjects as being to do with the effects of a (fictitious) vitamin compound, called 'Suproxin', on vision. All of the subjects were supposedly injected with Suproxin. In fact, the subjects in the experimental group were given epinephrine, which acts like adrenalin to create a state of physiological arousal similar to that which occurs when one is emotionally excited (hand tremor, pounding heart, etc.), and some in the control group were given a placebo of salt water, which does nothing. There were three experimental conditions: 'informed', in which subjects were correctly informed of the physiological side-effects that Suproxin (epinephrine) would have; 'misinformed', in which subjects were told that Suproxin would have side-effects but were given completely incorrect symptoms (itching feet, slight headache, numbness); and 'uninformed', in which subjects were not led to expect any side-effects of the injection. While individual subjects were supposedly waiting for the injection to take effect, before the study proper, another subject injected with Suproxin was also brought into the room to wait with the subject. In fact, the latter person was a confederate of the experimenter who had been trained to play one of two roles. With half the subjects, the confederate acted out the role of someone who was extremely happy and euphoric, behaving in a bizarre, slap-happy way, playing games, engaging in playful and ultimately frenzied antics. With the other half, the confederate acted out the role of someone who became more and more angry, becoming more and more annoyed with the personal and intimate questions contained in a questionnaire both subjects were completing, until finally tearing the questionnaire up and throwing it into the wastepaper basket. Half of the subjects in the control and experimental groups were exposed to the euphoric role and half to the angry role (except that no 'misinformed-anger' condition was run).

Schachter and Singer argued that misinformed and uninformed subjects would be uncertain of their emotional state compared to informed and control subjects. The former are experiencing a state of arousal that has no ready explanation, either because the symptoms do not fit what they have been told about the effects of Suproxin or because they have not been led to expect any effects. The latter are either experiencing arousal that they believe to be caused by Suproxin or have no arousal. Misinformed and uninformed subjects, therefore, being uncertain of what they are feeling, will compare with the confederate in the same situation to find the appropriate cognitive label for their experience. Depending on whether the other person is euphoric or angry, they will label their arousal differently and correspondingly come to feel (and behave) euphoric or angry. These predictions were reasonably well-supported. With a euphoric confederate, misinformed and uninformed subjects were significantly more euphoric than informed ones, as measured by both their own self-reports and by behavioural observation. With an angry confederate, uninformed subjects were significantly more angry than informed ones, judged by observation of their behaviour, but only non-significantly so in terms of their self-reports. Depending on the behaviour of the confederate, misinformed and uninformed subjects were more euphoric and uninformed subjects more angry than control subjects, as predicted, but only the difference on the behavioural measure between uninformed and control subjects in the angry confederate condition reached significance.

Interestingly, the control subjects showed relatively high levels of euphoria and anger, tending to fall between the informed subjects and the other conditions. These results tend to suggest that simple social comparison, even without physiological arousal or with only the arousal induced by the actions of the other, may be sufficient for emotional experience. Any state of emotional uncertainty may lead to emotional contagion on the basis of social comparison. Later studies on the misattribution of emotion have followed up the idea that cognitive labelling may be sufficient for emotional experience (Fiske and Taylor, 1984).

Subsequent research has neither unambiguously supported nor disconfirmed Schachter and Singer's theory of emotions (for reviews, see Cotton, 1981; Manstead and Wagner, 1981; Reisenzein, 1983). Emotional experience is probably not as generally labile and fluid as the above study implies (Marshall and Zimbardo, 1979; Maslach, 1979). However, there is support for some aspects of Schachter and Singer's analysis and their work has inspired much interest in the social cognitive basis of emotions (see Fiske and Taylor, 1984).

## Bystander intervention

Latané and Darley's (1970) research on helping illustrates that social comparison can sometimes inhibit morally appropriate behaviour.

They were interested in the conditions under which a bystander will intervene in an emergency to help a victim in some kind of distress. They wanted to show – in part explanation of some very unpleasant real-life instances – that sometimes the very fact that a large number of possible helpers is present in an emergency can reduce the chances of any single bystander helping.

In one experiment (Darley and Latané, 1968), the subjects were recruited for a discussion about the problems of urban living. The discussion was to be held over an intercom system with each participant in a different room. Initially, each person took a turn speaking for a few minutes introducing their problems. Each person was then to have a second turn commenting on what had been said. In fact, the first speaker was a confederate of the experimenters who had been trained to play the role of a 'victim'. During his initial remarks he mentioned that he was prone to seizures. During his second turn he acted out a realistic seizure, which the subjects could hear over the intercom. After a few relatively calm sentences, he began to stammer, choke and talk more loudly and incoherently; he muttered things such as 'I'm gonna die er . . . er . . . I's . . . gonna die er . . . help'. The question was would the other subjects try to help the victim.

In one condition, only one subject and the victim were present for the discussion; in another condition, two subjects plus the victim were supposedly present; in a six-person condition, five subjects plus the victim were supposed to be present. In reality, however, there was only one naive subject present in each condition, the presence of the other participants being faked by means of tape-recordings. The results were that 85 per cent of the subjects tried to help the victim when they believed they were the only other person present, 62 per cent helped with two possible helpers, and only 31 per cent helped with five possible helpers.

There are at least two ways in which social comparison processes can contribute to the explanation of this kind of result. First, before one helps, one must define the situation as an emergency, as one in which it is appropriate to offer help. Emergencies are often novel, ambiguous situations. In such situations, one may turn to others to compare reactions to find an appropriate definition of the situation. However, if others fail to react immediately or fail to react at all – perhaps because they too are engaged in comparative information-seeking – one may conclude that it is inappropriate to define the situation as an emergency requiring action. The situation may be defined as one in which nothing should be done. Latané and Rodin (1969) had subjects work on a questionnaire while a female experimenter worked in her office next door. The subjects heard a (fake) crash, screams and moans. A total of 70 per cent of the subjects who worked alone went to help the female experimenter, but only 7 per cent went to help if they were working with a confederate who had been trained to act calmly and passively as if nothing had happened. The social reality test of comparing with the confederate defined the situation as a non-emergency.

Even if there is a clear emergency, people may still be very uncertain as to the appropriate way to act. Here, too, the failure of others to help may define inaction as the appropriate response. Latané and Darley suggest that the more bystanders present the less responsibility any single bystander feels for helping the victim. Again, it is possible that as bystanders compare with each other to reduce their uncertainty about the situation, their failure to act immediately suggests that it is no-one's shared or personal responsibility to act. Consistent with social comparison theory, the presence of others does not lower the tendency to help if the others are not in the same situation of being able to help as the subject (Bickman, 1971).

Finally, we should note the positive effects of social comparison. The presence of a comparative model who helps has been shown to increase the tendency of subjects to help (e.g. Bryan and Test, 1967). Such models may define the situation as one in which it is proper to act, helping as the proper form of action and the enactment of such a norm as the personal responsibility of the subject.

## Informational and normative social influence

Deutsch and Gerard's (1955) theory of informational and normative social influence is an attempt to distinguish two processes underlying social conformity and their distinctive antecedent conditions. They suggest that these conceptually distinct processes often co-occur and for this reason have tended to be confused in prior research.

*Normative influence* is defined as an influence to conform to the *positive expectations* of another (another person, a group or one's self). Positive expectations are those whose fulfilment leads to positive feelings towards and solidarity with the other. In this process, conformity is motivated by the desire to please others. One conforms to gain social approval and acceptance and to avoid rejection. Deutsch and Gerard consider normative influence as 'the type of social influence most specifically associated with groups' (p. 635), and hypothesize that it is increased by group belongingness and social interdependence, surveillance of one's response by others and social pressure, and reduced by public and private commitment to some prior course of action producing countervailing expectations in others and oneself.

*Informational influence* is influence to accept information from another as *(trustworthy) evidence about objective reality*. One interacts with others in much the same way as one might with a 'measuring or computing machine' (p. 635) that produces reliable information about reality. In this process, conformity is motivated by the desire to form an accurate view of reality and to act correctly. It is increased by uncertainty about the correctness of one's judgement and the ambiguity of the stimulus situation, and reduced by the perceived uncertainty of the others.

Deutsch and Gerard (1955) varied Asch's paradigm to test their hypotheses. The face-to-face condition was exactly the same as in Asch's (1951, 1952, 1956) experiments, except that they used only three confederates and two series of 18-line judgements were made. In the visual series the lines were visually present when the subjects responded, but in the memory series the lines were removed before anyone made a judgement. The anonymous condition was the same as the face-to-face except that subjects made their judgements privately by pressing a button; similarly, the confederates' responses (which were faked – no-one else was present) were relayed to the subject by electronic means. The subjects in the anonymous situation were intended to realize that their judgements could not be identified as theirs by the group. The group (interdependence) condition was the same as the anonymous one except that the subjects were instructed that their group was in a competition with 19 similar other groups to win a prize by making as few errors as possible. There were also three commitment variations. In the face-to-face and anonymous conditions, some of the subjects wrote down their judgements on a sheet of paper before hearing the group's responses and then threw away the sheets afterwards (self-commitment). Others did the same but, instead of throwing away the sheets, they signed them and handed them to the experimenter after each series of trials (public commitment). In the Magic Pad self-commitment variation, the subjects in the anonymous condition wrote down their responses on a Magic Pad before hearing the group and then erased their responses by lifting the plastic covering after each trial — intended to be the ultimate private response.

In line with the concept of normative influence, the subjects showed less conformity to the group in the anonymous (private) than in the face-to-face (public) setting, less in the commitment conditions than with no commitment, and more conformity in the group than anonymous non-group condition. Also, as might be expected, public commitment and the more 'public' self-commitment variation produced less conformity than the Magic Pad variation. The concept of informational influence was validated by the finding of more conformity with the memory than visual series of trials, especially when the subjects did not write their judgements down first and hence were probably more uncertain. The group condition where the instructions made the subject 'feel that he was a member of a group faced with a common task requiring cooperative effort for its most effective solution' (Deutsch and Gerard, 1955, p. 629) produced about 52 per cent conformity on critical trials. It is striking that such conformity occurred even where the group goal had been defined explicitly as being as accurate as possible (i.e. not making errors). It is also striking that even where the subjects responded anonymously in the standard, no commitment condition, about 25 per cent of critical responses were still errors. This is not much lower than the 30 per cent error rate obtained in the usual face-to-face situation (although the difference was statistically significant). Deutsch and Gerard believed that the anonymity manipulation was faulty and that conformity would have dropped more if the subjects had been made fully aware that their responses could not be identified by the group.

Deutsch and Gerard use the term 'normative' in a much more specific sense than we have used it so far. They are implicitly defining social norms as shared expectations about appropriate behaviour to which one conforms to the extent that one is interdependent with others and seeks their social approval. They equate this process explicitly with the influence that depends on group membership. We shall employ their terminology for distinguishing between 'normative' and 'informational' processes, but it is not suggested that influence processes related to social norms and group membership are adequately summarized by this one process.

## Dual-process and multi-process models

There are definite parallels between the processes described by the three theories. Festinger's group locomotion seems identical to normative influence and to be a process of public compliance rather than private acceptance. The social reality function works through social comparison processes, represents informational influence and is plainly acceptance rather than compliance. The theories, in fact, suggest a two-process model of influence that has been widely accepted and which can be summarized as follows:

*Informational influence*: 'true' influence, i.e. influence leading to private acceptance and internalization, long-lasting attitude change, is informational in nature; others' responses are influential to the degree that they provide evidence about reality; others are informative to the extent that they are perceived as similar, expert, trustworthy, credible, etc.; the process is one of social comparison, motivated by the desire to be correct, to achieve subjective validity for one's beliefs.

The process has a causal structure as follows:

1 Objective stimulus ambiguity, difficulty or complexity, the difficulty of making direct tests of physical reality, leads to subjective uncertainty, a need for information to reduce uncertainty.
2 Uncertainty creates social dependence, dependence on others for valid information.
3 Informational dependence leads to influence; one conforms to the responses of others perceived to provide evidence about reality.

The need to know reality correctly leads to the development of shared social norms and group structure. The classic example of this process in its apparently pure form would be the autokinetic study of Sherif (1936). There is good evidence that this study represents an informational process of influence leading to internalization (Allen, 1965).

*Normative influence*: this is compliance, in which one conforms outwardly but not necessarily inwardly to the expectations of others; it is a specifically group process of conformity to social pressure, based on the power of others to reward and punish, and socially motivated by a desire for acceptance and approval and to avoid rejection and hostility. One is concerned with the consequences of one's actions in terms of how the group will react rather than the content of the action itself; it is 'conformity' in the sense of slavish submission to group pressure, but in the main it is tactical and instrumental more than irrational and emotional. Some conformers may have an irrational, emotional need to belong, but, in general, attraction to the group is based on mutual interdependence for shared goals. Conformity is assumed to be functional for the group to reach its goals.

The causal structure is as follows:

1  The power of others to reward or punish (e.g. to accept into or reject from the group) creates a need for their social approval and a fear of being different.
2  Therefore, under conditions of surveillance by others such that one can be personally identified and held responsible for any nonconformity,
3  one will tend to comply with their expectations or submit to other group pressures, producing conformity to the group norm.

One's dependence on others gives them power to control one's outward behaviour. The basis of influence is not the validity of others' behaviour but a social relationship of power and a motivation to be socially accepted. The classic example of this process is assumed to be Asch's (1956) conformity experiment in which one gives false answers in order to agree with the group. There is evidence that Asch-type conformity is overwhelmingly compliance and that explicit group interdependence and public identifiability increase conformity (Allen, 1965; Deutsch and Gerard, 1955).

The dual-process scheme is congruent with several other theories: Kelley's (1952) distinction between comparative and normative functions of reference groups; Thibaut and Strickland's (1956) 'task set' where others are 'mediators of fact' and 'group set' where the person 'is motivated to gain membership' in the group; and Jones and Gerard's (1967) distinction between dependence for information leading to 'comparative appraisal' (i.e. self-evaluation through comparison with others) and dependence for outcomes leading to 'reflected appraisal' (i.e. inferences of how others evaluate one based on their reactions).

This model can be reduced to a one-process dependence formulation (Moscovici, 1976; Turner, 1985) or expanded to three or even more components (French and Raven, 1959; Kelman, 1958, 1961). Both informational and normative influence reflect a person's social dependence on others (for information and other positive outcomes) and therefore can be seen as aspects of a wider theory that social interdependence is the basic process underlying social and group relationships (see Turner *et al.*, 1987). Kelman (1958), on the other hand, distinguishes three processes of influence: compliance, internalization and identification. He separates what we have called normative influence into *compliance*, which is based on others' power to mediate rewards and costs, and *identification*, which is based on attraction to the other and can lead to a form of acceptance of other's values so long as the relationship is maintained. French and Raven (1959) distinguish five (and Raven, 1965, six) influence processes reflecting different forms of dependence and power. By and large, the differences between the dual-process theory and the one- and multi-process theories are to do with the degree of detail specified about types of dependence and related characteristics of the influence process rather than the substance of the formulations. All accept the dependence/power formulation of influence and make some basic distinction between informational and compliance/ group-based processes.

The exceptions to this summary are possibly Kelman's concept of 'identification' and French and Raven's 'referent power'. These notions are interesting because they suggest types of influence in which reference group norms lead to a form of informational internalization. This was implicit in Festinger's concept of social reality testing, but the general trend has been to distinguish sharply between social and cognitive motives. They stand as possible exceptions to the general rule of a dichotomy between socially and cognitively motivated conformity. These theories and issues are discussed in more detail in Chapters 5 and 6.

## Social dependence and conformity

The dual-process model leads to a simple and powerful explanation of social conformity: conformity to the group increases with the normative and informational dependence of the individual on the group (the relative power of the group over the individual) with respect to a given stimulus situation. Conversely, the ability of the individual to influence (lead) the group increases with the dependence of the group on the individual (the relative power of the individual over the group).

This analysis points to three classes of variables determining conformity to the group: factors affecting the relationship of the individual to the group; the relationship of the group to the stimulus situation; and the individual to the stimulus situation. For example, is the group a relevant reference group for the individual? Does the person seek its approval and wish to be a member? Does he or she perceive the group as a trustworthy, credible source of information? Is the group consensual in its reaction to the stimulus? And does the person find the task cognitively difficult and unstructured? One can make the same kind of analysis from the perspective of the group to assess the likely influence of the person over the group.

The empirical results from a huge number of studies support these ideas extremely well. There seem to be at least five relatively firm empirical generalizations that emerge from conformity research congruent with the two-process model.

## 1 Reference group membership: Interdependence, similarity and group cohesiveness

The two-process model points to the importance of reference group membership in social conformity. One should tend to conform more to the norms of people to whom one feels psychologically attached through relations of interdependence, similarity and mutual attraction. The hypothesis is well-supported. Walker and Heyns (1962), for example, found that female students conformed more to a norm when it was attributed to their own sorority group than to other women on campus or sorority women in general. White (1957, in Allen, 1965) and Israel (1963) obtained evidence that subjects would sometimes refer their opinions to an absent reference group, such as family or friends, and that this would affect reactions to the physically present membership group. Allen (1975) found solid support for the idea that physically absent social supporters will lower conformity to the majority in the Asch paradigm under appropriate conditions (e.g. the supporter must not be perceived as having deserted the subject).

Deutsch and Gerard's (1955) study illustrates the importance of cooperative interdependence for a common goal between subjects and group. Jones et al. (1958) also found more conformity in interdependent than non-interdependent groups when the experimenter gave feedback confirming the incorrect group norm. Other studies (see Allen, 1965) have replicated this effect. Social interdependence, by definition, provides motivation for maintaining membership in a group, because it implies that significant goals are mediated by group membership. Also, however, it implies similarity of perspective between self and other, as one appraises the situation from the perspective of common efforts to reach a shared goal. A positive interdependence with respect to a goal can often easily be restated as a shared social value.

Since the studies of Festinger *et al.* (1950), Back (1951) and Schachter (1951), much evidence has accumulated for the importance of attraction to the group (Allen, 1965; Shaw, 1976). For example, Lott and Lott (1961) confirmed the positive relation (+0.54) between conformity to the group norm and attraction to the group across 15 natural friendship groups. Sherif and Sherif (1956) reported a study by Zeaman in which subjects in the autokinetic situation moved more towards a liked partner than a disliked partner. Conversely, Sherif and Sherif (1960) cite a study in which intergroup conflict between monks and novices in a monastery prevented convergence in autokinetic estimates taking place when monks and novices were in the same session.

There are also some noteworthy exceptions to the general finding that conformity is positively related to attraction to the group. Studies by Downing (1958), using Sherif paradigm, and Harper (1961, in Allen, 1965), using the Asch paradigm, both failed to find more conformity in high than low cohesive group conditions. It seems likely that attraction to the group may not always increase conformity if the influence situation is informational in character and visual/perceptual or other physical reality judgements are required. Presumably in such situations the basis of group cohesiveness may be irrelevant to the nature of the person–group discrepancy (Boyanowsky and Allen, 1973). Both friends and strangers may function as reference groups for physical reality testing. If such situations are redefined as normative in character by, for example, explicitly informing subjects that people tend to like each other better when they agree, then one would expect more conformity in high than low attraction conditions (e.g. Walker and Heyns, 1962). Jackson and Saltzstein (1958) found more conformity to high than low attraction groups only if the group accepted the subjects as members and a group response rather than individual responses were reported. We can conclude that people conform more to attractive than less attractive groups providing that they feel part of the group, define the majority's responses as a group norm, perceive the basis of group cohesiveness and the norm as relevant to the task, or believe that conformity is necessary to acceptance by the group.

Because there is evidence that people like similar others and perceive people they like as similar, much of the data concerning group cohesiveness are probably also support for (and in informational studies may actually be mediated by) the person's similarity to the group. Boyanowsky and Allen's (1973) study shows the importance of similarity in the sense of ingroup–outgroup membership. Other studies (e.g. Gerard, 1953; Linde and Patterson, 1964) make the same point. In general, the role of similarity in terms of relevant background attributes has been so taken for granted in, for example, the Asch paradigm, that surprisingly few studies have manipulated it. As Allen and Wilder (1977, p. 188) comment:

> An important feature of the situation is the strong degree of similarity on several dimensions among all the group members; and subjects are aware of the similarity. All of them are (usually) college students of similar age and race; the group is usually composed of same-sex members; all are presumably intelligent and rational individuals; they have had similar educational experiences; often all subjects have come from the same classroom (psychology course); they share a reasonably homogeneous cultural life and so on.

## 2. Consensual validation and social support

One of the most important findings to emerge from the Asch paradigm was the discovery that conformity dropped dramatically from about 33 to 5 per cent if just one social supporter broke the unanimity of the group. Conformity depends upon the perception that the group is consensual (of 'one mind') and the deviant isolated. Conversely, when a deviant minority becomes a consensual subgroup and the majority breaks ranks, so the power of the deviants to change the group increases (Kiesler and Pallak, 1975; Moscovici and Lage, 1976; see Chapter 4). A mass of studies have subsequently confirmed the importance of unanimity versus the disruption of the group consensus in increasing or decreasing conformity (Allen, 1965, 1975; Tanford and Penrod, 1984). The other Asch finding that unanimity is more important than the size of the group (that conformity levels off at around four persons, or five persons, see Gerard et al., 1968) is more evidence that it is the qualitative fact that there is an agreement in the group which is decisive. Gerard *et al.* (1968) and Wilder (1977) suggest that conformity may increase with the number of influence sources where sources are perceived as acting (and agreeing) independently. In this case, group size would function to increase the significance and persuasiveness of consensus.

Allen's (1975) careful review of the social supporter effect shows that the key issues in whether social support will reduce conformity and whether such reduced conformity will generalize have to do with subjects' perceptions that the supporter is genuinely disagreeing with the group (in the same psychological situation as the subjects) and never repudiates such dissent, and that other persons similar to themselves would also resist when under the same circumstances. There are several bases of the social supporter effect and, conversely, of the power of group consensus. A social supporter provides the possibility of an alternative, independent view of reality, gives an example of such independence (Nemeth and Chiles, 1988), and contributes to the 'cognitive restructuring' of the stimulus. At the same time, the supporter reduces the isolation and danger of the deviant and breaks the group consensus, implying both that disagreement is possible and that the group is fallible.

Probably the central factor in the power of group consensus to define reality lies in the causal attributions it attracts (Kelley, 1967). As Allen (1975, p. 19) states:

> The group may attribute deviation to personality characteristics of the individual when he is all alone. But idiosyncrasy of personality is not as plausible an explanation when disagreement with the majority is shared by more than one person. Asch (1951) observed that objective explanations were sought by the group when more than one deviate was present.

By extension, the power of the majority consensus itself to influence may reflect the fact that such agreement can only be plausibly explained in terms of the objective character of the stimulus – their behaviour is perceived to be an appropriate, valid reaction to the real situation. Newtson *et al.* (1973, cited in Allen, 1975; cf. Oakes *et al.*, in press) obtained data consistent with the idea that the larger some deviant subgroup, the more its behaviour is attributed to the situation and the less to dispositional (personality) attributes. Research on minority influence (Chapter 4) is also consistent with this inference.

In sum, the more consensual the group and the more isolated the individual (i.e. the less others agree with the deviant), the greater the power of the group to define reality, induce self-doubt in the deviant as to both her competence and social position, and threaten her with ridicule and rejection for being different.

## 3  Surveillance and public compliance (normative influence)

The idea that conformity to the group will be greater under public than private conditions, when the group can observe and identify any deviation, is central to the process of normative influence. The early studies of Asch (1956) and Deutsch and Gerard (1955) and later studies confirm that this is so (see Allen's, 1965, review). More recent studies in the minority influence tradition also provide evidence that majority influence tends to exert more effect in public than private conditions, whereas minority influence is more effective in private than in public (Maass and Clark, 1984; Moscovici and Lage, 1976). Studies in the impression management tradition also imply that public conditions of responding are preconditions for the presentation of self to achieve desired ends (Tetlock and Manstead, 1985). Both of these traditions will be discussed presently. It will suffice here to note Allen's (1965) point that more conformity in public than private need not always indicate a mere public compliance effect: 'in the more public situation the group may be regarded as more convincing, so that actual private change as well as public compliance could be greater in the public than in private conditions' (p. 146). Brown (1985, p. 27) also points out that studies tend to confound the public versus private character of the conformer's response with the face-to-face presence of the group; these may have independent effects.

## 4  Stimulus ambiguity and subjective uncertainty (informational influence)

The idea that stimulus ambiguity produces uncertainty leading to informational conformity to others was also confirmed early on by Sherif, Asch, and Deutsch and Gerard. Asch (1956) found a definite negative relationship between the clarity of the task and conformity: as the differences in length between stimulus lines decreased, conformity increased. Deutsch and Gerard (1955) found more conformity with the memory than visual series of lines. Festinger (1954) and Allen and Wilder (1977) cite examples of less conformity when more objective feedback of correctness and competence was provided to a subject. Allen (1975) found that an incorrect social supporter in the Asch situation, i.e. somebody who disagrees with the group but who is also incorrect, reduces conformity on visual but not opinion items, whereas a correct social supporter reduces conformity on both. Presumably on the more ambiguous opinion items the subject needs the agreement of the correct supporter to feel sufficiently confident to resist the group. On the unambiguous visual items, even an incorrect supporter is sufficient to make the group look uncertain.

By and large, the evidence suggests that ambiguity leads to uncertainty (e.g. Crutchfield, 1955; Wiener, 1958), and that uncertainty and certainty produce susceptibility and resistance to influence, respectively (e.g. Kelley and Lamb, 1957). The link between ambiguity of the stimulus and uncertainty has been so strongly assumed that variability of responses has been suggested as an operational definition of stimulus ambiguity (Wiener *et al.*, 1957). Assuming reasonably that competence, confidence and success on a task reduce uncertainty, and that task difficulty increases uncertainty, then much other data bearing on these factors also confirm the expected relationship between uncertainty and influence (Allen, 1965).

## 5 Relative subjective validity and relative influence

The dual-process model implies that mutual influence in the group will vary with the relative power of members. This idea is confirmed relatively unambiguously by many studies. Individuals will both tend to exert more influence and to resist influence more than others, the more they are perceived to be able, competent, credible, successful, correct, confident, certain and consensual compared to others (Allen, 1965). These individual differences are likely to represent variations' both in self-assessed informational power and in self-esteem and need for approval. These data, however, do not imply an enduring, consistent, 'conforming personality'. There seems to be no empirical evidence for the latter idea. It does seem likely that there are historical, cultural and subgroup differences in the tendency to conform in specific paradigms and tasks as a function of different social values, social roles and experiences. Such differences, however, do not call into question the universality of influence processes in human society so much as illustrate some of the complexities and subtleties that arise when general processes function in specific real-life social contexts.

## 6  The extremity of the norm

One other finding should briefly be mentioned as it can probably also be explained by the dual-process theory. Influence is related to the degree of discrepancy between the individual and the group (i.e. the extremity of the norm) and the relationship is probably curvilinear. That is, conformity will tend to increase the more the group's position differs from the individual's, but only up to a point, after which the group will tend to be derogated and lose credibility. The optimal point of moderate discrepancy and most influence will vary with the characteristics of the source, target and the task (Bochner and Insko, 1966). At some point, as discrepancy increases, the power of the source will be insufficient to counteract the existing information and established expectations that commit the individual to his or her position, and the individual is likely to find an alternative to conformity to cope with his or her dependence.

## Conclusion

Social conformity research has provided a solid body of knowledge about influence processes, well-tried research methods and an imposing theoretical edifice. The dual-process model commands wide acceptance and fits the main findings remarkably well. With the benefit of hindsight, however, there are some nagging doubts. The supposedly separate processes of normative and informational influence, for example, are rarely distinguishable in the research data. Many variables such as group interdependence, cohesiveness and unanimity seem capable of exerting their effects on conformity through one or both processes. A cohesive group, for instance, is influential both because one wishes the approval of people one likes and because one will perceive such a group as a more trustworthy source of information. It is the nature of science that we should wonder whether there might not be a simpler way of explaining such effects, in terms of one process rather than two. Also, the basic dichotomy between normative and informational processes seems the less reasonable the more closely it is examined. Do not social norms convey information? Isn't information validated at least in party by its congruence with existing social values?

In future chapters, we shall ask whether the variables controlling conformity work in the way that the dependence theory supposes they do. Is the effect of the face-to-face situation purely one of compliance, for example, as implied by the concept of normative influence? Is social reality testing something one turns to only in the absence of physical tests, as implied by the concept of informational influence? These and other questions related to the adequacy of the dependence theory are far from settled. Important challenges to the theory have also come from research on group polarization and innovation, suggesting that it presents a highly restricted view of influence phenomena. We turn to these areas in the next two chapters.

## Suggestions for further reading

Allen, V. L. (1965). Situational factors in conformity. In L. Berkowitz (ed.), *Advances in experimental social psychology*, Vol. 2, pp. 133–75. New York: Academic Press. An excellent review of the empirical literature on social conformity up to the mid-1960s.

Festinger, L. (1954). A theory of social comparison processes. *Human Relations*, 7, 117–40. Summaries of Festinger's theory abound, but the only way to be sure of what he said is to read the original.

Goethals, G. R. and Darley, J. M. (1987). Social comparison theory: Self-evaluation and group life. In B. Mullen and G. R. Goethals (eds), *Theories of group behavior*. New York: Springer-Verlag. An up-to-date, lucid and scholarly review of the theoretical and empirical developments since 1954. An excellent source of references for those who wish to read about social comparison theory and research in more detail.

Latané, B. and Darley, J. M. (1970). *The unresponsive bystander: Why doesn't he help?* New York: Appleton-Century-Crofts. Latané and Darley's illuminating application of social comparison ideas to understanding when people do and don't help.

Levine, J. M. (1989). Reaction to opinion deviance in small groups. In P. B. Paulus (ed.), *The psychology of group influence*, 2nd ed. Hillsdale, N. J.: Lawrence Erlbaum Associates. A useful, careful and contemporary discussion of the literature.

# 3 / GROUP POLARIZATION

## From risky shift to group polarization

In 1961, James Stoner discovered the 'risky shift'. He found an exception to the generally assumed tendency of groups to converge and compromise on the average position of their members. He employed a Choice Dilemma Questionnaire (CDQ) and a procedure for comparing the individual and group responses of subjects that has become standard. A choice dilemma is a fictional situation presented to subjects in which the 'hero' has to choose between more or less risky alternatives. The subjects select the degree of risk they would accept to obtain some desirable outcome. Summing across 12 such CDQ items, Stoner found that on average groups tended to make riskier decisions than individuals. This is what he called the risky shift.

During the 1960s and early 1970s, much work was addressed to replicating and explaining the risky shift. However, at least two CDQ items produced a group shift to caution instead of risk. Thus something more general seemed to be involved than merely a uni-lateral shift towards risk. Moscovici and colleagues (Doise, 1969, 1971; Moscovici and Zavalloni, 1969) clarified the nature of this more general process with their concept of 'group polarization'. They proposed that groups tended to become more extreme in the direction to which they were already tending.

Moscovici and Zavalloni (1969) demonstrated group polarization in two experiments on attitudes to President de Gaulle and attitudes to Americans, instead of on the usual risk-related decision-making materials. Their French secondary school students initially tended to evaluate de Gaulle positively and Americans negatively. Group discussion to consensus produced significant shifts towards more extremely positive and negative attitudes, respectively. Myers and Bishop (1970, 1971) reported group-induced polarization of racial attitudes and similar effects in imaginary decision situations. Fraser *et al.* (1971) also provided clear evidence in favour of the group polarization hypothesis, showing shifts-to-risk on initially risky items and shifts-to-caution on initially cautious items. Gouge and Fraser (1972) extended these results to eight social issues unrelated to risk. Myers and Lamm (1976, p. 603) have since defined the group polarization hypothesis as 'The average postgroup response will tend to be more extreme in the same direction as the average of the pregroup responses.'

Group polarization, then, is the finding that group discussion or some related group manipulation tends to strengthen the prevailing response tendency within a group. The mean response of members tends to become more extreme after group interaction in the same direction as the mean response before interaction. For example, people divided into different groups on the basis of their prevailing attitudes will tend to become more extreme in line with their shared attitudes (Myers and Bishop, 1970), and a sample of people who are already on one side of an issue will become even more extreme in that direction as a function of group discussion.

It is where groups stand with respect to the psychological midpoint of a scale that determines whether they will polarize and the direction of the polarizing shift. For example, after discussing feminism, a group of moderately 'pro' feminists would tend to become, on average, more 'pro' than they had been initially. A group of moderately anti-war people would tend after discussing the issue to become even more anti-war. Polarizing shifts tend to be negligible and unreliable where there is no initially dominant tendency. Key empirical support for this idea is the finding that the direction and magnitude of polarizing shift across items is predicted by the pre-test trend in the sample on those items. There is a very high positive correlation (around +0.9) between the pre-test mean and shift across items (Myers, 1982; Teger and Pruitt, 1967).

What this makes clear is that the so-called risky shift has, in fact, nothing at all to do with risk. We are not dealing with some 'content-bound exception to the normal tendency toward "averaging" in a group', but a general propensity of groups to polarize –

'society not only moderates ideas, it radicalizes them as well' (Moscovici and Zavalloni, 1969, pp. 126 and 134).


## Theoretical significance of group polarization

Reconceptualizing risky shift as group polarization has great theoretical significance. It calls into question the informational dependence model of conformity discussed in Chapter 2. The basic idea of this model – derived from the findings of F. H. Allport, Sherif, Asch and Festinger's theory of uniformity pressures – is that social norms form through a process of *interpersonal averaging or convergence* within groups. The model assumes that people tend to become uncertain of the appropriateness of their opinions under conditions where reality is complex or ambiguous. This uncertainty produces a need for information from others. People tend to be persuaded by others and conform to the behaviour of others to the degree that others' responses are perceived to provide information about reality. It is supposed in the group situation, therefore, that where people are uncertain and discussing some issue, they will tend to exchange the information at their disposal. As each individual exchanges his or her private stock of information with each other individual, they will each tend in part to be persuaded by the others and in part to persuade others. Thus, on balance, people will tend to move towards each other and will end up at the average of their initial individual views. This agreed position produced by interpersonal averaging is assumed to be the group norm, the position the group defines as appropriate and correct in relation to the issue. This theory of norm formation is widely accepted and there is good evidence to support the idea that people do converge under certain conditions. Polarization, however, plainly contradicts it. Under some conditions, people do not converge on their pre-test mean, but converge on a more extreme position.

There is also a metatheoretical issue. The interpersonal averaging theory is individualistic (Turner and Oakes, 1986). It implies that social influence is simply a 'change in individuals induced by individuals' (Kiesler and Kiesler, 1969, p. 26), i.e. that nothing qualitatively different or new emerges from group interaction and that the group norm is nothing more than the sum or (in this case) average of the individual properties of members. Group polarization raises the classic problem of the relationship of the individual to the social group. Is group psychology reducible to the psychology of the individual or is there something special, distinctive, irreducible about group psychology? It seems to show that something special does happen in the group, that groups produce emergent normative tendencies that are not reducible to an aggregation of individuals' responses as they exist in isolation. A phenomenon that seems directly at odds with theoretical tradition and defies an elegant, satisfactory explanation is of great interest to science, for it must call into question established ways of thinking.

Under what conditions do groups polarize and under what conditions do they converge on their pre-test mean and why? These become the new theoretical issues. We have a general empirical answer to the former question – where there is a pre-test tendency favouring one pole of the response dimension or not – but what does this represent in terms of the determining mechanism?

## Some empirical details

Before looking at theories of group polarization, it is useful to clarify some points of detail. The standard group polarization experiment comprises three stages:

1 A *pre-test* in which group members' initial individual views on an issue are measured (producing a *pre-test group mean*, i.e. the average of members' initial views).
2 A group discussion to *consensus* (in which subjects are instructed to reach a unanimous group agreement).
3 A *post-test* in which members' individual views are re-recorded (producing the *post-test group mean*, i.e. the average of members' views after discussion).

The precise finding where polarization has taken place is that the consensus and post-test mean tend to be more extreme than the pre-test mean but in the same direction (i.e. towards the pole of the attitude scale that is closer to the pre-test mean). It is this polarizing shift from pre-test to post-test mean (and consensus) that poses the explanatory problem for theorists of social influence.

Although polarization involves extremitization, it is not the same thing. Polarization implies a shift in the direction of the prevailing tendency, whereas extremitization implies a shift in any direction. Also, polarization is an average change in the group. Not all individuals may polarize in a polarizing group. In fact, some may become more moderate (Fraser *et al.*, 1971).

Myers and Lamm (1976) argue that polarization is purely a sample and not a 'group' effect, i.e. it is the pre-test mean of a *sample of groups* on an item which predicts shift. The sample effect tells us what the average group does but not necessarily that each group tends to follow its own pre-test mean. The positive correlation between the pre-test mean and shift across items does not necessarily imply such a correlation within items across individual groups. This issue is not settled. Fraser *et al.* (1971), for example, report data that do suggest a group effect.

Finally, polarization seems to be an extremely robust and general phenomenon. A mass of studies (Lamm and Myers, 1978; Myers, 1982) show that it can be obtained across a range of issues and response dimensions and in naturalistic and field settings as well as laboratory contexts. Groups may become riskier in making decisions about gambling, more extreme in their social and political attitudes, or more polarized in their judgements about individuals' physical attractiveness. They even polarize in ambiguous factual judgements (e.g. 'How far is the Dead Sea below sea level?'). The one exception that has been mooted is that of established groups. Fraser and Foster (1984) suggest that possibly the phenomenon has to do with the formation of group norms rather than the application of established ones. Nevertheless, it does seem that groups can polarize on any response dimension at all.

## Theories of polarization

There are several classes of theory. Some were specifically addressesd to the risky shift (such as the idea that people become less responsible for their actions in group contexts) and so have been discarded as too limited to cope with polarization. Some have been rejected on empirical grounds. There are some that still seem promising but have been little developed (e.g. leadership theories). Of the theories that currently seem viable and are attracting attention, there are three major classes: social comparison/value theory (which I shall abbreviate to 'value theory'), informational influence/persuasive arguments theory and social conformity theory. There are variants of each class.

The distinction between conformity theory and the others can be confusing, as all theories make some use of processes that have been previously discussed in the conformity chapter and, as already pointed out, one of the significant things about polarization is that it tends to contradict a simple conformity model. The difference is that the value and persuasive arguments theories tend to assume that the group norm is the average position and try to explain why groups polarize beyond the norm, whereas conformity theory explains polarization by showing that it represents conformity to a norm that is extremitized. In other words, the former focus on explaining shift beyond the norm, whereas the latter focuses on explaining why the norm is displaced beyond the pre-test mean. For this reason, conformity theory (in this context) does not adopt an averaging model of conformity, but, for example, an 'Asch' model of conformity to a majority (see Chapter 1) or some other notion.

Another point of confusion is that social comparison and informational influence are opposed to each other, whereas in the conformity literature they are closely related. Readers should pay attention to the substantive ideas and pay little attention to labels for the moment. In concluding, I shall try to relate the theories to the conformity field.

### Social comparison/value theory

Brown (1965) explained risky shift by assuming that a 'cultural value for risk' (in the USA) became salient in discussion, that people compared in terms of this value and, finding that they embodied less of it compared to others than they had supposed, shifted to risk. This was the origin of value theory. Once cautious shifts and then group polarization came along, the model was modified from a one-value (the value for risk) to a general-value theory.

There are now several different versions of the theory. Levinger and Schneider (1969) emphasize 'pluralistic ignorance': that people initially underestimate the average position of other group members, compromise at the pre-test between their ideal position on some issue and their (under-) estimate of the group norm, and are allowed to shift closer to their real position by exposure to the true group norm in discussion. Pruitt (1971a, b) suggests that comparison with extremists in the group 'releases' people to shift to valued positions.

Myers and Lamm (Myers, 1982) emphasize the role of social differentiation and intragroup competition in group interaction. They hypothesize that people are motivated to be positively different from others and shift competitively towards more extreme positions to achieve the appropriate valued difference from others.

Following Festinger (1954), Jellison and Riskind (1970) propose that people compete to be better than others on dimensions related to the social comparison of abilities and that group decision-making is perceived to correlate with valued abilities. Jellison and Arkin (1977) suggest that people try to look better than others on ability-related attributes in order to be rewarded by the group (an impression-management explanation – see Chapter 5). Baron *et al.* (1975, cited in Lamm and Myers, 1978) also creatively adapt Festinger's social comparison theory. They argue that social comparison on dimensions unrelated to values, or *accuracy evaluation*, will produce the averaging effect, but that comparison on dimensions related to values, or *rank-order evaluation*, leads to polarization. In rank-order evaluation, one is concerned with being better, i.e. more valued, than others, as in Festinger's model of ability comparison. With accuracy evaluation one wants to be right, correct in some judgement, as in Festinger's model of opinion validation. However, they propose that it is the context of evaluation (rank-order versus accuracy) that predicts polarization or averaging, rather than whether group discussion is overtly concerned with opinions or abilities. Even the comparison of factual judgements can sometimes take place on valued attributes, leading to rank-order evaluation (Baron and Roper, 1976).

Sanders and Baron (1977, p. 304) summarize value theory as follows:

> . . . people often value opinions more extreme than those they personally espouse. People fail to adopt these ideal (extreme) positions as their own due to fear of being labeled an extremist or deviate. . . . However, during a group discussion, in which members may compare their positions, relatively moderate members may realize that relatively extreme members hold opinions closer to their most admired position than they themselves do. This realization either 'releases' the moderate members from their fear of appearing extreme, or motivates moderates to 'compete' with the extreme members to see who can come closest to espousing the most admired position. In either case, the moderates are motivated to adopt more extreme positions, while there is no corresponding pressure on extreme members to moderate their opinions (although, of

course, simple conformity pressure may lead to some small amount of moderation by extreme members). The net result is an overall polarization of opinions.

In sum, value theory proposes that (1) people are shifting to some socially approved, valued pole; (2) they are seeking to be positively different from their fellows; (3) the process is one of comparison; (4) the relative positions of others are underestimated at the pre-test; and (5) people are motivated to gain a positive evaluation of themselves and to look good to others. People compare themselves with others in the group in terms of the salient value and shift to maintain and enhance their positive distinctiveness from others. What does the research show? The picture is mixed.

## Research on social comparison/value theory

### 1 The foundational assumption

Lamm and Myers (1978, p. 176) point out that there is much evidence for what they call the 'foundational assumption' of value theory that 'people are motivated to see and present themselves as better embodiments of socially desired abilities, traits, and attitudes than are most other members of their groups.' For example, people tend to perceive themselves as superior to the average member of their group on relevant attributes (Codol, 1975). Most businessmen see themselves as more ethical than the average businessman. Most people think that they are less prejudiced than others and so on. Much evidence in social psychology suggests that people evaluate themselves positively and are motivated to maintain a positive self-evaluation. Self-evaluation being comparative, we typically evaluate ourselves as at least better than average.

### 2 Abstract cultural values

There is little evidence that people are comparing in terms of some *abstract* cultural value, i.e. one that has any kind of tangible existence outside of the group context (Wetherell, 1983). The value concept has gradually been reduced to the idea that the response dimension in terms of which polarization takes place is value-laden, that the group prefers one pole to the other, as indicated by the pre-test trend. Although it is reasonable to suppose that the response dimension is associated with value, this is problematic as an explanation of polarization or as a demonstration of the causal role of values. To say that the group is shifting in the valued direction, has become operationally the same as saying that it is shifting in line with the pre-test trend. Plainly, then, the former idea has little use as an explanation of the latter.

Baron and Roper (1976), however, have shown a causal link between an imposed social value and polarization. They experimentally associated perceptual judgements in the autokinetic paradigm with social value by defining larger estimates of movement as indicating more intelligence. This manipulation produced polarization (towards larger estimates) in a setting where convergence is normally the rule.

Other studies, on the other hand, have found polarization in factual judgements that seem unrelated to cultural values. Vidmar (1974) obtained polarization in judgements of category width – where the subjects did not apparently see broad or narrow width judgements as any more admirable. Wetherell (1987) reports a study that manipulated the context of evaluation in Baron et al.'s (1975) sense and found that obscure factual judgements associated with accuracy evaluation produced as much polarization as those associated with rank-order evaluation.

If people are shifting towards more valued positions (which seems a plausible assumption), it is not proven that abstract cultural values are the causal factor in this shift. In factual judgements, for example, the valued response is the one perceived as correct, competent and accurate, but it makes little sense to suppose that there is some abstract social value that defines which particular response that is. It also seems possible that polarization does take place in accuracy contexts. A conceptual problem for Baron et al. here is that surely, in any case, accuracy itself is valued. One wants to be more accurate rather than less, and more accurate than others, just as one wants to be more intelligent.

Value theory suggests that subjects can deviate from the group norm and still be valued because there are cultural values external to the group shared by group members. This made sense when one could point to a specific cultural value-for-risk to explain the risky shift. As soon as cautious shifts made their appearance, however, and it seemed that cultures could have opposing values in the same domain applied in varying situations, the concept of value became *post hoc.* If the existence of a cultural value is inferred from the direction of shift, then the concept is explanatorily circular. It is a redescription of the fact that, and the direction in which, groups shift but not an explanation of *why* they shift. It simply restates that in specific situations group members value positions more extreme than their average choice. One now has to explain why this is so and why people adopt which values in which situation.

## 3 Fake norm studies

The point that there is little evidence that people are shifting to an abstract value external to the group is reinforced by the reliable finding that people confronted by a manipulated group norm – pro or anti the supposed cultural value – shift towards the fake norm. Most studies suggest that people shift to the norm to the same extent, whether or not it is pro or anti the cultural value (Baron *et al.*, 1971; Blascovich and Ginsburg, 1974; Cecil *et al.*, 1970; Clark and Crockett, 1971; Roberts and Castore, 1972; St. Jean and Percival, 1974). Baron *et al.* (1973) found that people will shift more in the valued direction, but only on the private post-test, where, by definition, conformity pressure is reduced.

The fake norm studies strongly suggest that the group norm and not abstract cultural values define the valued direction in the group context. They question the basic idea of value theory that subjects are compromising between conformity to the group norm and wanting to be more distinctive from others in the valued direction (as inferred from the pre-test trend). It is not problematic for the theory that subjects are influenced by a fake norm, but it is problematic that they are not less influenced by the norm when it conflicts with the supposedly valued direction.

## 4 Own, average other and ideal responses

Better, but again partial, evidence for value theory comes from subjects' estimates of others' responses. There is evidence from risky shift research that if subjects estimate the positions of the 'average peer' and those they 'admire most' on CDQ items before group discussion, then their own position is more extreme in a valued direction than the estimated average response, but less extreme than the most admired, ideal response (Myers and Lamm, 1976). This is what one would expect from the theory. However, the effect is only found where the self is rated first. Sanders and Baron (1977) suggest that this is compatible with value theory, as rating self first makes the later ratings implicitly comparative with self. Subjects assume that others also rate their ideal response as more extreme than their own. It is true, therefore, that subjects in group discussion would tend to discover that they are not as extreme as they think compared to others and do value even more extreme positions than their own. Subjects also do perceive other persons who have actually responded more extremely than themselves (in the most valued, ideal direction) as more socially desirable than persons who have not (Myers and Lamm, 1976).

Perceived differences between one's own and one's ideal position (self-ideal discrepancies) seem to predict the degree of shift (Myers and Lamm, 1976). Composing groups on the basis of self-ideal discrepancies led groups whose members perceived themselves as further from their ideal to shift more towards the ideal than groups whose members saw themselves as closer.

More important for value theory are the effects of self–other discrepancies. It is these that are supposed to motivate shift. People who most want to be positively distinctive presumably have the largest self–other discrepancies and suffer the most disconfirmation of their supposed positive distinctiveness in the group. It is the shift motivated by such disconfirmation that is at the heart of the theory. Unfortunately, such discrepancies do not predict shift; they appear unrelated to the degree of polarization in the group.

What is the real picture here? Is it more or less extreme members in the group who are shifting? The data show that the net result of shift is convergence (e.g. Singleton, 1979). It is the most extreme persons who tend to become more moderate and the least extreme who shift the most. What matters is not the disconfirmation of one's expectations of being distinctive, but one's actual position relative to others. One shifts not to maintain distinctiveness but to become closer to others. This is a conformity pattern, not a social differentiation pattern. Singleton (1979) argues convincingly that shift is produced mainly by the movement of deviants towards the dominant norm of the group, against their personally held values (as inferred from their pre-test responses). Thus the shift does not represent an intensification of the salient values in the situation as suggested by value theory, but arises from a *change and reversal of the initial values of deviants*.

## 5 Mere exposure versus the exchange of persuasive arguments

The main evidence for value theory is that simply being exposed to others' positions – social comparison information without group discussion (the exchange of persuasive arguments) – is sufficient for polarization. It makes sense to discuss this material in conjunction with studies supporting persuasive arguments theory. The latter argues that shift is caused by the exchange of persuasive arguments in group discussion. Relevant arguments are persuasive when perceived as novel (original) and valid (Burnstein, 1982). Moreover, persuasive arguments theory suggests that influence is related purely to the informational content of discussion (understood as the direction, pro or anti an issue, validity, originality and relevance of exchanged arguments) and has nothing to do with the position of the source of the information. The debate between value and persuasive arguments theories has come to be a debate over the importance of positions versus arguments, comparison versus information, the comparison of members' positions on an issue without group discussion versus the exchange of information/arguments without knowledge of others' positions. Both theories have come to suggest that the group interaction process itself is not important for polarization. What is important for one is the comparative positions of members inferred from group interaction and, for the other, the information provided by the group, as merely one medium among others for the effective dissemination of persuasive arguments. Persuasive arguments theory is explicit that, for the purposes of obtaining polarization, merely reading arguments, for example, should be able to substitute for group discussion (Vinokur and Burnstein, 1974).

Readers may feel that the distinction between social comparison and informational influence is odd and forced. Doesn't knowing someone's position on an issue clarify the meaning and affect the perceived validity of their arguments? Doesn't one decide where someone stands on an issue on the basis of the kinds of arguments they propose? The evidence, too, questions such a sharp dichotomy. Recently, some theorists have argued for a reintegration of social comparison and informational processes (Isenberg, 1986; Myers and Lamm, 1976; Sanders and Baron, 1977; Turner, 1985; Turner and Oakes, 1986, 1989; Wetherell, 1987; Witte, 1987), but this is to run ahead of the story.

A number of early studies supported the idea that exposure to others' positions without group discussion or interaction produced polarization, but the effect was weak. Myers (1982) suggested that the pre-test had the effect of making subjects feel committed to their initial responses and so reduced subsequent shifts. He eliminated the pre-test in several studies and demonstrated mere exposure effects. The implication is that what matters is not the exchange of information in discussion, but simply the possibility of comparing one's own choice with the choices of others.

For example, Myers et al. (1974) had subjects respond to three risky CDQ items without a pre-test commitment. They were merely informed of the distribution of responses of 40 subjects in a control condition. The subjects, therefore, simply compared their own implicit position with the responses of control subjects without group interaction and discussion. The result was significant shift to risk among experimental subjects (comparing their post-test choices with the observed pre-test choices of the control subjects). The subjects moved significantly beyond the control group norm.

Burnstein and Vinokur (1977; Burnstein, 1982), arguing for persuasive arguments theory, have attacked the mere exposure idea in several ways. They claimed that (a) information without social comparison is sufficient for polarization, (b) information is more important than social comparison, and (c) social comparison only leads to shift to the extent that it stimulates thinking about arguments. In support of (a), Burnstein and Vinokur (1973) had subjects arguing against their own positions and still found shift. To test (b), Burnstein et al. (1973) manipulated 25 arguments and five positions independently and found an effect of arguments but not positions. For (c), Burnstein and Vinokur (1975, cited in Burnstein and Vinokur, 1977) showed in a distraction experiment that only people allowed to think about arguments in response to comparison shifted.

Burnstein and Vinokur are suggesting that social comparison is neither necessary nor theoretically sufficient for polarization. Their response to the mere exposure effect is to argue that exposure is not 'mere', but, in fact, functions to stimulate cognitive activity and the generation and mental rehearsal of persuasive arguments. They are arguing that persuasive arguments theory is exclusively correct.

However, several counterarguments can be made. Sanders and Baron (1977) point out with respect to (a) that positions, i.e. comparison information, can be inferred from arguments, and, on the basis of a reanalysis of Burnstein and Vinokur's (1973) data, suggest they probably were. They note with respect to (b) that the comparison information provided in Burnstein *et al.*'s (1973) study was haphazard and did not provide information about the group consensus (norm). The information presented about people's positions lacked coherence and meaning. St. Jean and Percival (1974) manipulated exposure to arguments and information about group consensus independently. They found no effect for arguments but an effect for comparative positions forming a group consensus. This is one of the fake norm studies and it argues clearly for the importance of social comparison information. It is of little comfort to value theory, however, because, like the other fake norm studies, it points to the importance of the normative position of the group. It suggests a conformity rather than a social differentiation process.

There are three responses to (c), i.e. the claim that social comparison only leads to shifts when it stimulates thinking about persuasive arguments. First, Sanders and Baron (1977) suggest that social comparison also depends upon cognitive activity and so distraction should interfere with this process as well as the generation of persuasive arguments. Secondly, mere exposure effects have been demonstrated in 'argument-poor' settings where the concept of rational persuasion based on informed argument seems meaningless, e.g. in judgements of obscure factual issues, ratings of people's physical attractiveness, or gambling on matters of pure chance (Baron and Roper, 1976; Blascovich *et al.*, 1975; Isenberg, 1986; Myers, 1982; Vidmar, 1974).

For example, Blascovich *et al.* (1975) formed three experimental conditions for playing blackjack: an individual condition, a group-without-discussion condition and a group-with-discussion condition. Their subjects played 20 hands of blackjack alone to establish a baseline, and then played another 20 hands in their experimental condition. In the group-without-discussion condition, the subjects heard each others' bets but did not discuss them. In the group-with-discussion condition, the subjects placed collective bets after trying to reach a consensus. The size of the bets did not increase (the measure of risky shift) from the first to the second series of 20 hands in the individual condition, but it did in both group conditions. However, polarization was not significantly greater in the with-discussion than without-discussion group conditions. Group discussion did not seem to add anything to mere comparison with others' bets.

Burnstein and Vinokur (1977) have attempted to argue that even in such settings persuasive argumentation is taking place. For example, they suggest that in Baron and Roper's (1976) autokinetic study, people are saying to themselves: '"I am intelligent, intelligent people make large estimates, therefore . . ." or "Intelligent people tend to be correct, I want to be correct, therefore . . ."' (p. 327). Such 'persuasive arguments', however, seem nothing more than a restatement of the salient social values in the situation and of a person's motivation to present themselves in terms of them. If a persuasive argument can be a subject's statement to self of a need to present oneself in terms of a social value, then 'information' can be information about others' comparative positions and social values, and persuasive arguments theory ceases to be a distinctive viewpoint.

This is not an unreasonable idea. Singleton (1979) makes the cogent point that the crucial information exchanged in discussion may be information about norms and values; it may be the appeals to, indications of and references to norms and values contained in arguments that make them persuasive and informative. For Festinger (1950, 1954), social comparison provides information through the consensual validation of responses; social comparison validates information. Why shouldn't information be about social comparative relationships and related norms and values? Burnstein and Vinokur themselves operationalize the validity of persuasive arguments in terms of social comparison with others. Vinokur and Burnstein (1978a, cited in Burnstein, 1982), for example, define validity in terms of judges' ratings of 'the extent to which the argument is true and accepted as such by most people' on a scale from 'Definitely untrue, completely invalid and implausible, nearly everyone would reject it as untrue' to 'Definitely true, completely valid and plausible, nearly everyone would accept it as true' (p. 116). A persuasive argument is thus one with which most people would agree. This revision of the idea of the informational content of persuasive arguments leads away from persuasive arguments theory and back to a more classical link between social reality testing and informational influence.

The third response of social comparison theorists to (c) is to show, as have Cotton and Baron (1980), that social comparison information mediates shifts even under conditions where it does not lead to the generation of persuasive arguments and that Burnstein and Vinokur's (1975) data may have been artifactual. Cotton and Baron also refute Jellison and Arkin's (1977) hypothesis that polarization reflects impression management and the public presentation of self.

There for the moment the issue rests. In line with value theory, mere exposure does seem sufficient for polarization and it has not been shown compellingly that the effect is mediated by the implicit generation of persuasive arguments. Some form of social comparison, such as that implicit in the perceived validity of persuasive arguments, may even be necessary.

## 6 Similarity between group members

The last issue, little pursued, has to do with the effects of similarity between group members on polarization. Does similarity increase polarization, as would be expected by value theory (as it will increase social comparison)? Apparently, it does (e.g. Goethals and Zanna, 1979). However, the effect of similarity between group members is consistent with either value or conformity theory. It does not distinctively confirm value theory, because for reasons detailed in Chapter 2, similarity can also be expected to increase conformity to group norms.

## Social comparison considered

In sum, there is good evidence that people shift to socially desirable, valued positions, but little evidence that this reflects the causal impact of abstract cultural values as opposed to a more group-based definition of value, i.e. group norms. Shift is a function of people moving towards agreement and their most admired position. There is no evidence of intragroup differentiation. Social comparison, with or without thinking about persuasive arguments, is sufficient for shift and some kind of social comparison is probably necessary for shift if one assumes that the perceived validity of information is related to social comparison (as in Burnstein, 1982, p. 116).

It is striking how little attention has been paid to group belongingness variables such as social interdependence, similarity and group cohesiveness. The reason is presumably because, although conformity pressures are accepted, it is taken for granted that they must predict convergence on the mean and therefore cannot in principle explain polarization. Something extra is needed, that something being the value significance of attributes such as abilities, which introduce a competitive element into comparison. The social comparison of opinions, it is assumed, only predicts pressures towards uniformity.

The difficulty for value theory is that polarization does occur with opinions and also where factual accuracy is important. All the evidence fits the social comparison of opinions model better than that of abilities in that there is evidence for uniformity pressures but not for competitive processes. Complicating matters theoretically is the fact that holding an accurate opinion would also seem to be associated with value. To be correct, competent, right, is to conform to a social norm and attract approval (see Chapter 1). The outcome of uniformity pressures with respect to factual opinions is a social value – just as much as with subjective preferences – that is, a group-based norm that specifies the appropriate, desirable opinion that members *ought* to hold. Three issues present themselves. If only uniformity pressures are at work, why does polarization occur? If polarization is due to the comparison of valued attributes, why does it occur with opinions in accuracy contexts? If the comparison of opinions is also value-laden (as I have just argued), why do we sometimes find convergence on the mean? The nice idea of Baron *et al.* (1975) that accuracy evaluation leads to convergence and rank-order evaluation leads to competitive differentiation does not quite work. What is different about situations that produce convergence on the mean and those that produce polarization and how can conformity lead to both? These are the issues that emerge as central.

## Informational influence/persuasive arguments theory

Some theories propose that polarization derives from informational influence in line with the balance of persuasive material that becomes available in discussion. The most important representative of this class is the persuasive arguments theory of Burnstein and Vinokur.

Their theory states that there is a 'cultural pool' of persuasive arguments, pro and anti an issue, that is sampled by experimental subjects and reflected in the sample pre-test trend. Thus the more the pre-test trend is 'pro', the more it is assumed that the balance of persuasive arguments in the pool is 'pro'. These arguments are produced and exchanged in discussion and people shift in line with · the persuasive arguments that are novel to them. The group polarizes in the direction of the balance of arguments (towards the dominant pole, say X rather than Y) predicted by the pre-test trend, because the dominant pole produces more and better arguments than the non-dominant pole (the balance, both quantitative and qualitative, favours $X$) and these also tend to be more novel.

Vinokur and Burnstein (1974) state explicitly that, although the balance of arguments in the pool predicts the pre-test trend and the balance raised in discussion, *this alone is insufficient* to produce polarization. The crucial factor is that the persuasive arguments generated in discussion favouring $X$ over $Y$ should be more *novel*. It is strongly implied that, in general, persuasive arguments favouring the dominant pole will tend to be more novel than those favouring the non-dominant pole, but it is never explicitly explained why this should be so. Burnstein and Vinokur (1977, p. 317) illustrate the crucial role of novelty in their analysis with the following example:

> Consider a choice in which the culturally given pool contains six pro-X arguments, a, b, c, d, e and f, and three pro-Y arguments, l, m, and n. If three equally pro-X individuals discuss the issue, one of several distinct outcomes would be predicted, *depending on the distribution of arguments among members*. Say all three of our discussants had thought of the same arguments. In this case, discussion would produce no change in their attitudes towards X. On the other hand, if a, b, and m had come to mind in one; c, d, and m in the second; and e, f, and m in the third (i.e., if each has different pro-X arguments, but the same pro-Y arguments), then the discussion would produce marked polarization towards X. Finally, polarization towards Y would be predicted if one member had generated a, b, and l, another a, b, and m, and the third a, b, and n (i.e., if each had initially thought of the same pro-X but different pro-Y arguments). Normally, individual argument samples are representative of the larger pool. Therefore, average prediscussion preferences can be estimated from the balance of pro-X and pro-Y arguments in the pool. Post-discussion preferences can also be predicted if, in addition, we know the degree of overlap among individual samples.

Thus, if novelty were to favour the non-dominant pole, then depolar-ization (shift away from the pre-test trend) would take place.

What exactly are persuasive arguments? They are characterized by direction (pro or anti), validity, novelty and relevance. The usage adopted here is that a persuasive argument is a valid argument that may or may not be novel. Such arguments have been characterized as indicating the informational content of discussion (Myers and

Lamm, 1976), and this is correct in the sense that they are perceived to provide 'evidence about reality' (Chapter 2). It is not correct and is misleading in terms of the actual substantive content of group discussion. Novelty, relevance, validity and even to a degree the direction (see Eiser and van der Pligt, 1984) of arguments are psychological properties of information as perceived and judged by people. They are value judgements. We might say of arguments with which we disagree that they are 'irrelevant', 'wrong' and 'unoriginal', that 'we have heard it all before'. We might discount and reject them, saying 'I do not find them compelling, persuasive or believe that they say anything new', etc. Similarly, arguments for views we accept might be judged as 'cogent', 'sound', 'highly relevant', 'logical', etc. Of course, people are sometimes influenced to change their minds (that's what this book is about), but the point is that we can describe a position as original, valid and relevant without providing any information about what the position actually is. We can manipulate whether arguments are pro or con risk, and this certainly gives us some idea as to what kind of discussion is taking place, but this is primarily a manipulation of people's judgements of the arguments and only secondarily of their intrinsic informational content.

Burnstein and Vinokur, in fact, operationalize these properties in terms of people's perceptions and value judgements, not the objective content of persuasive arguments. Burnstein (1982) has theorized about the properties of validity and novelty in information-processing terms, but his suggestions are speculative and do not relate directly to the research operationalizations. In this context, then, informational influence indicates the exchange of arguments that induce shifts because of these judged properties. It is important to bear this in mind because at times the impression is created that these properties are somehow intrinsic to the arguments (that they are inherently rational, logical, sound, etc.). Vinokur and Burnstein (1974, p. 306), for example, cite with approval a statement of Thorndike's to the effect that:

> for certain types of question at least, there is a certain inherent logic and plausibility in the right choice, which makes it more possible to build up a good argument on that side. Thus in a mathematical problem, as an extreme example, one might not be able to achieve a solution himself, but might have no hesitation in recognizing the correctness of one that was demonstrated to him.

## Research on persuasive arguments theory

### 1 Exposure to persuasive material

There is good general evidence that exposure to or exchange of persuasive material affects shifts (e.g. Ebbesen and Bowers, 1974; Kaplan and Miller, 1977; for reviews, see Isenberg, 1986; Lamm and Myers, 1978). Indeed, given the operationalization and definition of persuasive arguments discussed above, it would be extraordinary if this were not so. Vinokur and Burnstein (1978a) have shown that one shifts towards novel, valid arguments, but is uninfluenced by material that is either valid but not new or novel but invalid. Other studies support the importance of novelty, but some caution is needed here. Might not the repetition of persuasive arguments, i.e. the presentation of non-novel persuasive arguments, sometimes have an effect? This seems very possible (Anderson and Graesser, 1976; Kaplan, 1977; Lamm and Myers, 1978). An impact of the repetition of persuasive arguments across people is more consistent with the process of consensual validation discussed in Chapter 2 than a purely informational process. Data on the importance of social consensus (see Chapter 2) and 'consistency' (see Chapter 4) indicate two major traditions pointing to the influence of repetition of material across and within individuals. These effects imply that under some conditions shared and repeated responses can probably acquire persuasive power by virtue of their sharedness and repetition.

It is also important to note that information that goes against the group norm ceases to be persuasive. St. Jean and Percival's (1974) study has already been noted. Turner et al. (1988, 1989) cite several studies showing that influence varies with the ingroup versus outgroup source of the message and not simply with the information it contains. For example, people shift more towards similar and ingroup others than different and outgroup others on exactly the same items and when presented with exactly the same information (Turner et al., 1988). The effects of similarity and group cohesiveness were shown in Chapter 2. It is worth recalling that the social relationship between the source and target of influence and the relationship of information to the shared norms of the group are basic to the process of social influence. These are aspects of a fundamental idea – which seems to be missing from persuasive arguments theory – that the subjective validity of information that cannot be physically tested is socially tested.

## 2  Information exchange versus social comparison

There are studies attempting to show that information exchange and not social comparison is necessary and sufficient for polarization. These have been discussed. The conclusion was that information exchange does not seem necessary. It does appear to be sufficient, but this may be because persuasive arguments imply social comparison or some other process. If a valid argument is one with which most people are perceived to agree, then social comparison information is implied. Perhaps information is about norms, and persuasive arguments are those judged to be pro-normative. It may not be meaningful to equate the informational validity of material with its substantive informational content.

## 3  Correlational relationships implied by persuasive arguments theory

Other studies show the correlational relationships implied by the theory: that the balance of persuasive arguments in a sample predicts the pre-test trend; that more and better arguments favour the dominant pole (Vinokur and Burnstein, 1974); that the pre-test trend predicts the balance of arguments raised in, and the trend of, discussion (Myers and Lamm, 1976); and that the trend of discussion predicts the degree of shift (see also Isenberg, 1986). Vinokur and Burnstein (1974) also report that subjects passively exposed to a sample of arguments from the 'cultural pool', i.e. a sample generated by other subjects responding to the same items, reproduce the shifts displayed on those items in group discussion. However, no control group of subjects responding to the items without exposure to previously generated arguments was included in this study.

These are important correlations suggesting that the exchange of arguments in discussion is correlated in some way with shift. The power of the pre-test mean to predict shift is captured almost entirely by the content of discussion, according to Myers and Lamm (1976). This is too optimistic. The statement is fine given that we remember (a) that the obtained relationships are correlational and not causal and (b) that the content is not substantive information but the exchange of value judgements. It would be most surprising if a group spent its time arguing against the direction in which it subsequently moved. For example, there is evidence that the expression of arguments in public discussion is more polarized than in private (Lamm and Myers, 1978). It may be that social influence processes work to ensure that the balance of arguments in discussion reflects the emerging consensus rather than vice versa. Similarly, the fact that subjects generate more arguments in line with the dominant pole and rate them as more persuasive, may simply reflect the fact that they are already committed to the dominant pole. Surely arguments may be perceived as more persuasive because they are congruent with the side to which subjects are naturally tending rather than vice versa? The opposite causal direction to persuasive arguments theory, from shift to rated balance of arguments rather than from arguments to shift, seems just as plausible here, if not more so. One naturally tends to rate arguments whose implications one agrees with as better than those whose implications one rejects.

Vinokur and Burnstein (1974) have found that persuasive arguments are partially diffused in a sample and have tried to show that they can predict shift across items by taking into account the relative number and persuasiveness of $X$ and $Y$ arguments in the sampled pool (the balance) and their likely novelty in groups of five persons (see also Bishop and Myers, 1974). In effect, they tried to predict shift from a mathematical model that derived shift from the relative balance and impact of $X$ and $Y$ arguments in the pool, defining impact in terms of the mean persuasiveness and degree of novelty of arguments. The model did successfully predict shift, but so did a simple persuasion model (one that simply looks at the balance of $X$ and $Y$ arguments in the pool). Taking the estimated novelty of $X$ and $Y$ arguments into account did not add predictive power to the simple persuasion model. They were forced to conclude that the findings 'do not favour the partially shared information model over a simple persuasion model' (Vinokur and Bernstein, 1974, p. 314). Both models were very good. The difficulty is that Vinokur and Burn-stein's model is largely confounded mathematically with the simple persuasion model (as they acknowledge), and so in this study not only were the predictions of the two models almost identical, but in practice the success of their model may actually result from this confounding.

The problem is also theoretical. The simple persuasion model can predict polarization, but it cannot explain it. Group polarization is of interest precisely because it contradicts such a model. The same might also be true of the partially shared (novel) arguments model, i.e. persuasive arguments theory. It might be argued that it can predict, because it is tapping into relationships correlated with the causal process, but that it might not actually be able to explain. Here we are entering into an important but neglected theoretical issue. What seems to be missing from these data is any direct evidence for a heuristic mechanism that would explain why groups polarize rather than simply converge upon the pre-test mean, that would explain why and how the balance of arguments in the pool translates into $X$ arguments being more novel on average than $Y$ arguments in the sample. Before elaborating this point, other difficulties should be noted.

## 4 Effects of group discussion

Active discussion of material produces more polarization than passive receipt of arguments (Myers and Lamm, 1976). The implication is that the group is not simply a passive medium for the diffusion of information, as Vinokur and Burnstein (1974) suggest. The finding can be explained in terms of socially motivated cognitive processing and rehearsal of material, but it also fits the ideas of conformity theories about group belongingness and 'normative commitment' (Moscovici and Zavalloni, 1969). The group context does play a role.

## 5 Effects of group membership

Other data imply more directly the importance of group membership. The mode of interaction, similarity and cohesiveness of group members and the salience of their social identity have all been found to affect shift (Wetherell, 1987). Doise (1969), Reid (1983) and Skinner and Stephenson (1981), for example, found that subjects tended to adopt more extreme positions in line with, and relevant to, their ingroup identity after comparison with an outgroup. Conflicting data (Reid and Sumiga, 1984; Vinokur and Burnstein, 1978b) that intergroup comparison (or comparison between what may be subgroups) can produce intergroup convergence (or the depolarization of subgroups), is plausibly explained in terms of the salience of a superordinate group identity. It seems likely that the degree of salience of the subgroup boundaries will determine whether divided subgroups converge towards each other (as one group seeking consensus) or polarize away from each other (Wetherell, 1987). Turner *et al.* (1989) found that categorizing people as members of risky or cautious *groups* produced polarization in line with the normative tendency that defined the group, but that defining them as risky or cautious *individuals* did not (cf. Spears *et al.*, 1990).

## 6 Polarization without rational persuasion

Also, as noted earlier, polarization takes place in settings where the idea of persuasive argumentation seems meaningless (unless one redefines a persuasive argument to be the assertion of a social value). Vinokur and Burnstein (1974) imply that a persuasive argument is supposed to have some intrinsically compelling content.

### Informational influence considered

It is evident that some kind of informational influence is an important part of group polarization. The pre-test trend is related to what goes on in discussion, which is related to the shift. People shift in line with the perceived balance of arguments, but this is not conclusive for persuasive arguments theory, since shift takes place without argumentation, and the perceived balance of arguments may *reflect* rather than *determine* shift. The group context is not merely a passive medium for the exchange of information.

The main objection to persuasive arguments theory, I believe, is not that it does not describe what is going on in discussion but that it does not satisfactorily explain why people actually polarize. There are three points here: (a) the heuristic mechanism is only vaguely specified; (b) the *ad hoc* assumption that substitutes for such a mechanism is implausible; and (c) the model of the persuasion process is unsatisfactory and in contradiction with the assumptions of the informational influence tradition from which it derives.

The theoretical fascination of group polarization derives from the fact that it contradicts a simple persuasion model (the idea that mutual influence simply reflects the relative number and persuasiveness of X and Y arguments in the sampled pool, i.e. the initial balance of persuasive material). If individuals' pre-test choices are determined by the balance of X/Y information available to them, then, to be consistent, the group decision should be determined by the balance in the group. This balance is best described by the pre-test mean, arising from combining members' individual $X/Y$ balances. The group should converge on the mean, but it does not. To explain this, one must assume that $X$ arguments have disproportionately greater impact than $Y$ in group discussion, *not* an impact proportionate to the balance in the pool (which predicts convergence on the mean). What is it about group discussion or exposure to it that gives a disproportionate advantage to the dominant tendency? Kaplan (1977, 1987), Lamm and Myers (1978, pp. 171–2) and Sanders and Baron (1977) have also noted this issue.

Vinokur and Burnstein (1974) acknowledge that a simple persuasion model cannot explain polarization and introduce the idea of differences in novelty between $X$ and $Y$ persuasive arguments to account for the disproportionate impact of the former. For the novelty hypothesis to do the job, there must be a systematic explanation of why and how the balance of $X$ and $Y$ arguments in the cultural pool is associated with or produces a greater average novelty of $X$ than $Y$ arguments in the average group. This is what is lacking.

One idea might be that simply because there are more $X$ than $Y$ persuasive arguments in the pool, there will be more novel $X$ than $Y$ persuasive arguments in the average group (sample). If all persuasive arguments were completely novel (i.e. unique to one person and existing in only one form), then there would be more novel $X$ than $Y$ arguments in the sample by definition. In fact, however, what matters is not the preponderance of novel $X$ arguments but the average novelty of $X$ relative to $Y$ arguments (how novel the average $X$ or $Y$ argument is in the average group). For example, if all persuasive arguments were completely novel, then they would be weighted equally in the influence process as a function of their novelty. One would be in the same situation as if novelty did not matter, i.e. back to a simple persuasion model in which novelty did not change the relative impact of $X$ and $Y$ persuasive arguments. The fact that the balance of completely novel arguments favoured $X$ would only predict convergence on the mean. The same is true if $X$ and $Y$ arguments are of the same degree of average novelty in the sample. In this case, too, there would be no difference in the average impact of $X$ and $Y$ arguments as a function of novelty. For persuasive arguments theory to be genuinely heuristic, therefore, it must explain how sampling from the cultural pool leads to $X$ persuasive arguments being on average more novel than $Y$ persuasive arguments.

The assumption made by the theory of representative sampling from the cultural pool, however, means that the relative novelty of any argument will be the same on average in the sample as in the pool. Taking the relative novelty of X and Y persuasive arguments into account therefore adds nothing to the explanation of the average difference in impact between X and Y arguments *unless* the initial assumption is made that X arguments are for some reason already on average more novel in the cultural pool than Y arguments.

One must wonder whether the predictive success of persuasive arguments theory has much to do with its supposed explanatory kernel, which seems to rest on nothing more than an *ad hoc* assumption. This is not to say that group polarization is not produced by persuasive argumentation, but rather that the theory lacks the heuristic mechanism to provide a systematic explanation of why majority arguments have a disproportionate effect. It may be that in group discussion arguments in line with the dominant tendency are perceived as disproportionately more persuasive and novel just because they are in line with the dominant tendency. If we make such an assumption, we have accepted that the perception of persuasive arguments merely reflects the polarization of the dominant tendency that is already taking place and the explanatory task shifts to understanding the latter. Persuasive arguments theory works in so far as we make an assumption that majority arguments are on average more persuasive and novel than minority ones. The problem is that such an assumption is *ad hoc* and not derived from the theory. The solutions to this problem proposed by Kaplan (1977) and Lamm and Myers (1978) suffer, I believe, from the same basic difficulty of being *ad hoc* and essentially redescriptive.

Nor does the assumption that cultural majorities are more novel than minorities seem plausible. The model of social reality implied here is one where disagreement and conflicts of opinion simply reflect the partial diffusion of information (i.e. degrees of ignorance), and the full sharing of easily recognized 'facts' would lead to agreement. In fact, of course, this holds true only under extremely limited conditions of cultural and ideological homogeneity. In reality, society is full of social conflicts arising from real differences in social identity and group memberships, social location, basic values, goals and interests. People differ from each other sociologically, occupying different positions in the social structure and belonging to different social groups with varying aspirations and objectives. Disputes over facts and information are often only symptomatic of underlying social and political tensions. We can be fully aware of and share all relevant information and still disagree. Minorities disagree with majorities often only after rejecting majority interpretations and resisting their arguments. Societal minorities usually know and reject majority arguments, whereas the majority may never be confronted by the minority view. If we take a social conflict rather than a partial diffusion model of disagreement, then minorities are surely *more* novel than majorities. Moscovici (see Chapter 4) takes just such a view. Persuasive arguments theory attempts to explain group polarization with the idea that majorities are more novel than minorities. Moscovici explains innovation and social change as the work of minorities. The latter view seems more plausible.

Finally, there is the problem of informational validity as a perceived and cognitively processed property of the arguments, somehow independent of social reality testing. For Festinger (1950, 1954), the subjective validity of complex information is a function of the social relationship of the source to the recipient, shared reference group memberships, the relevance of the information to the goals, values and norms of the group, and the extent to which any message has consensual support. The validity of information derives from reality testing and measures the degree to which it provides evidence about reality. Burnstein and Vinokur, in contrast, assume that validity is somehow contained in the semantic content of messages (what the message is actually saying) as it matches and interacts with cognitive structures. Validity is a matter of information processing rather than social reality testing. The classic studies (e.g. Asch, 1956) suggest that neither information nor information processing can be self-validating except within the framework of established norms and social conventions. It can only be true indirectly where the cognitive structures involved are representations of social reality tests. Thorndike's mathematical solution is easily recognized as correct because it is measured against the socially shared and internalized conventions of the science – no idiosyncratic rules are allowed. Any piece of information can be socially presented to be perceived as invalid. And, as Gestalt psychology and attribution theory have shown, the very meaning of information is a function of the socially defined context.

Persuasive arguments theory raises the issue of why information in line with the dominant tendency of the group should be perceived as more persuasive than information not so in line? The answer provided in Chapter 2 is that it is more consensual. However, the most

consensual information has been assumed to be average information. The next question, then, is why should the consensual position
of the group be perceived as more extreme but in the same direction
as the group mean? In effect, is there any way in which group
polarization can be explained as social conformity, as movement to
the norm of the group?

## Social conformity theory

A straightforward application of social conformity ideas cannot
work for reasons already stated: it has been assumed that the group
norm forms at the average. Yet, by the same token, there is little
problem if we can explain why the norm might be extremitized.

## Majorities, normative commitment and the Zeitgeist

One solution is to take conformity to the majority (as in the Asch
paradigm, where the majority is not influenced by the minority) as
the model and assume that people converge on the mode rather than
the mean position. If the distribution of positions is skewed so that,
for example, a definite majority favours risk and only a deviant
minority favours caution, the shift by the minority without any
corresponding compromise by the majority would predict polarization (Fraser and Foster, 1984). Zaleska (1978), for example, found
that 38–68 per cent of group decisions over five studies represented
convergence on the mode. However, it is now generally agreed that
the evidence does not make such a simple solution possible. Problems
with the majority model include the facts that skewness does not
predict shift, that members of the majority can shift and that there is
shift in dyads where there cannot be a majority (Myers 1982; Myers
and Lamm 1976; Wetherell, 1983).

Moscovici and Zavalloni (1969) argue that the mode of interaction in group discussion increases 'normative commitment' and
that normative commitment polarizes the group. They argue that 'in
the course of intellectual work, when the group or individual carefully considers the different alternatives and the arguments attached
to them, the whole cognitive field becomes better organized, and the
dimensions which earlier had less prominence become more salient'
(p. 128). The members become more involved in the issues,
more certain, and particular aspects of the stimuli become more

meaningful and salient. This *commitment* process produces a shift of judgement towards extremity, but at the same time the 'direction of shift is a function of the values and dominant attitudes of the group or in the society; the values and attitudes have a selective effect' (p. 128). Moscovici and Lecuyer (1972) suggest that any disruption of group interaction and communication between members will weaken the commitment process.

Similarly, Doise (1969) explains his data that the evocation of the presumed opinion of a rival outgroup polarizes individuals' judgements of their own group by suggesting that such an evocation makes the defining features of one's ingroup more salient, and that salient attributes are perceptually extremitized.

Paicheler (1976, 1977, 1979) suggests that individuals not only interact 'horizontally' within the group but also 'vertically' in relation to the wider social codes and norms in society. She distinguishes between progressive ('norm-oriented' deviants) and reactionary ('anti-norm-oriented' deviants) minorities, i.e. those arguing for and in advance of the social norms evolving in society and those opposing the direction of social change, respectively. She shows that groups tend to polarize in the direction of the Zeitgeist. Groups containing an extreme norm-oriented confederate tend to polarize more towards the evolving norm (say feminism) than those without such confederates. Consistent confederates are more effective than inconsistent ones. Anti-norm-oriented confederates influence members with moderate views but do not influence and may even produce resistance among more committed (progressive) members (this 'bipolarization' produces a slight overall depolarization in the group).

## Self-categorization theory and prototypical ingroup norms

Most recently, Turner and colleagues (Turner *et al.*, 1987; Turner and Oakes, 1986, 1989; Wetherell, 1987) have proposed a self-categorization theory of group polarization. They argue that people are conforming to a shared ingroup norm, but that the norm is not the pre-test average but rather the *prototypical* position of the group. They demonstrate that the prototype coincides with or is more extreme than the mean in the same direction, depending on the social context within which the group defines itself. It tends to differ more from the mean as the group moves towards the extreme of the comparative context. In essence, the prototype is the position that best defines what the group has in common compared to other relevant outgroups. A person becomes more prototypical as he or she differs less from ingroup members and more from outgroup members. Thus the most prototypical, normative position need not be the one most similar to other ingroup positions (the mean position, which on average is least different from other ingroup positions), because a *less* similar position may differ *even more* from the contrasting outgroup. It is the person with the highest *meta-contrast ratio* (produced by dividing the individual's average difference from outgroup members by his or her average difference from ingroup members) who is defined as most prototypical of the ingroup.

Self-categorization theory is described in more detail in Chapter 6. For the moment, it suffices to note that it explains convergence on the mean or polarization as arising from the same basic process of members moving towards what they see as the consensual position of their group. The difference is simply that in different social contexts the consensual position may or may not be perceived as coinciding with the mean, depending on varying intergroup as well as intragroup comparisons. It is assumed that the response scale represents the social frame of reference, i.e. it operationalizes the salient comparative context. People are making social comparisons, in fact, meta-comparisons between intergroup and intragroup differences, to determine what best defines them as a distinct group and what they have in common, and it is this norm that validates people's ideas and arguments and ensures that material in line with the dominant tendency is perceived as more persuasive. An advantage of the theory, therefore, is that it integrates social comparative, normative and informational influence processes into one unified explanation of both polarization and convergence on the mean.

Several studies (Hogg *et al.*, 1990; McGarty *et al.*, 1990; Turner *et al.*, 1988, 1989) show that the ingroup prototype (the position that best defines what a group has in common in contrast to other groups) does tend to be more extreme than the pre-test mean in the same direction, i.e. *polarized*. There is also correlational evidence (McGarty *et al.*, 1990) that the magnitude of group polarization is a function of the degree to which groups actually shift towards their prototypes and the degree to which those prototypes are polarized. These relationships are obtained both within and between items.

Other data show that the same information is more persuasive coming from ingroup or similar others than outgroup or different others; that the salience of ingroup–outgroup membership (based on, for example, competition between groups) does lead subjects to perceive the ingroup norm as more extreme than the pre-test mean (the ingroup norm is perceptually polarized in appropriate comparative settings); and that, for group polarization to occur, group members must perceive their initial tendency as a shared group norm rather than as an aggregate of individual tendencies (Mackie, 1986; Mackie and Cooper, 1984; Turner *et al.*, 1988, 1989). Also relevant is the study by Doise (1969), in which students at a Parisian school of architecture became more polarized in their opinions about themselves when confronted by the presumed opinions of a rival school. Thus there is evidence that comparing one's ingroup with an outgroup does lead members to polarize in the opposite direction.

Self-categorization theory not only hypothesizes that intergroup comparison produces polarization, but also that the *direction of polarization on an item can be reversed* by changing the comparative context. Hogg *et al.* (1990) have confirmed this prediction in a decision-making context. Subjects perceived the ingroup norm as riskier than the pre-test mean when confronted by a more cautious outgroup, but as more cautious than the pre-test mean when confronted by a riskier outgroup.

## Conclusion

Social comparison, informational influence and social conformity all seem to be involved in group polarization. There is little evidence for intragroup differentiation or the role of abstract cultural values. People converge on an extremitized, consensual position. This does not seem to be simple conformity to a majority. Information in line with the dominant tendency of the group is perceived as more persuasive. One explanation may be that information is validated by its congruence with the ingroup norm and that this norm is perceived as more extreme than the pre-test mean in certain comparative contexts.

In relation to Chapter 2, value theory has extended Festinger's theory of the social comparison of abilities, seeing shift as a compromise between uniformity pressures and social differentiation. The researchers have stressed aspects of social comparison related to normative influence and the positive presentation of self – not social comparison *to be correct*, but *to look good and better than others*.

formity in order to function smoothly and effectively. Individuals who do not conform can achieve nothing – they are merely 'deviants', a disruptive aberration. Moscovici argues that conformity can be maladaptive; that times, situations, and the needs of the group change, and that social norms therefore *must* change to be adaptive in new conditions. If conformity were the only process of influence, then groups could not function effectively to meet these changes.

He cites a study by Kelley and Shapiro (1954) to illustrate the problem with the conformity viewpoint. They argued that where the group norm was more and more detrimental to the group, leading to failure, people in highly cohesive groups would conform less than in low cohesive groups. People for whom the group is attractive and important are likely to want their group to succeed. Therefore, we might expect such people to conform less to the old norm as they seek to move the group in a new direction. The hypothesis was not supported. There was a slight tendency in the opposite direction, i.e. for more conformity to the detrimental norm in high than low cohesive groups, implying that groups depended (for an adaptive change of norms) upon those who were less attached to the group and cared less about their membership. Here was a turning point in the literature: traditional concepts and paradigms of influence led to paradoxical findings of counterproductive conformity to maladaptive norms.

The issue was raised of how to understand the process of social change, an issue that traditional theory seemed incapable of addressing. In group life, there is *innovation* and *normalization*, other forms of influence, as well as conformity. We need theories that address these phenomena. Influence functions to produce social conflict and change as well as stability and social control. We need a 'genetic' model that sees social conflict and change as being at the heart of the influence process. Moscovici (1976, pp. 3–6) describes this model as 'genetic' (in contrast to functionalist) to emphasize that growth and innovation are fundamental processes of social existence, that influence does not merely *adapt* people to a given social system, but continually *produces* and changes that system.

## Minorities and social change

The dependence theory, Moscovici continues, implies unilateral influence 'from the top down' and is, therefore, incompatible with the facts of social change. In the theory, influence is based on power, prestige, authority, material resources, information, etc. This influence is exerted unilaterally by those with resources – the leaders, the experts, the majority, or their representatives – upon those who are dependent because they lack these things, those at the bottom of the social hierarchy – the marginals, deviants, low status groups, the societal 'minorities'. Minorities (i.e. deviant subgroups) lack the things that make influence possible by the very terms of the theory. They cannot innovate; only the majority, the normative, dominant subgroup, can change things. However, according to Moscovici, social change 'from the top' is implausible and an inadequate description of historical realities. Social change 'from the bottom', from minorities, is a widely acknowledged fact. It is the 'have-nots', the outsiders, the oppressed, not the ruling elites, who change society. By their nature, then, theories of conformity are inadequate to explain social change by minorities.

## Social and physical reality

Moscovici goes on to argue that even as a theory of conformity the dependence formulation is flawed. It explains influence (private acceptance) as an informational process activated by uncertainty and the need to reduce uncertainty. We look at the world and usually see things much as they are; sometimes, reality is ambiguous, unclear; we become uncertain; we need more information; we turn to others with information, the experts, or other people in the same situation. Or, seeing that the group is wrong, we conform, nevertheless, to be liked, to be popular. This picture painted by the theory seems like common sense, but, in fact, it is wrong. It divides the individual from society and makes an artificial dichotomy between the physical and the social worlds. Social influence is merely a substitute process for reducing uncertainty, where the individual cannot test reality directly employing objective, physical means. The implication is that the individual can perceive and know the world directly without the mediation of society and resorts only to society as a function of the uncertainties that sometimes arise from the primary process of individual perception.

There are several objections to this view. Individual perception and cognition of even the physical world are in actuality socially mediated. What we take to be the evidence of our senses is often and perhaps usually the evidence of our culture. When we hear a thunderclap, for example, is it the sound of an angry god, two clouds bumping one another, or the delayed sound of lightning striking? The answer will vary with the beliefs of our culture and time. Perhaps what we hear is the same, but we give it different meanings according to our culture? It is doubtful that one can draw a sharp dividing line between perception and 'meaning'. Understanding influences perception and understanding of even the physical world is a product of society (Tajfel, 1969a). We know how science (a social institution), for example, has changed radically our perception of the physical universe.

More concretely, consider the lone individual in Asch's control condition (see Chapter 1), matching lines to the target stimulus. Is this an asocial, purely individual perceptual activity? When we say the subject answered correctly, was this a purely physical judgement? No, Moscovici suggests, the person is acting as a representative of a group, a society, a culture, applying established rules, standards, procedures and norms. The person may be physically isolated, but, psychologically, he or she is making fully social and normative judgements, replying on the basis of shared cultural conventions that include everything from the meaning of words to the appropriate system of measurement (Moscovici and Faucheux, 1972). The person could, of course, have used a ruler, checked the cards physically, etc. This is true, but it would have made no difference to the social nature of the judgements. Moscovici points out that rulers and other technological devices for inspecting the world are themselves the material embodiments of a cultural consensus. They are useful because we agree about what they show and they already represent standardized, conventionalized, consensual procedures. If a telescope did not produce the same results across astronomers, we would put no trust in the telescope and reject its data.

Is uncertainty a product of stimulus ambiguity? In Sherif's autokinetic situation, is one uncertain and in need of influence because the point of light is objectively variable? If reality is *objectively* unstructured, ambiguous and variable, then 'uncertainty' is a veridical and valid representation of the stimulus. In this case, why does one want information, why does one want to agree? Any agreement must be arbitrary and pointless. If I am not sure of something because I cannot trust my eyes, but the problem is not in my eyes but 'out there', then everybody else will have the same problem and there is no reason to trust anybody else's judgements more than my own.

The only point of seeking agreement is if one assumes that, despite one's own uncertainty, the world is perceptually structured, a correct answer possible, and that *subjective* uncertainty does *not* reflect *objective* ambiguity. The subjects in Sherif's study think that the light is *really* moving, that perception, not reality, is ambiguous. To illustrate this, Moscovici cites an experiment by Sperling (reported in Asch, 1952). Sperling employed the autokinetic paradigm, but told his subjects that the movement of the light was an optical illusion. The result was that convergence (mutual influence) was reduced. In fact, many of the subjects did not believe that the effect was an illusion and continued to be influenced but, among those who were convinced, mutual influence disappeared. Thus convergence depended on uncertainty in the context of a reality perceived, paradoxically, as objectively unambiguous. Similar results to Sperling's have been reported by Alexander *et al.* (1970). Informing subjects that the movement of the light was illusory reduced convergence.

Moscovici (1985) has since stated that he has not been able to replicate the Sperling effect. What he now seems to be arguing is that it is not objective reality that is important, but what he calls the *norm of objectivity*, the shared belief that there are objective, valid, correct answers that require and imply agreement.

If uncertainty is not produced by the objective ambiguity of the world, what does produce it? Moscovici's answer is society, social relationships. Consider the Asch paradigm. The disagreement, contrary to fact, of a unanimous group creates uncertainty in the naive subject. Subjects share an implicit belief that similar people facing an identical stimulus ought to agree (Asch, 1952; Turner, 1985). If they do not, then there is a cognitive conflict, there is uncertainty about the correct answer. People try to puzzle it out, to explain the social and cognitive conflict. One possible explanation is that they are wrong. Without the agreement of similar others, as Festinger points out, there cannot be subjective validity; the difference is that Festinger assumes that one only needs agreement if reality is too ambiguous to be tested physically. The Asch study shows that disagreement creates uncertainty even where reality is unambiguous and easily tested perceptually. It is the social conflict between the individual and the group, not any supposed difficulty of testing reality objectively, that produces uncertainty and initiates the influence process.

Who reduces uncertainty? Moscovici is less clear about this in that to shift to the new point of view. The minority can exploit the majority's dislike of conflict and its need for consensus. Here we have arrived at Moscovici's genetic theory of influence. The basic notions are that influence is not unilateral but reciprocal, that every group member, irrespective of rank, both influences and is influenced, that influence creates social change as well as control, is related to the production and resolution of conflict, follows shared norms of objectivity, preference and originality, and that effective influence depends upon the behavioural style of the source, the way its behaviour is organized and patterned.

The key empirical factor in the way the minority creates conflict and has influence is its *behavioural style*, the 'rhetoric' of behaviour, including the 'self-presentation of the sender, the sequence of arguments, and other oratorical devices that are symbolic variables' (Moscovici and Faucheux, 1972, p. 158). The most important behavioural style is *consistency*, both intrapersonal consistency across time and situations (including the simple repetition of a message) and interpersonal or social consistency across individuals, i.e. consensus. Consistency is a sign of certainty and commitment to a coherent choice. It ranges from 'persevering repetition . . . through the avoidance of any contradictory behaviour, to the elaboration of a logical system of demonstration' (p. 158). A consistent minority is distinctive and visible, creates conflict, doubt and uncertainty about established norms, signals that it will not compromise or budge, that it is confident, committed, certain (it must feel strongly to stand out) and provides an alternative norm, a new way of looking at things, which would resolve the conflict if the majority will move.

In sum, the genetic theory suggests that a consistent minority (1) disrupts the established norm and produces doubt and uncertainty in the mind of the majority, (2) makes itself visible, focuses attention on itself, (3) shows that there is an alternative, coherent point of view, (4) demonstrates certainty, confidence, and commitment to this point of view, (5) signals that it will not move or compromise, and (6) implies that the only solution to restore social stability and cognitive coherence is for the majority to shift towards the minority. Minority influence is seen as a complex social psychological process with various facets. What exactly is the basis of persuasion in the theory? Is one simply persuaded by rhetoric, does behavioural style influence how the message is perceived, or does it imply that the minority possesses an alternative norm and somehow induce acceptance of it? There are several possible answers. It is also important to note that

Moscovici's theoretical analysis changed radically in 1980 when he proposed a dual-process model in place of the original genetic model, complicating the theoretical picture.

## Evidence for the genetic model of minority influence

1  *The impact of a consistent minority: The 'blue–green' and other studies*

The initial studies conducted by Moscovici and his colleagues looked at the impact of a consistent minority on colour perception. There is now a collection of studies employing what can be called the 'blue–green' paradigm (Doms and Van Avermaet, 1980; Moscovici and Lage, 1976, 1978; Moscovici *et al.*, 1969; Moscovici and Neve, 1973; Moscovici and Personnaz, 1980, 1986; Personnaz, 1981; Sorrentino *et al.*, 1980).

Moscovici *et al.* (1969) looked at the responses of female students to consistent minority influence. Each experimental group comprised four naive subjects and two confederates. They were seated in a row before a screen on which were projected a series of six blue slides in six different orders. Each slide was shown for 15 seconds. The subjects were told that they were in an experiment on colour perception and that their task was to state out aloud the colour of the slide (and judge its light intensity). In the experimental trials, both confederates (the minority) consistently described the blue slides as 'green'. In 12 groups, the confederates were seated next to each other and responded first and second. In 20 groups, they were separated and responded first and fourth.

A second experiment (10 groups) not only measured changes in the verbal responses of the majority but also looked at more private, lasting changes on their 'perceptual thresholds'. At the end of the slide judgements, the subjects were asked to participate in another, supposedly independent experiment. They were shown 16 disks in the blue–green zone of the Farnsworth 100-hue colour perception test. Three disks were unambiguously blue and 3 green, but 10 were more ambiguous, i.e. blue–green. The 16 disks were presented 10 times in random order and the subjects privately judged their colour (the discrimination test). It was assumed that minority influence might result in a shift of subjects' perceptual threshold so that more blue–green disks would be designated green than previously. A third experiment (11 groups) varied the consistency of the minority. They responded 'green' 24 times and 'blue' 12 times, the blue responses being randomized over the 36 colour slide trials. A control group comprised four groups of naive subjects who took the discrimination test after the perceptual (slide) task.

In the control group, 0.25 per cent of responses designated the slides as 'green' (i.e. the blue slides were seen and described as blue). However, 8.42 per cent green responses were made in the presence of a consistent minority, but only 1.25 per cent with an inconsistent minority. The subjects changed their responses (giving four or more green responses) in 43.75 per cent of groups containing a consistent minority (representing 32 per cent of the subjects). The seating position and order of the minority had no effect. There was also evidence that the consistent minority significantly lowered the perceptual threshold for green, leading to a greater readiness to designate ambiguous blue–green disks as green on the discrimination test. This change in the 'perceptual code' of subjects was a general effect, not limited to subjects who were publicly influenced by the minority. In fact, there was a significant tendency for groups that did not modify their public judgements to make even more green responses on the discrimination test than those that did. Moscovici *et al.* suggested that the impact of the consistent minority was greater at the perceptual than public, verbal level. These experiments testify that a consistent minority (but not an inconsistent one) has a definite and significant (but not very large) influence.

Moscovici and Lage (1976) replicated and extended these results. Using the same blue–green paradigm, they created six conditions. The *control* group of subjects simply responded to the stimuli in writing, without exposure to influence. The *consistent* and *inconsistent minority of two* conditions were the same as in Moscovici *et al.* (1969), the confederates responding first and fourth in groups of six. The *consistent minority of one* responded green throughout all trials, being first in a group of four (three naive subjects). The *unanimous (consistent) majority* condition comprised three fully consistent confederates responding green in groups of four, the one naive subject responding last. In the *non-unanimous (inconsistent) majority* condition, four confederates always responded green (in differing orders) in the presence of two naive subjects (the latter were expected to support each other and disrupt the unanimity/consistency of the overall majority of five confronting each subject).

The percentages of green verbal responses obtained (with percentages of influenced subjects in parentheses) were as follows: control,

1.22 (6); consistent minority of one, 1.22 (15); consistent minority of two, 10.07 (42.5); inconsistent minority, 0.75 (11); consistent majority, 40.16 (50); inconsistent majority, 12.07 (35). The only clear evidence of influence on the perceptual code (measured by the discrimination test) was obtained with a consistent minority of two. The perceptual effect of the consistent minority was the same for subjects who had and who had not been influenced verbally. There was some evidence for a perceptual impact of the majority, but only on verbally influenced subjects in the consistent condition, and on the variability of subjects' responses in the inconsistent one.

Moscovici and Lage (1976, p. 163) concluded that:

> minority and majority influences differ in nature. A minority, without obtaining substantial acceptance of its point of view at the manifest level, can nevertheless influence subjects to revise the very basis of their judgements, while a majority can make them almost all accept its point of view, if it is unanimous, without affecting the underlying perceptual-cognitive system. In other words, majority influence works on the surface while minority influence has deep-lying effects.

It is worth noting that the data suggest that given ambiguous stimuli (blue–green disks), people in the consistent, consensual minority condition modified their perceptual categories to some degree. These discrimination test data, however, do not tell us what subjects actually 'saw' when they were making their verbal or written responses. We do not know that minorities did or that majorities did not have a private effect when subjects were making green verbal responses. A series of studies conducted to provide direct perceptual evidence of minority influence employing the phenomenon of the 'complementary colour after-image' has as yet proved inconclusive (Doms and Van Avermaet, 1980; Moscovici and Personnaz, 1980; Personnaz, 1981; Sorrentino *et al.*, 1980).

## 2 *The meaning of consistency*

The above studies show that consistency is important for both minority and majority influence. Other studies illustrate that what matters for influence is not the simple repetition of a message, but the psychological meaning attributed to consistency, i.e. how it is interpreted in the situation (Allen and Wilder, 1978; Nemeth and Wachtler, 1973, 1974).

The point is made most strikingly in a study by Nemeth *et al.* (1974). They used the same paradigm and stimuli as Moscovici *et al.* (1969). There were 96 male students in five experimental conditions who judged 28 slide presentations, half of which were 'bright' and half 'dim' in luminance, but all of which were of the same blue colour. In conditions 1 and 2, the two confederates (who responded first and fourth) were repetitive, consistently responding 'green' (1) or 'green-blue' (2). Conditions 3, 4 and 5 involved the 'patterning' of minority responses. In the random condition (3), the minority responded 'green' to 14 slides and 'green-blue' to the other half in a predetermined random order. In two correlated conditions, the minority either responded green to the bright slides and green-blue to the dim slides (4), or green to the dim slides and green-blue to the bright slides (5). It was hypothesized that 'correlated', non-repetitive ('inconsistent') minority influence would be just as effective as repetitive influence, because the patterning of the former responses with an objective variation in the stimulus (luminance) would lead them to be perceived as consistent. In other words, consistency is not a matter of simple repetition, but of the interpretation of the minority's behaviour in relation to the environment.

There was no significant difference between the two correlated conditions in the influence of the minority on subjects' 'green' responses. The mean number of green responses in conditions 4 and 5 was 5.84. This was significantly larger than in the control (0), random (0.06) and repetitive/green (0.69) conditions, but did not differ from the repetitive/green-blue condition (4.00). Correlated minorities were also seen as more confident in their judgements than the random and repetitive/green minorities. Thus repetition and the intensification of conflict it fosters is not necessary for minority influence. Minority responses that vary with an objective property of the stimulus are judged favourably and as more confident and exert more influence than repetitive consistency that is relatively arbitrary. It is worth noting that the more objectively realistic judgement of 'green-blue' was more effective than that of 'green' in the repetitive minority conditions. Unlike in the studies described above, the repetitive/green condition did not produce significant influence.

Thus it is not arbitrary repetition, but patterning, the systematic relationship of responses to reality, and the meaning attributed to them that are important. Responses need not be objectively consistent but they must be *perceived* as consistent. The message must be perceived as coherent, different, plausible, natural, corresponding to reality, and objective and the minority as confident and committed (Moscovici, 1985). The studies described below on the difference between consistency and 'rigidity' are also relevant here.

## 3  The importance of consensus

Minorities must be consensual as well as consistent. A consistent minority of one is likely to be ineffective. For example, Moscovici and Lage (1976) reported that a consistent minority of one had no influence at all compared to their control condition.

Nemeth *et al.* (1977) varied the number of minority confederates facing a group of six naive subjects from 1 to 4 (i.e. there were either 1, 2, 3 or 4 confederates in the experimental conditions and none in the control groups of varying, matched size). They hypothesized that, as the size of the minority increased, their attributed competence would increase, but the confidence attributed to their judgements would decrease – so that, for example, a minority of one would be perceived as very confident but incorrect. This is what they found. Consistent, too, with the idea that influence is a function of both perceived competence and confidence, a minority of three (both competent and relatively confident) exerted significantly more influence than minorities of one or two (mean 'green–blue' responses out of 25 slide presentations being 2.25 versus 1.35 and 1.31) and non-significantly more than four (1.88). Although the experimental conditions as a whole differed from the control group (where the mean influence was 0), it is clear that the influence of minorities less than three is negligible (0.05 per cent). This is the more striking because the minority response was not 'green', but the less arbitrary 'green–blue'.

Arbuthnot and Wayner (1982) found that a minority of one was less effective than either a minority of two or a minority of one who gained a convert (the latter conditions did not differ) and that, in fact, a minority of one, seated at the head of the table and arguing consistently (as in Nemeth and Wachtler, 1974), did not have a significant influence on the majority's position.

Kiesler and Pallak (1975) report what Moscovici and Mugny (1983) call a 'snowball effect' – people are persuaded by the emerging, developing consensus. A minority has more influence where majority members compromise with or defect to the minority, but not where minority members compromise by moving to the majority. Bray *et al.* (1982) found that minority conflict across three issues produced substantial influence (measured on the last issue) with a minority of two, but little or no influence with a minority of one; a minority of one was effective if he followed the strategy of agreeing on two but disagreeing on the last issue and demonstrated competence by solving rather than failing to solve a difficult word puzzle. The main problem for a minority of one is perceived incompetence, the attribution of their dissent to personal defect.

## 4 Compromise or social conflict?

The studies of Bray *et al.* (1982) and Nemeth *et al.* (1974) imply that a compromising minority (i.e. one that acts flexibly, makes concessions, is less conflictual, and promises the possibility of reaching agreement) can sometimes be more effective than an uncompromising one. Kiesler and Pallak's (1975) study implies that more important than minority compromise may be the perception that the minority can induce compromise on the part of the majority, that it is becoming the focus for a new consensus.

Nemeth and Brilmayer (1987) investigated the impact of consistency and early or late compromise on the part of the minority on public responses and both direct and indirect private measures. They defined compromise as 'a change in position in the direction of the opposing faction' (which may be interpreted as inconsistency or a strategy of negotiation). In a simulated jury setting, groups of three naive subjects and one confederate (or without the confederate in the control condition) discussed the amount of financial compensation to be received by the victim of a ski-lift accident. The consistent minority argued for the same very low amount over 10 public rounds of discussion in the group. The compromising minorities shifted towards the majority position either on rounds 2 (early) or 9 (late). By round 10 of the public judgements in the groups, it was found that the consistent minority had had no effect compared to the control condition, but that both compromising minorities had had significantly more influence on public responses than the consistent confederate. There were no differences between conditions on a private measure of responses to the case discussed. However, on related personal injury cases (indirect measures), there was more shift in the minority direction with consistent and late compromise minorities than in early compromise and control conditions. It appears that at least at the level of public responses, compromise rather than a consistently conflictual stance may be the best strategy for a minority.

Moscovic and Mugny (1983, p. 59) accept that compromise on the part of a minority can sometimes even facilitate private acceptance of its position. Wolf (1979) found on both direct and indirect private measures that an inconsistent minority who can be rejected from a high cohesive group has more influence than a consistent one in the same situation. This finding is interpreted by Moscovici and Mugny (1983) as evidence for the role of minority compromise in reducing the danger of social divisiveness and the exclusion of the minority person. Wolf also found more minority influence in high- than low-cohesive groups, and that a consistent minority has most influence in a high-cohesive group where she cannot be rejected. As Festinger (1950) might predict, the cohesiveness of the group mattered more than simple consistency for minority influence.

A compromising stance on the part of the minority makes sense as part of the idea of the genetic model that influence represents a collective negotiation of reality, in which people work out their social differences and reduce conflict, but it is at odds with the specific hypothesis that minorities exercise influence through the production of social conflict. The social conflict model of minority influence implies that an uncompromising, socially divisive stance should be more effective (Mugny and Perez, 1987; Perez and Mugny, 1987). A problem is that there are many possible interpretations of the difference between a compromising and uncompromising style. A compromising style can be seen as less consistent, dogmatic, discrepant, cognitively distinctive, visible, antagonistic, or as a sign of weakness or goodwill. One reasonable interpretation is that a minority must be cognitively distinctive and consistent but not appear socially divisive or rejecting (Moscovici and Mugny, 1983). It is unclear how far these aspects of disagreement have been varied independently. It may be the socially divisive nature of minority conflict that explains the generally low level of direct influence. Also, the issue arises of how exactly can a minority remain consistent while compromising, if consistency is to be understood as to do with behavioural style and rhetoric rather than the informational content and coherence of the message.

## 5  The style of negotiation

Studies by Mugny and Papastamou on the 'flexibility' or 'rigidity' of the style of negotiation adopted by minorities raise similar points. They generally find that a flexible style is more advantageous than a rigid, more dogmatic style (Mugny, 1975a, 1982; Mugny and Papastamou, 1980, 1982; Moscovici, 1980; Moscovici and Mugny, 1983; Papastamou, 1983; Ricateau, 1971).

Mugny (1975a, p. 211) defines the difference between a rigid behavioural style and a flexible, negotiating style as follows:

We define a style of negotiation with the population which is 'consistent to the extreme', in that its propositions are unalterable and its demands go beyond the bounds of possible acceptance by the population, a style which refuses compromise on any point whatsoever, as *rigid* (R). A style which, on the contrary, is more flexible and adapts to the population, accepting certain compromises but not calling into question the fundamental consistency of the minority, will be defined as a *negotiating* style (N).

The basic idea is that a consistent minority must be willing to compromise and negotiate with the population, i.e. the people it is trying to influence, if it is not to 'lose influence and be labeled as dogmatic, extremist and unrealistic' (p. 211).

He found in two experiments that when minorities are equally consistent, a flexible style of negotiation has more influence than a rigid style and that rigid minorities attract a more negative social image. In these studies, Mugny is drawing a distinction between the 'cognitive' consistency of a minority in terms of the content of its message and its 'interpersonal' style of negotiation. It seems a moot point, however, whether rigidity and flexibility were manipulated as social styles independent of the perceived content of the minority position. The rigid minority, for example, was presented as politically more extreme (see Mugny, 1975a, p. 217).

Mugny and Papastamou (1980) varied whether there were one or two minority sources, which were either flexible or rigid. A single minority had more influence when it was flexible but two sources had more influence when they were rigid. In general, a single, rigid minority had least influence. In a second study, subjects rated the authors of a rigid left-wing tract in terms of either 'political' or 'psycho-political' adjectives. Moderate subjects were influenced in the political but not psycho-political situation. The authors argue that, in the latter situation, the rating task 'psychologized' the rigid minority (i.e. they were derogated as idiosyncratic and psychologically deviant) and so reduced its influence. In the first study, subjects were likewise able to 'individualize' a single rigid minority group, i.e. interpret its differences from the majority in terms of its unique, deviant characteristics. Individualization and psychologization are closely related strategies by which minorities are invalidated and their authentic message rejected as the product of cranks, fanatics, lunatics, extremists, etc. (Papastamou, 1983, 1986).

The important point is that there must be cognitive conflict but not social antagonism (Moscovici and Mugny, 1983). Moscovici and Mugny have never interpreted these findings as being at odds with the social conflict model of innovation, but they would seem to indicate a definite limitation of the effectiveness of minority conflict, at least in terms of 'direct' influence (i.e. immediate, public effects on directly relevant measures). Other studies (Moscovici, 1980) suggest that rigid minorities tend to have more indirect than direct influence (delayed, private effects on related, more general measures). A solution that Moscovici and Mugny seem to have adopted is to argue that a socially conflictual stance of the minority produces better results than a less conflictual stance, but at the level of *indirect* influence. This work contributed to the development of the theory of minority conversion (see below).

## 6 Social identity and minority influence

A natural step under the influence of social identity research (Tajfel and Turner, 1986; Turner, 1982) was for Mugny (1984a; Mugny *et al.*, 1984; Mugny and Papastamou, 1982) to propose that social identification with a minority facilitates its influence. In the style of negotiation studies, Mugny and Papastamou have shown that minorities must not allow themselves to be individualized or psychologized. If perceived as idiosyncratic deviants, they will have less influence. Similarly, following Turner (1982), Mugny has argued that if minorities are categorized as members of an outgroup, their influence will be less. Being influenced by a minority involves redefining one's social identity and taking on some of the attributes that define the social identity of the minority. Assuming that minority identity is defined negatively, and that people seek positive social identity, it follows that minorities categorized as (positive) ingroup rather than (negative) outgroup members will be more influential. The same prediction has also been derived from the lower credibility of outgroup minorities perceived as arguing in their own self-interest (Maass and Clark, 1984; Maass *et al.*, 1982) and is made on more general grounds by self-categorization theory (Turner, 1985; Turner *et al.*, 1987; see Chapters 3 and 6). The latter interpretations imply private acceptance of ingroup influence. Mugny's analysis seems gradually to have changed to imply that the influence of ingroup minorities is one of compliance (Mugny and Perez, 1987).

With one possible exception (Nemeth and Wachtler, 1973), the data are consistent in showing that ingroup minorities exert more influence than outgroup minorities (Davidson, 1988; Clark and Maass, 1988a,b; Maass and Clark, 1982, cited in Maass and Clark 1984; Maass *et al.*, 1982; Martin, 1988a,b,c; Mugny *et al.*, 1983; Mugny and Papastamou, 1982; Perez and Mugny, 1987). Maass *et al.* (1982) exposed 120 conservative males to either a male (ingroup) or female (outgroup) minority of two, who argued for liberal positions on the issues of abortion and the death penalty, representing pro- and anti-Zeitgeist positions respectively. Neither minority was influential on the death penalty issue where its position ran counter to the Zeitgeist. However, on the pro-Zeitgeist abortion issue, outgroup minorities were perceived as more self-interested and had less influence than ingroup minorities. Maass and Clark (1982) replicated these results, finding that a gay minority arguing for gay rights had less influence on a straight majority than a straight minority arguing for gay rights.

Mugny and Papastamou (1982) manipulated the similarity of subjects' views (close or distant) to a minority message about the cause of pollution, the flexibility or rigidity of the minority and whether subjects believed they had one or five social category memberships in common with the minority (e.g. we are intellectuals, of the same sex, are young, etc.). The subjects were more influenced by minorities sharing five than just one common category membership ($p < .06$), an effect which was significant among close, but not distant, and with rigid, but not flexible, minorities. Interestingly, subjects facing a rigid outgroup minority and 'close' subjects facing an outgroup minority were little influenced.

Martin (1988a) explored the effects of ingroup and outgroup minorities on public and private influence. British secondary school pupils read a text on 'grants for pupils' attributed to either a minority of pupils from their own school or from a school against which they discriminated. Their attitudes before and after reading the text were measured either publicly (other pupils from their class would see their responses) or privately (by means of an anonymous ballot box procedure). Ingroup minorities had more public influence than outgroup minorities, but there was no significant difference in private. Both ingroup and outgroup minorities had more private than public influence, but this difference was significant only in the outgroup condition. The least influence was obtained on public responses to an outgroup minority. Thus enhanced social identification with the minority increased its public but did not significantly decrease its private impact, either in absolute terms or relative to the outgroup minority. These findings were replicated in a second study (Martin, 1988b). Other studies exploring ingroup–outgroup effects (Clark and Maass, 1988a,b; Perez and Mugny, 1987) are better discussed below in relation to the dual-process model.

Ingroup–outgroup effects are found in minority influence in line with other studies applying social identity and self-categorization ideas (Turner and Oakes, 1989) to social influence (see Chapters 3 and 6). Contrary to Mugny and Perez's (1987; Perez and Mugny, 1987) 'positive social identity/intergroup comparison' interpretation, the effect of the ingroup does not seem to be one of compliance, i.e. limited to public influence. The data seem more supportive of a social reality testing process (Turner, 1985) in which people categorized as similar to self are more persuasive than those categorized as different from self in relevant areas (see Chapter 6). However, unlike in other research areas, which show more ingroup than outgroup private influence (e.g. Hogg and Turner, 1987a), outgroup minorities do seem capable of private influence even when their influence is not acknowledged in public. These data lead us into the more general issue of the role of group membership and social norms in minority influence.

## 7  Group membership and social norms

The idea of behavioural style and rhetoric implies that it is the way the minority behaves – how they say something – that matters more than what they say or who they are, but the evidence cautions against such a view. *Why* the minority behaves as it does, *who* they are, *whom* they are seeking to influence, and *what* they are saying all seem to matter, not simply the way their behaviour is organized.

For example, minority responses must be plausible, patterned ('distinctive' in Kelley's, 1967, attribution terminology) and 'objective' (Moscovici, 1985) – they must be attributed to external causes (reality) rather than to personal idiosyncrasies and subjective biases. The minority must comprise ingroup rather than outgroup members, be part of a cohesive, shared reference group (Wolf, 1979), and they must form a consensual subgroup rather than be seen as unique 'psychologized' deviants. Their message must also be congruent with underlying norms and values and the Zeitgeist (Maass *et al.*, 1982; Paicheler, 1976, 1977, 1979). The minority must be basically 'on the same side' as the majority group (e.g. anti- rather than pro-pollution), pro-normative rather than counter-normative, 'concordant' rather than 'discordant' (Mugny, 1975b, cited in Maass and Clark, 1984). In the majority of studies, minority and majority are part of an implicit shared group membership (Davidson, 1987). Just as in conformity studies where similarity with the majority is usually assumed, so in minority influence studies it is implicitly an ingroup minority that is involved (e.g. in the blue–green studies).

It needs to be emphasized that these are the conditions for successful minority influence. Part of the reason why real-life minorities must often engage in a protracted struggle to exert influence and why it is so frequently a difficult and bitter exercise, is that they will often begin without these advantages. Much of their work will be directed to counteracting the propaganda of the majority and influencing how they are defined by the population, just as the dominant group will work constantly to define them as deviant, immoral and different. The conditions for effective minority influence are not givens in real life as they can be in experimental studies, but must be actively created over time by the minority. We should not forget the simple point that real minorities often fail.

The point need not be laboured. A minority, especially a unique individual, belonging to an outgroup, arguing directly against the core norms and values of the ingroup, is unlikely to be influential, no matter how consistently the message is presented. Such consistency will doubtless be psychologized as rigidity, dogmatism, etc. The behavioural style adopted is likely to work only if it brings about a redefinition of the person's social image and relationship to the group. This is the implication of Mugny's distinction between behavioural style and style of negotiation – that it is the production of cognitive and *not* social conflict that facilitates minority influence. There is an alternative view: Social conflict may be ineffective in terms of direct influence, but what about indirect influence? This brings us to a consideration of the two-process model presented by Moscovici in 1980.

## The dual-process model of majority compliance and minority conversion

One effect of minorities reported early on was the stimulation of original, creative, divergent thinking. Even if the minority did not have direct, overt influence, it had indirect influence in the sense of stimulating thinking about new alternatives (Nemeth, 1986; Nemeth and Kwan, 1985; Nemeth and Wachtler, 1983; Wachtler, 1976). Minorities seem to stimulate enhanced cognitive activity and deeper information processing (Nemeth and Mayseless, 1987).

In 1976, Moscovici and Lage suggested from the results of their study that majorities and minorities produce different forms of influence. Majorities exert social pressure and produce compliance, while minorities have a cognitive, informational impact leading to private change. In 1980, Moscovici drew together various lines of evidence to argue for a theory of minority conversion. He suggests that majorities tend to produce compliance rather than conversion, whereas minorities tend to do the opposite, i.e. the former tend to produce a direct, immediate, but temporary, public effect, whereas minorities produce an indirect (appearing on related, more general measures), delayed and private effect. His explanation is that majorities induce *conformity* by means of a *comparison* process and minorities *conversion* by means of a *validation* process.

Thus Moscovici (1980) writes that the arguments of a majority are accepted passively with little cognitive activity – that their 'credibility presented an obstacle to the processing of information' (p. 214). One simply assumes that they are correct. When an individual disagrees, he or she will not focus on the object of disagreement, but will think 'Why do I not see or think like them?' All the person

> can do is engage in a *comparison process* to detect a possible flaw in the alternative judgement . . . to understand why he [*sic*] has made a mistake. . . . For lack of a satisfactory solution, he is

tempted to make concessions, moved by the urge to correct his mistake and be acceptable to others. This compels him to concentrate all his attention on what others say, so as to fit in with their opinions or judgements.

(Moscovici, 1980, pp. 214–15)

By contrast, when one disagrees with a minority, 'its answers are from the start considered deviant and require supplementary verification. Each one wonders: "How can it see what it sees, think what it thinks?" If the minority is insistent', then people undertake a *validation process*, 'an examination of the relation between its response and the object or reality just because a single pair of eyes is supposed to see less well than several' (Moscovici, 1980, p. 215). One tries to see what the minority sees, to understand what it understands. With a discrepant majority, all attention is focused on the others and one's preoccupation is to resolve a 'conflict of responses'. With a discrepant minority, all attention is focused on reality and one works to resolve a 'conflict of perceptions' by trying to understand the minority's point of view. Disagreement with the minority stimulates one to think actively about why it is wrong, how it might seem to be right, and one's own views, and such thinking unconsciously leads one to see things differently (i.e. it converts).

It is plain that these are essentially the two processes of normative and informational influence that we have discussed in previous chapters. The comparison/conformity process is concerned with the presentation of a positively valued, public self and represents a submission to social pressure. The validation/conversion process is a private, cognitive process of thinking about and validating the content of minority views to arrive at a subjectively valid, correct understanding of the world.

The theory of minority conversion represents a change from Moscovici's earlier, genetic model in some important respects:

1 Conformity is redefined from an influence back to a power process, reflecting dependence and social motives for approval and acceptance.
2 It is, in fact, defined as *more* of a power process than it had been hitherto in the conformity literature, for being in a majority is supposed causally to reduce one's informational impact and conformity is seen solely as compliance.
3 The idea of influence within the group as fully reciprocal, a collective negotiation where every person irrespective of position

is both the source and target of influence, seems to have been rejected.

4 The behavioural style of the minority and the conflict it induces are held to lead to *thinking about* and *understanding* of the minority point of view, which generalizes to related material, and thus there seems more emphasis on the *cognitive processing* of the informational content of minority views than on the *social co-ordination* of relationships.

Mugny and Perez (1987; Perez and Mugny, 1987) have developed this model further by integrating it with social identity theory (Tajfel and Turner, 1986) and Turner's (1982) concept of referent informational influence. Mugny and Perez elaborate Mugny's (1984a) earlier views to suggest that social identity and intergroup comparison processes relate to public or direct influence, whereas validation, cognitive processing of the minority message to understand it in relation to the objective world, underlies indirect influence or conversion. An interesting construct is being developed here that normative influence/compliance is a process in which one takes on the positively valued attributes of the ingroup majority to achieve a positive social identity in comparison with the negative outgroup minority. Accepting direct influence becomes a form of intergroup discrimination for positive social identity in which one moves publicly towards to the positive majority and rejects the negative minority. Informational influence/conversion is a process in which conflict with and rejection of the outgroup minority leads one to think about, understand and process more deeply their ideas and accept the core values that underlie them. Because conformity to the majority is motivated by the desire for a positive social identity, there is no cognitive conflict or need to think about their point of view; the influence is superficial. Because the minority are categorized and socially rejected as outgroup members, the social conflict is intensified, cognitive activity and validation are stimulated, and indirect influence increased.

In sum, social or intergroup conflict with a minority reduces direct influence but increases indirect influence. Social identification with a minority, like social acceptance of the majority, leads to direct but decreases indirect influence. Contrary to Turner's (1985) self-categorization theory of the role of social identity in influence, which assumes that shared ingroup identity is the basis of private acceptance and that compliance is a reaction to the outgroup identity of others (see Chapter 6), Mugny and Perez hypothesize that shared social identity actually *reduces* true informational influence while categorization of others as an outgroup actually *increases* it.

Both Moscovici and Mugny seem to agree that social conflict with a minority reduces direct influence but stimulates thought, whereas the majority, assumed to be correct, induces superficial, unthinking agreement that does not last beyond the immediate public situation. These are interesting but paradoxical ideas in that (a) one is *less* influenced by those one thinks are correct, (b) it is their *perceived correctness* that inhibits thought and prevents their influence, and (c) the public and private worlds are not merely split but inversely related. Let me confess that I do not find these ideas plausible. Neither do I find the theory fully convincing. I do not see why one would try to validate the viewpoint of a deviant minority, especially a negative, outgroup minority. I do not see why increased cognitive processing should lead to acceptance rather than rejection. I do not see why disagreement with a majority perceived as correct or similar to self should not create more cognitive conflict and activity, just as Moscovici (1976) himself argued in relation to the Asch study. I cannot see how the effect of a majority can be characterized as pure compliance.

Nevertheless, I am fully persuaded that Moscovici, Mugny and others have produced some fascinating and compelling data, which any alternative theory must confront. This is not, however, to suppose that the relevant data provide unambiguous support for the dual-process model.

## Evidence for the dual-process model

Moscovici (1980) cites a number of lines of evidence for the two-process model. Much of it is suggestive rather than conclusive. For example, he cites studies by Nemeth and Wachtler (1973) and Wolf (1979) – and one can add Kiesler and Pallak (1975) – showing that minorities produce both private and public influence. If one accepts the logic of the 'inverse rule' (that the private impact of minorities is due to the same 'conflict of perceptions' which rules out any public influence), this seems weak support. Then there are studies by Mugny and Papastamou showing that a rigid minority sometimes produces less direct and more indirect influence. This finding can be accepted, but there is the problem that social conflict and the cognitive distinctiveness of the minority message are probably correlated, confounded effects of rigidity. Conflict may reduce direct influence, but cognitive distinctiveness may increase attitude change once the immediate conflict is psychologically attenuated. It is not proven that the social conflict leads to later cognitive change; the causal process is not established. Also, Papastamou (1979, cited in Moscovici, 1980) seems to show that under the right conditions rigidity can produce both more direct and more indirect influence. Another problem is that these studies look only at the effects of the minority; they do not address the full model.

One study that did is the 'sleeper effect' study of Moscovici *et al.* (in Moscovici, 1980, pp. 226–8). After a delay of three weeks, the minority, especially a rigid minority, had more impact than the majority on indirect measures, while the majority and a 'fair' minority had more impact than the rigid minority on direct measures. However, the majority had no more immediate influence on subjects than the minority and, in fact, had little influence at the outset (which Moscovici explains as being due to the absence of social control). It is difficult to see, therefore, how the delayed effect of the majority on direct measures can be described as a compliance effect 'which disappears over time'. A follow-up study showed that a majority exercising collective control over subjects did produce immediate influence, but no minority nor delayed measurement conditions were included (Papastamou, 1979).

The most relevant studies are those that have manipulated the presence of both the majority and the minority and obtained measures of both direct and indirect influence.

## 1 The blue–green studies

The predicted pattern of majority compliance and minority conversion is most convincing in Moscovici and Lage (1976), but it is not reliably replicated. Moscovici and Personnaz (1980) found evidence for minority conversion but not majority compliance. In two attempted replications, Doms and Van Avermaet (1980) found conversion but not compliance for both majorities and minorities. Sorrentino *et al.* (1980), using only minority conditions, failed to replicate the conversion effect reported in the other studies. Personnaz (1981) did replicate minority conversion using a spectrometer method, but there was only very slight evidence of majority compliance. In a recent study, Moscovici and Personnaz (1986) also found little evidence of compliance. What small sign of majority compliance there was in one phase was eliminated by the 'psychologization' of the task, i.e. when it was made more subjective and ambiguous by being represented as having to do with the relationship between colour perception and personality. 'Psychologization' also increased the indirect influence of majorities and decreased that of minorities (as in Mugny, 1984b).

## 2 The creativity studies

Nemeth (1986), Nemeth and Kwan (1985), Nemeth and Mayseless (1987), Nemeth and Wachtler (1983) and Wachtler (1976) all show that subjects tend to converge with little thought more on majority responses, but that minorities tend to stimulate divergent, novel, creative thinking and more active information processing. These creative effects of the minority differ from the usual idea of indirect influence in the sense of shifting towards the minority position, but they do imply that there is a qualitative difference in reactions to a disagreeing majority and minority. They are consistent with the dual-process model and inconsistent with suggestions that majority and minority effects differ only quantitatively (Latané and Wolf, 1981).

## 3 Simultaneous exposure to majority and minority

Maass and Clark (1983, 1986) have reported studies testing the dual-process model. In one study (Maass and Clark, 1983), subjects were exposed to a summary of a five-person group discussion on gay rights. In the majority-con/minority-pro condition, four group members presented eight arguments opposing gay rights and the one minority member presented eight arguments in favour of gay rights. In the majority-pro/minority-con condition, the four-person majority and one-person minority took opposite positions to those just described. Unlike in other studies, therefore, the subjects were exposed to majority and minority arguments at the same time. The control group subjects were not exposed to a group discussion. Half of the subjects in all three conditions had their post-discussion attitudes measured in private and half were informed that they would be participating in a future group discussion and that they should indicate the position they would be taking on the attitude measure so that the information could be passed on to the group (the public condition). The subjects were 84 female students selected for their relatively moderate attitudes to gay rights.

In the majority-con/minority-pro condition, attitudes were more positive towards gay rights on the private than public post-test, but the effect was not significant. In the majority-pro/minority-con condition, attitudes were significantly more positive in public than private. Also, private attitudes were significantly more positive when the minority was pro than con. There were no differences in control group ratings. Apparently, then, the majority tended to have more impact than the minority in public, and the minority tended to have more impact than the majority in private.

In a second study, Maass and Clark replicated these findings and also found that minorities stimulated subjects to think of more pro-arguments and fewer counter-arguments than majorities (i.e. pro and counter the position of the influence source) and that cognitive activity (the number and direction of arguments generated about gay rights) mediated attitude change in the private but not public condition.

Maass and Clark (1986) replicated the design of their 1983 studies (exposing experimental subjects to group discussions comprising majority and minority participants and also using control groups) but added a parallel set of *majority-only* conditions in which no mention was made of a deviant minority and the relevant arguments were deleted from the group discussions. Again, subjects were more influenced by the majority in public than private and by the minority in private than public when exposed to both majority and minority opinions. However, when there was no minority in conflict with the majority, the subjects were more positive towards gay rights when the majority was pro rather than con, and this difference was significantly stronger in private than public. For example, when the majority-only condition was con, attitudes to gay rights were more negative in private than public. As the authors point out, in the absence of a minority, the majority produced conversion, both public and private influence. This result is not consistent with the dual-process model and suggests that the majority compliance observed in these studies may be more a function of the conflict beweeen majority and minority than a simple reaction to the power of the majority. The implication is that the minority is polarizing the group discussion into a social/intergroup conflict that reduces the private influence of the majority as well as the public influence of the minority.

An even less supportive set of results is reported by Mackie (1987). She conducted a series of four studies on private attitude change in which subjects were exposed to simultaneous majority and minority influence in experiments 1 and 2, majority-only and minority-only conditions in experiment 3, and consensus information about the majority and minority (without persuasive messages) in experiment 4. There was consistent and significant evidence for majority conversion in the first three studies, which was *stronger* with simultaneous exposure than in the majority-only conditions. Experiment 4 also produced evidence for private majority influence, but it was short-lived and did not generalize. There was little sign of minority influence in these studies (subjects in experiments 1 and 2 who mildly disagreed with the minority showed some slight indirect influence).

These studies offer mixed support for the dual-process model. Maass and Clark's (1986) study must condition our interpretation of their otherwise supportive pattern of results. The finding of majority conversion in the absence of a minority implies that majority compliance in their experiments may be a function of the minority's conflict with the majority polarizing the situation in more complex ways than hitherto suspected. Mackie's studies show that majorities can produce conversion even in the simultaneous exposure paradigm and seem completely inconsistent with the model.

## 4 Characteristics of majority influence

Mugny (1984b, 1985) conducted two interesting studies employing a modified Asch paradigm. In one study (Mugny, 1984b), subjects judged the lengths of lines, as in the Asch paradigm. They were presented with the consistently incorrect responses of 88 per cent (majority) or 12 per cent (minority) of an imaginary sample of subjects. In additional majority and minority conditions, they were informed that the study involved an optical illusion. There was also a control condition in which no source responses were provided and an 'authority' condition in which the experimenter gave the incorrect responses and the idea of the illusion was introduced. Direct influence was measured as movement to the incorrect source on test trials; indirect influence was assessed as a subsequent tendency to underestimate the length of the standard line relative to a stimulus line (as did the minority) in a later series of judgements without overt influence.

The results for direct influence (the mean number of items out of 12 where influence was shown) were that the majority (4.27 without illusion, 3.52 with illusion) and the authority (4.6) conditions had significantly more impact than the control (2.17) and minority conditions (2.35 without and 2.36 with illusion). The minority sources did not have a significant influence compared to the control condition. The magnitude of indirect influence (mean number of changes from pre-test to post-test) decreased from majority with illusion (+0.33), minority without illusion (−0.22), authority (−0.6), majority without illusion (−0.73), control (−1.22) to minority with illusion (−1.23) conditions. The first three conditions differed significantly as a whole from the latter three. Thus there is clear evidence of a majority condition that produces direct influence and conversion (majority with illusion) and a minority condition that has no significant direct or indirect influence (minority with illusion). Making the task ambiguous by introducing the idea of an optical illusion seems to increase the indirect influence of a majority without greatly reducing its direct impact, and to reduce the indirect influence of the minority without improving its minimal direct impact. These results provide little support for the idea that compliance and conversion are inversely related.

In a second, similar study (Mugny, 1985), subjects were exposed to an incorrect majority source described as being the same age, older or younger than themselves. The older the majority (and, therefore, presumably, the more it was perceived as valid and competent), the more direct influence was obtained. The younger majority tended to produce more indirect influence than the other conditions. However, the older source led more subjects to make both direct and indirect changes. Mugny (1985, p. 460) acknowledges that 'direct influence is not always, nor necessarily, an obstacle to latent changes'. Other studies also report that majorities can have more influence than minorities and that such influence can represent conversion, i.e. influence which is internalized, delayed or indirect (e.g. Mackie, 1987; Moscovici and Personnaz, 1986).

## 5 Ingroup–outgroup studies

Manipulations of the social identity of the majority and minority have obtained at best partially supportive results. The general predictions here are that ingroup minorities (and majorities) should have more direct than indirect influence and that outgroup minorities (and majorities) should have more indirect than direct influence. According to the logic of the dual-process model, ingroup membership should encourage a *comparison process* and outgroup membership should intensify social conflict and the *validation process*.

Aebischer *et al*. (1984) found more indirect influence of a social minority (i.e. low status outgroup) than a social majority (high status ingroup), but no differences on a direct measure. Both the majority and the minority produced some direct influence.

Perez and Mugny (1987) exposed 165 female, high school students to either an ingroup (female) or outgroup (male) minority that argued for abortion and was explicitly opposed by an ingroup or outgroup majority. The subjects responded on measures of attitudes to abortion (direct influence) and to contraception (indirect). On the direct measure, subjects were most influenced by the minority where both majority and minority were outgroup members. Interestingly, this condition also produced the least indirect influence, reversing the usual pattern of minority influence. On the indirect measure, too, there was an interaction between the group membership of the majority and minority. When the majority was an ingroup, there was no difference between the impact of ingroup (mean attitude change: −0.02) and outgroup (+0.07) minorities. When the majority was an outgroup, the ingroup minority (+0.19) had significantly more impact than the outgroup minority (−0.25). Thus an ingroup minority confronting an outgroup majority tended to have more indirect than direct influence and an outgroup minority confronting an outgroup majority tended to have more direct than indirect influence. It is difficult to see how these data can be construed as support for the dual-process model or the more specific idea that categorization of a minority as an outgroup facilitates conversion. The striking finding of a minority producing more direct than indirect influence in the outgroup–outgroup condition provides some support for the idea that the typical minority influence pattern (of more indirect than direct influence) reflects an ingroup–ingroup situation (see Clark and Maass, 1988b).

In a series of studies already partly described, Martin (1988a,b,c) found that an ingroup minority had more public influence than an outgroup minority and that this influence did not tend to decrease in private. He also found that an outgroup minority had more private than public impact, but only slight evidence that an outgroup minority had more private impact than an ingroup one. In one study (Martin, 1988c) exploring public influence, subjects were informed that an ingroup or outgroup (by a trivial criterion unrelated to the attitude measure) minority was similar or dissimilar to them, or were provided with no information. The ingroup minority had more influence than the outgroup minority where subjects assumed or had been told that they were similar to the minority, but there was no difference between the various outgroup minority and the dissimilar ingroup minority conditions (where there was much less influence). Consistent with self-categorization theory (see Chapter 6) and the idea that ingroup minority influence represents conversion, it seems that people are only influenced by ingroup others who are categorized as similar to self.

Other evidence along these lines is provided by Clark and Maass (1988a,b). Clark and Maass (1988a) found that ingroup minorities have more impact than outgroup ones in both public and private. In their later (1988b) paper, they investigated this issue in relation to the perceived credibility of the minority source. Using the simultaneous influence paradigm of Maass and Clark (1983), subjects with moderate attitudes to abortion were exposed to majority-pro/minority-con and majority-con/minority-pro conditions. The majority were always presented as ingroup members (same university) and the minority as either ingroup or outgroup (different, rival university) members. The subjects responded to the attitude measure in public or private and also judged the credibility of majority and minority. In this study, the ingroup–outgroup categorization was not directly relevant to the abortion issue.

There were several findings. The majority was perceived as more credible than the minority, but only where the latter comprised outgroup members. With an ingroup minority, the basic pattern of influence found in Maass and Clark (1983) was replicated: the subjects were more influenced by the majority in public than in private and by the minority in private than in public. With an outgroup minority, however, the subjects tended to shift away from the outgroup position and towards the majority in both private and public. In fact, the ingroup minority had significantly more private impact than the outgroup minority, regardless of its position on abortion. Ingroup minorities were perceived as more credible than outgroup minorities and the influence of the minority source was related to its perceived credibility, but ingroup minorities had more impact than outgroup minorities on attitude change even when their greater credibility was held constant statistically. Thus the ingroup membership of the minority increased independently both its credibility and its influence. The authors noted that the supposed superiority of outgroup over ingroup minorities for producing conversion seems only to have been reported on latent (i.e. related, more general) measures.

These studies show that an ingroup minority can have more direct influence than an outgroup one without any necessary reduction in its indirect influence, and that an outgroup minority can have less direct influence without necessarily any more indirect impact than an ingroup one. It still remains true with some complications (Perez and Mugny, 1987) that an outgroup minority facing an ingroup majority tends to have more influence in private than public. In sum, the bulk of evidence does not support the model in any straightforward way. Much of it seems directly inconsistent.

## Some reasonable inferences

It seems clear that minorities can stimulate cognitive activity (and creativity) and indirect influence. The fact that they may fail to exert influence at the direct level does not imply that they will have no impact at the indirect level. I do not think it is established, however, that they have indirect influence *for the same reason* that they do not have direct influence, i.e. that it is the social rejection of the minority that produces the indirect effect. It may be that conflict suppresses the direct effect and at the same time makes the minority message more cognitively distinctive, which subsequently facilitates influence under conditions where the minority is less categorized as deviant and rejected (Davidson, 1987).

Under the conditions of the studies reviewed above, it seems true that minorities will probably have as much or more indirect than direct influence, but social identification with the minority increases direct influence without weakening indirect influence, and disidentification does not significantly increase the indirect influence of outgroup minorities compared to ingroup minorities. The one instance of an atypical pattern, where the minority had more direct than indirect influence, is in Perez and Mugny's (1987) study, where an outgroup minority faced an outgroup majority. I suspect that this is evidence that the more typical pattern (of more indirect than direct minority influence) is facilitated and not weakened by the situation in which both majority and minority belong to an ingroup. I suggest that conflict with an ingroup majority reduces direct minority influence and that the reduced salience of the conflict in the indirect situation reinstates the influence of an ingroup minority.

Majorities do tend to have more direct than indirect influence in some of these studies, but in others they have no more direct impact than minorities, and in still others they have as much or more private influence than minorities. Under the conditions expected by conformity theory, i.e. where the stimulus situation is subjective, ambiguous and people are uncertain, majorities can certainly have an informational impact (Hogg and Turner, 1987a; Mackie, 1987; Moscovici and Personnaz, 1986; Mugny, 1984b, 1985).

I think we must conclude that:

1  Under certain experimental conditions, majorities tend to have more direct than indirect influence and minorities more indirect than direct influence, just as Moscovici suggests.
2  Depending on conditions, majorities may have no influence, both direct and indirect influence, or as much as or more indirect influence than minorities.
3  Minorities may have no influence, both direct and indirect influence, or as much or as little direct influence as majorities (e.g. Aebischer et al., 1984; there seems to be no study in which the minority had *more* direct impact than the majority).
4  Therefore, although there is a modest correlation between the majority or minority status of the subgroup and the direct or indirect form of influence, this is a function of specific, limited experimental conditions and not evidence for exclusive causal processes (i.e. comparison versus validation) linking majorities to compliance and minorities to conversion.

It seems plausible that majorities are more likely to have a public than private effect where their position is perceived as unambiguously contrary to the majority norm actually shared by subjects or perhaps is assimilated to the subjects' own position and so is not perceived as discrepant at all. They are likely to have both direct and indirect influence where their position is seen as moderately and plausibly discrepant from subjects' initial positions in a socially unstructured situation where subjects are uncertain of the normative response. To some degree, the notion of majority compliance may be an artifact of experimental situations that have either minimized or exaggerated the discrepancy of the majority position from the real majority position shared by subjects. The studies of Moscovici, Mugny and their colleagues are beginning to show this.

Minority impact is more likely to be indirect than direct unless measures are taken to reduce the polarizing, socially divisive stance of the minority. It seems unlikely that increasing their public effect weakens causally their private effect. There is probably a confounding of two things which go with a consistent minority stance, namely *social/intergroup conflict*, which prevents direct influence, and the moderate *cognitive distinctiveness/discrepancy* of the message, which facilitates influence at a later stage when the social conflict has dissipated. Disagreement with an ingroup subgroup is likely to produce more cognitive activity and private influence the more persuasive the subgroup is immediately. A plausible, not too arbitrarily discrepant ingroup majority, for example, is likely to produce much processing and cognitive conflict. Thus, minority conversion without compliance may be produced by the polarization of intragroup disagreement into a social division in the immediate, public situation, and the reverse, the subsuming of the social division into a broader, superordinate ingroup membership in comparison with the wider society, in the private situation (Davidson, 1987). There is a conversion effect, but it seems unlikely that it is produced by validating the message of an outgroup one rejects; nor do the data confirm that factors which improve public impact must weaken private influence, or vice versa.

## Conclusion

Do majority and minority influence embody qualitatively different processes? Does the former represent compliance and the latter conversion? The dual-process model has not been unambiguously supported and indeed is called into question by much recent evidence. The research shows that both majorities and minorities can induce either compliance or conversion under the right circumstances. Majority influence is not primarily a compliance process, for there is majority conversion too, and minorities can have overt as well as hidden effects. Moreover, the theory underlying the dual-process model leaves open important questions and is not conceptually fully plausible.

This is not to say that the difference between majority and minority influence is purely 'quantitative'. There seems little doubt that majorities and minorities are capable of producing qualitatively different effects in particular circumstances – whether it be majority compliance versus minority conversion or some other pattern. Is it possible to derive these different outcomes, when observed, from a common set of basic principles? Qualitatively different effects do not always require explanation in terms of distinct processes. The answer must depend on the availability of adequate theory. The general issue of one or more processes is open until research unambiguously supports some specific theoretical analysis. An attempt will be made in Chapter 6 to show how minority influence and conformity can be seen as outcomes of the same basic processes.

Nevertheless, the dual-process model and the original genetic theory have raised important questions, provided lasting insights and produced fascinating research. The framework has provided a heuristic and fertile way of thinking about influence and the whole genetic perspective remains a fundamental contribution. The researchers have established the fact of minority influence and created a research tradition of indisputable value.

## Suggestions for further reading

Maass, A. and Clark, R. D., III (1984). Hidden impact of minorities: Fifteen years of minority influence research. *Psychological Bulletin*, 95, 428–50. A good review of the empirical literature up to the early 1980s.

Moscovici, S. (1976). *Social influence and social change*. London: Academic Press. Moscovici's major statement of his position. A very important book, original, brilliant and provocative.

Moscovici, S. (1980). Towards a theory of conversion behavior. In L. Berkowitz (ed.), *Advances in experimental social psychology*, Vol. 13, 209–239. New York: Academic Press. Moscovici's presentation of the dual-process model of majority compliance and minority conversion.

Mugny, G. (1984a). The influence of minorities: Ten years later. In H. Tajfel (ed.), *The social dimension: European developments in social psychology*. Cambridge: Cambridge University Press/Paris: Editions de la Maison des Sciences de l'Homme, Vol. 2. A useful summary of Mugny's early thinking about the relationship between social identity and minority influence.

# 5 / POWER, COMPLIANCE AND SELF-PRESENTATION

## The meaning of power

The concept of power is used in some overlapping and some contradictory ways in social psychology. There are at least four important usages. Deriving from Lewinian research on group dynamics (e.g. Cartwright and Zander, 1968; French and Raven, 1959) and also 'social exchange' theories of social interaction (e.g. Thibaut and Kelley, 1959) is the idea of power as the capacity or ability to exert influence. In this formulation, influence is power in action and power is the basis of influence. Most recently found in the writings of the minority influence theorists (but reflecting a long-made distinction) is the idea of power in contrast to, and as the opposite of, influence. This is the idea of power as, in the extreme, naked coercion or compulsion – the control of others' behaviour through domination, forcing submission and compliance on the part of others. This is power as opposed to persuasion. As Moscovici (1976) puts it, if one has power, one does not need influence; if one can influence, one need not resort to power. This is the 'influence' process usually described as compliance or submission to social pressure. Lewinian theorists also distinguish compliance from other forms of power.

Next, there are two forms of power related to the idea of hierarchical social structure, shading into a more social structural or sociological conception of power. There is power as a leadership position (Hollander, 1985), as a social role in a social system defined by the exercise by the occupant of more effective influence than others. Leadership as a role position is defined by power over followers. Then there is power as legitimate authority, influence based on 'legitimate power' (French and Raven, 1959). Authority often goes with a leadership role, but it need not. Like leadership, it can be informal or formal, imposed or emergent, legitimate or illegitimate. Normally, when we speak of someone in a group or institution as having the authority to control and influence others, we mean legitimate authority, but social psychological theory is little developed in relation to this concept.

Authority may be defined as the power to influence (or control) based on social norms, traditions, values and rules (generally the social structure) that prescribe that one has the right to such power. Social norms not only arise from influence processes but also specify that certain persons or positions in a social hierarchy should have influence, be obeyed and even believed (Collins and Raven, 1969).

Sometimes, then, we might speak of persuasion, social control, leadership and authority as forms of power and, at other times, of power, persuasion and authority as influence processes. For consistency, except where appropriate in describing a theorist's ideas, I shall usually employ the concept of power to mean the compliance process and distinguish power (compliance), influence (persuasion) and authority (legitimate power) as the three main processes of influence (in the widest sense). Leadership represents either a formal social role or a differential exercise of influence by one or more group members, which in either case may involve one or more of the three influence processes. Distinctions can still be made within the power or influence processes. Moreover, there are also philosophical, political, economic and other psychological definitions of power (Ng, 1980). Thus one may think of the 'will to power' as a basic psychological motivation. We are only concerned in this chapter with power as a social psychological relationship between people. First, we shall review early thinking about the concept of compliance.

## Compliance and theories of influence

Asch (1952, 1956) argued that influence was not just slavish submission to social pressure and was unlikely to be a unitary process, i.e. that a distinction needed to be made between influence and power. In his conformity research, he found that subjects faced with the unanimous disagreement of an incorrect majority would sometimes change their overt behaviour and distort their judgements even when there had been no change in their perception. The implication was that this pattern reflected socially and emotionally motivated compliance with the majority. The subjects conformed in order to avoid ridicule and rejection and to win social approval.

Festinger (1953) theorized that attraction to the group (group cohesiveness) was the basic determinant of whether members internalized group norms or merely complied publicly. The role of group cohesiveness in his 1950 theory was not merely to increase compliance with the group to facilitate locomotion to group goals, but also to increase uniformity pressures in general, including those serving social reality testing. Thus the effect of group cohesiveness on conformity reflected and indeed determined an informational process of private acceptance. Uniformity pressures for group locomotion indicated a compliance process only in the case where members were not attracted to the group.

Deutsch and Gerard (1955) took a different line. They hypothesized that informational influence depended upon uncertainty. Normative influence, the specifically group process of conformity, represented compliance in that it depended on surveillance. It was based upon shared group membership and social interdependence and was motivated by the desire for social acceptance and approval. To the degree that one was attracted to the group, the more one would want its approval, and the more likely one was to comply with its expectations in order to gain such approval. Thus group cohesiveness determined compliance.

As discussed in Chapter 2, the compliance process has been identified with normative influence and the assumption has been that the motivational basis of such influence has been the desire to gain rewards and avoid costs and particularly to gain social approval and avoid rejection. The usual view is that group cohesiveness increases the normative power of the group, but that in so far as attraction to others is associated with trusting and feeling similar to them, it could also imply informational influence (persuasion).

This formulation was refined in the theories of Kelman (1958, 1961) and French and Raven (1959). Kelman (1958, 1961) distinguished three processes: *compliance*, based on others' power to mediate rewards and costs; *identification*, in which liking for another induces private acceptance of their opinions for just so long as the social relationship with them is maintained; and *internalization*, influence based on the content and credibility of the information provided (informational influence). Identification is a new category of influence in which attraction to the other is neither simply the basis of a power process nor related to the other's credibility, but implies a form of acceptance of the other's values motivated by a desire to be similar to the other. The identification notion harks back to Festinger (1953) and Freud (1921).

French and Raven (1959) theorized that influence reflects the psychological forces that one person can induce on another. Power to induce forces does not directly equate with influence; the counter-vailing power of the other to resist and other factors intervene. However, these complications aside, power is assumed to be the basis of influence. French and Raven (1959; Raven, 1965) distinguished five and then later six bases of power, i.e. six types of social psychological relationship between one person and another that allow one person to influence another. In general theoretical terms, the dependence of one person (P) on another (O) provides O with power over P, which allows O to influence P. French and Raven's contribution is to systematize and classify the different types of dependence and the distinct forms of influence they produce.

The six influence processes are *reward* and *coercive* power (the powers to reward and punish another), which they call public dependent types of power (i.e. these induce compliance), *referent*, *expert* and *informational* power, which are subdivisions of what we have called informational influence, and *legitimate* power, i.e. legitimate authority. Referent power is based on identification with the other, but, unlike in Kelman's system, it is a strongly informational process. Collins and Raven (1969) define it as more or less equivalent to Festinger's social comparison theory of social reality testing. Referent power is not compliance, nor is it just the motive to be like another. It represents the power of liked others to define reality for the individual. Expert and informational power both lead to internalized influence, but are based more on the perceived knowledge and information possessed by the other than on reference group identification. They represent a more rational, cognitive and less social process of influence. Expert power relates to the acknowledged competence and credibility of the other in a specific area. Informational power is very similar to what Burnstein and Vinokur (Chapter 3) seem to mean by informational influence, influence mediated by the actual content of messages.

As Collins and Raven (1969) point out, the direct evidence for compliance, reward and coercive power, is surprisingly thin on the ground. Researchers have regarded these processes as so obvious as not to need demonstrating. Moreover, reinforcement theory and social exchange ideas are so widely known in social psychology that it is a truism to suppose that behaviour can be controlled by the promise of rewards. There is a problem, however, in that what is a reward (or cost) for human beings is not defined by some objective class of stimuli. For example, one may think of money as a reward, but, under certain conditions, it may be perceived as a 'bribe' and found aversive (e.g. Schlenker *et al.*, 1980). What is found rewarding depends on the psychological meaning of the stimulus in the specific situation (how an objective stimulus is actually cognized) and this is often much easier to infer *post hoc* from the behaviour that one is supposed to be explaining than to predict in advance. Reinforcement theories of human conduct are notoriously unfalsifiable precisely because they rarely specify in advance what will be found rewarding and why. Even where rewards and costs are a plausible explanation of social control, they may not be a distinctive explanation. The 'conditioning' of verbal responses, for example (i.e. making desired responses more frequent by 'reinforcing' them with noises of approval), may be alternatively explained by supposing that subjects simply become aware of what the experimenter expects or wants (Collins and Raven, 1969). It is often a moot point whether reinforcement or some more cognitive process is the more plausible explanation of what is going on.

It is a platitude that in some sense in some situations one can control another's behaviour through the control of rewards. Reinforcement and social exchange theories explain all social interaction as controlled by rewards (Ng, 1980). Schlenker (1980) assumes that one acts in any social situation to achieve favourable reward/cost ratios. There is a danger of tautology in such generality. The key point is that in some situations one's behaviour is controlled through making one's compliance instrumental to the achievement of some subjectively defined goal. In other situations, such control may produce 'reactance' (Brehm, 1966), aggression or some other response. Some argue that reactance and non-compliance are also instances of reward maximization. Plainly, if everything is to be explained as reward maximization, then we need to predict exactly how and why individuals pursue which kinds of rewards in one way rather than another.

It is less evident that threats will always produce compliance. It can be assumed plausibly that the use of *coercive power* may produce a negative evaluation of the other, and other negative reactions likely to lead to a loss of influence (Collins and Raven, 1969; Worchel and Brehm, 1971). Evidence for *referent power* has been discussed in Chapter 2. A usefully detailed model of the operation of referent power is provided by Collins and Raven (1969).

An illustration of *expert power* is provided by Bochner and Insko (1966). A message attributed to a Nobel Prize-winning physiologist was able to persuade subjects that they needed much less sleep per night than when it was attributed to a less prestigious and credible source. Because the subjects found it difficult to derogate the credibility of the expert source, his influence tended to increase with the extremity of the position advocated until the bounds of plausibility were finally passed (i.e. where the message began to state that almost no sleep was needed).

Moscovici (1985) distinguishes between three methods of settling conflicts: rational demonstration of the truth or falsity of an opinion (e.g. offering proof employing agreed procedures), the use of power to impose a solution, and mutual influence to negotiate the conflict. *Informational power* is the power to change people's opinions using variations of the first method. One presents facts and evidence that are sufficient in themselves to change opinions. Is such power, then, really influence at all in the theoretical sense? It changes behaviour but only in the context of pre-established sets of norms, values and rules. Information can have an impact only given that other influence processes are already operating. One is influenced by valid information rather than just information, and one can always raise the question of whether such and such information is valid. Informational power must always depend on some other process that defines the information as valid or imply, implausibly I believe, that there can be information that is intrinsically valid (these issues are discussed more fully in Chapter 6).

Milgram's (1974) studies of obedience to authority provide the best known example of *legitimate power* and will be described presently.

Kiesler and Kiesler (1969) have sought to integrate the ideas of Festinger (1953), Kelman (1958) and French and Raven (1959). They suggest that their explanations of private acceptance can be made compatible if we assume that *legitimate*, *referent* and *expert* power increase the attraction of the source and that the effect of attraction on private acceptance depends on a continued social relationship with the source. Thus they accept that positive reference group membership can lead to private acceptance and not merely compliance. The more usual conception, however, is that group interdependence and attraction to others lead to compliance, and that the similarity or credibility of others is more important for acceptance. There is a close empirical link in that attraction relates to credibility through the perceived similarity and trustworthiness of liked others.

In general, there is agreement that compliance reflects outcome dependence: where the other controls desired outcomes and one is under surveillance by the other, compliance results. Attraction to the other may facilitate acceptance directly (where it is an expression of reference group identification) or indirectly (e.g. where it influences the other's perceived credibility), and it also increases the outcomes over which the group has control (e.g. the more one is attracted to the group, the greater the costs of rejection).

## Power versus influence

All the above theories can be assimilated to the dependence theory of influence (see Chapter 4). It will be recalled that Moscovici criticizes the confusion between power and influence that is inherent in the dependence theory. He argues that the dependence theory reduces all influence to a form of unilateral submission to those with the power of resources, knowledge or numbers. He believes that influence is primarily about social conflict and the collective negotiation of a shared, stable world rather than dependence for information.

Nevertheless, in discussing the modalities of influence he goes on to define conformity as submission to the social pressure of the majority. His argument, therefore, seems not to be that conformity is not a power process (which seemed to be his earlier position) but that the conformity model is not the *universal* process. Normalization and conversion also operate. Interestingly, this view of conformity now stresses its compliance aspects much more strongly than did the original dependence theorists. One can say that the dependence theorists adopt a 'power' theory that concedes that conformity has informational aspects, even if they are one-way. By contrast, Moscovici proposes a genetic model of the collective and reciprocal negotiation of social relationships, but characterizes conformity as purely a power process.

There are other views, too. Some seek a unified conception of influence processes in terms of 'social impact' (Latané, 1981; Latané and Wolf, 1981), social identity (see Chapter 6), or the 'subjective expected utilities' inherent in acceptance of a message (see Ng, 1980). Research on impression management and the public presentation of self is currently the most active and novel attempt to explore the power process from the perspective of the conformer.

## Social impact theory

Latané (1981; Latané and Nida, 1980) proposes a theory of social impact that specifies the effect of other persons on an individual. Social impact is defined as 'the great variety of changes in physiological states and subjective feelings, motives and emotions, cognitions and beliefs, values and behavior, that occur in an individual, human or animal, as a result of the real, implied, or imagined presence or actions of other individuals' (Latané, 1981, p. 343). The theory states that when other people are the source of impact and the individual is the target, impact should be a multiplicative function of the 'strength', 'immediacy' and number of other people. It is assumed that the marginal impact of each extra person is less than that of the last additional person, but the exact function is not specified. Similarly, when other people stand with the individual as the target of forces from outside the group, impact should be divided such that the net result is an inverse function of the strength, immediacy and number of the people standing together. The 'strength' of a source refers to its 'salience, power, importance, or intensity' (i.e. prestige, age, socio-economic status, relationship to and power over target). 'Immediacy' implies closeness in time or space and the absence of intervening barriers or filters.

Latané (1981) has applied the theory to research on social conformity and influence but finds only mixed support from studies of the effect of group size on conformity. For example, in the Asch paradigm (and in minority influence studies), the 'impact' of a minority of one tends to be minimal. The presence of a definite consensus within the influencing subgroup seems more important than its size (Moscovici and Lage, 1976). Latané and Wolf (1981) have employed social impact theory to try to integrate the influence of majorities and minorities, arguing that differences between the two are purely quantitative, a function of differences in the relative strength, immediacy and number of their members. This perspective implies that majorities should tend to have more impact than minorities (Wolf, 1985) and that the influence of a subgroup should increase at least marginally as it increases in size compared to the size of the target group. There is reasonable evidence for the latter prediction (Latané and Wolf, 1981; Mullen, 1983; Tanford and Penrod, 1984). There seems to be only weak evidence, however, for the effects of the other determinants of impact specified by the theory, i.e. strength and immediacy (Mullen, 1985, 1986).

More generally, the explanatory value of social impact theory is ambiguous. Latané (1981, p. 343) states explicitly that the 'theory' is not 'very specific. It does not say when social impact will occur or detail the exact mechanisms whereby social impact is transmitted. It does not purport to "explain" the operation of any of the number of particular social processes that are necessary to account for all the effects I have labelled "social impact" or to substitute for theories that do.' In other words, it seems primarily to be an attempt at the quantitative description of a number of empirical relationships rather than a theory of the underlying processes. The difficulty is that describing both majority and minority influence as instances of social impact, for example, does tend to imply that they embody a unitary psychological process. It is also not clear how the model can cope with the evidence that majorities and minorities can in specific conditions produce qualitatively different effects, or with the effects of other variables on the influence process apart from strength, immediacy and number. The 'immediate' (public, direct) impact of a minority, for instance, depends upon whether it is categorized as ingroup or outgroup (e.g. Martin, 1988a). There is a danger that the deliberate vagueness of concepts such as impact, strength and immediacy will allow the model to gloss over the detailed complexities of the influence process.

Mullen (1985, 1986) has also called into doubt the predictive precision of the theory, stating that the model is predictive only in the sense of specifying the direction of effects but not their precise value. He points out that the exact function specifying the effect of number is derived *post hoc* from observed data and varies greatly from study to study. His view is that the model is wholly descriptive, *post hoc* and not explanatory. Latané (1981) does not apparently dispute these points — his aim seems to be to search for and summarize a wide range of empirically similar relationships pertaining to the effect of the group on the individual. It may be that the perspective will prove more useful in summarizing across a variety of domains than in explaining social influence.

## Impression management and self-presentation

Impression management or self-presentation is the process of presenting a public image of the self to others. It is assumed that people seek to maximize rewards and minimize costs in a situation and, in particular, to obtain social approval and avoid disapproval. To this end, they seek to present themselves to others in such a way as to obtain favourable reactions or more generally to look good in terms of cultural ideals or their private values. Baumeister (1982), for example, defines self-presentation as 'the use of behavior to communicate some information about oneself to others' and suggests that the two main self-presentational motives are 'to please the audience and to construct (create, maintain, and modify) one's public self congruent to one's ideal' (p. 3). He argues that these motives to please the audience and construct one's generalized (ideal) public self will sometimes overlap and sometimes conflict with one another. Tetlock and Manstead (1985, p. 60) define the basic assumption of impression management theories as that 'People are highly sensitive to the social significance of their conduct and are motivated to create desired identities in interpersonal encounters.'

The link with power is clear. If compliance depends on surveillance by the group or 'audience', then one way to gain rewards or desired ends is not so much to conform privately but to look publicly as if one is enacting appropriate and desirable attributes. The distinction between the private and the public self is fundamental: it is the public self that is varied, controlled and observed. It is the public identity implications of actions in a given context that actively constrain and select our social behaviours. The difference from the power process as discussed so far is that self-presentation is not seen as passive conformity but as an active process of constructing a social identity and self-concept that enables one both to counter the power of others and to control others' actions by manipulating how one is perceived by others. If one can win others' approval, for example, one not only gains direct access to rewards, one also increases others' dependence on self and accrues power to shape their actions in turn. This theory also sees social influence as a process of reciprocal bargaining and negotiation, but based on mutual dependence. Self-presentation is the power of the dependent to change or modify the unilateral flow of influence (Schlenker, 1980).

The link between public self-presentation and conformity is explicitly acknowledged and related to findings that there tends to be more conformity in public (fact-to-face) than private (anonymous) conditions (Baumeister, 1982; Greenwald and Pratkanis, 1984; Tetlock and Manstead, 1985) and that individual differences in public/private self-consciousness and self-monitoring and situational differences in self-awareness (as induced by an audience or camera) produce differences in conformity (Greenwald and Pratkanis, 1984). The point that social behaviour changes importantly as the person moves from the private to the shared public setting is also made in the polarization and minority influence literatures (and in others such as research on cooperation in mixed-motive settings). For Asch (1952), the public setting embodied the 'shared psychological field', the field of 'mutual reference' between people, and was fundamental to the process of psychological group formation and mutual influence.

Illustrative studies showing that people manage others' impressions of self to create desired images are reported by Schneider (1969), Schlenker (1975), Baumeister and Jones (1978) and Baumeister et al. (1979). Schneider (1969) explored the effects of success and failure on a series of tests on self-presentation where another person either could or could not give the (male) subject feedback on his presentation. Failure subjects were more positive and success subjects more modest about themselves in the feedback condition than no-feedback condition. Presumably, failure subjects tried to gain approval from the other by counteracting the effect of their failure, while success subjects sought to preserve the status they had gained by not appearing too immodest.

Baumeister and Jones (1978) had subjects describe their attributes to a target person who supposedly did or did not have some prior information about their personalities. If the prior information was unfavourable, the subjects described themselves in terms consistent with it, but compensated by enhancing their self-descriptions on other traits. If the prior information was favourable, the subjects were generally modest and self-deprecating. The subjects who were assured that the target person would not have access to the prior information about their personalities did not show these self-enhancement effects. The effect on self-description of receiving a self-evaluation depended on whether the information was public or confidential.

Baumeister et al. (1979) showed that people conform to expectations only when such conformity puts them in a desirable light. Female subjects took a fake personality test that established either publicly or privately that they had a particular desirable or undesirable trait. They then performed an anagram task after being informed that persons with this trait usually performed poorly on such tasks. The subjects publicly informed that they had the desirable trait performed significantly worse on the task than the subjects in the other conditions. There was also evidence that when poor performance was linked to the undesirable trait, the subjects sought actively to disconfirm the expectation. Thus the subjects used performance on the task, confirming or disconfirming public expectations, to present a desirable image of themselves.

Other studies (Baumeister, 1982; Tetlock and Manstead, 1985) suggest that self-presentational concerns may underlie a whole range of phenomena: giving and receiving help, conformity, psychological reactance, attitude expression and change, reactions to evaluations, aggression, self-serving and counter-defensive attributions, task performance, ingratiation, emotional expression, group polarization, equity-seeking and de-individuation.

For example, Satow (1975), studying helping, found, perhaps not surprisingly, that people will give much more when they are making public rather than secret and anonymous donations to some cause. The public donations were on average seven times larger. Gottlieb and Carver (1980) found, in a modification of Darley and Latané's (1968) study of the effect of group size on bystander intervention (see Chapter 2), that a group of physically isolated, unacquainted people were much more likely to help (and to help quickly) a victim of an apparent seizure if they expected to meet and talk to each other later than if they expected to remain anonymous.

At the other end of the spectrum, Borden (1975) found that the type of audience, and therefore the kind of behaviour that was likely to be approved of, influenced the degree to which subjects were aggressive. They were more aggressive when they perceived themselves to be in the presence of a karate instructor than a pacifist. Moreover, the difference between the groups of subjects disappeared when the observer left the study half-way through, implying that it was not caused by any internal change produced in the subjects.

More generally, Zimbardo (1969) argues that de-individuation, reflecting submergence in the group and anonymity, tends to increase aggressive and other anti-social responses, because it leads to a loss of personal responsibility and removes fear of public censure. The process of de-individuation based on anonymity implies that anti-

social behaviour results from the failure of people to regulate their
actions in terms of the shared, public and constraining standards of
society. Reicher (1984a,b) contends that anonymity can affect the
content of the self-concept, and increases conformity to the norms of
the specific social (group) identity that it makes salient. He makes the
neglected point that submergence in a crowd, for example, may
mean that one cannot be observed by *outgroup* members, but one is
not anonymous with respect to *ingroup* (crowd) members. The
so-called effects of anonymity, therefore, may often reflect greater
conformity to ingroup norms and less to outgroup norms rather than
simply behaviour unregulated by norms.

Baumeister (1982) illustrates the distinction between 'pleasing the
audience' and 'public self-construction' with studies on conformity
and reactance. He points out that while people presumably conform
in specific situations in order to please the immediate audience, it is
nevertheless the case that 'conformists' are evaluated negatively. Our
(Western) culture values autonomy, integrity, independence of
mind, and so forth. One solution is to flatter the audience by agreeing
that one has been persuaded by their point of view but to deny to
society at large that one has changed one's mind. Braver *et al.* (1977)
found that subjects in their study admitted most yielding to a
persuasive speech when they were in the presence of the persuader
alone. They admitted least yielding when the persuader was absent
but when an observer was present (who might perceive yielding as a
sign of gullibility and lack of intelligence) and an intermediate
amount of yielding when both the persuader and the observer were
present. Baumeister (1982, p. 9) contends these data imply that
public conformity 'is born out of concern with maintaining a desirable public image for oneself rather than out of specific fear or threat
of punishment', and he argues that the opposing effects of persuader
and observer reflect the conflict between pleasing the audience and
generalized self-construction.

This interpretation also helps to explain why people will sometimes conform less to an audience that makes overt threats of
rejection, censure or punishment. To conform in such circumstances
might please the audience but it would represent an extreme loss of
face in terms of cultural values. Worchel and Brehm (1971) have
shown that increasing threat can lead to less conformity. Their
interpretation is in terms of reactance theory: according to this
theory, threats to one's behavioural freedom produce a state of
motivational arousal (psychological reactance) that motivates one to

take the threatened course of action. Baer *et al.* (1980) varied whether subjects received a high- or low-threat persuasive communication, whether subjects had had a previous opportunity to exercise their freedom by expressing a position contrary to that advocated in the threat and whether this opportunity was public or private, and whether subjects' attitudes after the communication were expressed publicly or privately. It was not simply the case that high threat led to less influence except when subjects had already had an opportunity to assert their freedom (the reactance prediction). They found, consistent with a self-presentation theory of reactance, that high threat decreased influence only under conditions of the public expression of attitudes and that prior exercise of freedom mitigated this effect only when it had also been public.

In many respects, impression management research has developed as a series of alternative explanations of phenomena predicted by existing theories (such as cognitive dissonance, reactance, equity, causal attribution, and instinctual or learning theories of aggression). In other words, much that has been explained in terms of intra-personal cognitive and motivational processes may be better explained as public conformity to the salient norms and values held by the subject, the audience or the culture at large. It may be behaviour enacted to protect and enhance one's public identity. Rather than people having needs for consistency, equity, etc., they may only be trying to *appear* consistent, equitable, free, competent, and so on.

Arkin *et al.* (1980) and Tetlock (1980), for example, have applied self-presentational ideas to 'self-serving' and 'counter-defensive' biases in causal attribution. Arkin *et al.* found the usual self-serving tendency to take credit for success and to refuse the blame for failure among subjects who did not expect future interaction. The tendency was reversed, however, among those who were high in social anxiety and who anticipated having their performances evaluated by experts. Self-serving attributions were also weakened by more private than public measures of attribution. It may be that the standard finding also reflects more a desire to avoid publicly embarrassing admissions than subjects' true (private) opinions. Tetlock (1980) found that observers do tend to evaluate positively moderately 'counter-defensive' teachers (who take the blame for pupils' poor performance) in situations where research has shown that teachers do make such attributions. Taking the blame will sometimes gain one credit with others. Morse *et al.* (1976) and Reis and Gruzen

(1976) have done the same for equity theory, explaining equity-seeking in terms of impression management.

Most of the research along these lines has been done in relation to cognitive dissonance theory. This theory explains cognitive changes (including private attitude change) as being motivated by a need to reduce an aversive motivational state of dissonance (i.e. psychological inconsistency between cognitions). One important finding (Festinger and Carlsmith, 1959) is that counter-attitudinal behaviour can induce more attitude change in line with the behaviour under conditions of low than high incentives for the behaviour. Tedeschi et al. (1971) argue that these and other dissonance findings can be explained in terms of the social rewards that accrue to people who appear consistent to others. Gaes et al. (1978), for example, obtained dissonance-type shifts towards counter-attitudinal behaviour only on standard (relatively public) paper-and-pencil scales, but not on a much more private measure (using a 'bogus pipeline'). Moreover, even the former attitude shifts were only obtained if subjects had behaved publicly inconsistently with their initial attitudes rather than anonymously. Schlenker et al. (1980) have shown that the social meaning of the monetary rewards for counter-attitudinal behaviour affect the relationship between incentive magnitude and reported attitude change.

Baumeister (1982, p. 13) summarizes a number of old and new studies implying that 'dissonance may be considered a person's attempt to adjust his or her general public self so as to be compatible with the counterattitudinal behavior'. His argument is not that dissonance phenomena do not have intrapsychic aspects, but that the experience of dissonance and the motive to reduce it are produced by the fear of the potential damage to one's reputation that could follow a public display of inconsistency. One response of impression management theorists to data showing that dissonance is not just superficial but is associated with unpleasant, internal states of arousal has been to incorporate such concepts into their own explanations of attitude expression. There is now wide agreement (a) that both dissonance and self-presentation processes are likely to be at work in attitude change studies (and that the task is to explore the conditions that influence each and how they interrelate) and (b) that impression management theory in this area may be moving towards a formulation that is becoming less distinguishable from dissonance theory (Chaiken and Stangor, 1987; Cialdini et al., 1981; Cooper and Croyle, 1984; Tetlock and Manstead, 1985).

Studies on anticipatory attitude shifts and the expression of attitudes reinforce the general point that attitude statements may often be interpersonal communications rather than reports of internal states (e.g. Cialdini *et al.*, 1973; Cooper and Jones, 1969; Hass, 1975).

Tetlock and Manstead (1985) have pointed out that in practice it is often difficult to discriminate between impression management and 'intra-psychic' (cognitive, motivational, etc.) explanations of research findings and suggest that the dichotomy may be arbitrary. A basic problem of interpreting the research is that impression management manipulations tend, inevitably, to confound processes affecting both the public and private self, identity implications and intra-individual processes. The public setting is complex; it does not merely vary the fact of being under observation by others. This in itself changes social relationships and introduces new processes. It may affect the content of the self and not simply whether it is private or public. Let us recall from Chapters 2 and 4 that it is by no means clear that conformity in public is purely compliance. The public situation may modify the private self. This is implied, for example, by Duval and Wicklund's (1972) theory of objective self-awareness, which hypothesizes that audiences can make personal standards and values more salient and hence affect private self-evaluation.

Self-categorization theory (Turner *et al.*, 1987; see Chapter 6) argues that the crucial fact about the public setting is that it is *shared with others* and provides a comparative context within which people can categorize themselves as identical to or different from others. Such contexts, therefore, change the level and content of self-identity in terms of *how people perceive themselves* and not merely how they look to others. Effects such as more conformity to others in public than in private may reflect *private* adherence to the norms of a shared, social categorical self (social identity) that is salient in the situation (Turner, 1982; Wilder and Shapiro, 1984). This analysis implies at minimum that whether the effects of the public setting are purely to do with the presentation of self or reflect real, situation-specific changes in the private self is likely to be a function of who the others in the situation are, and, in particular, whether they are ingroup or outgroup members by some relevant criterion.

The weaknesses of impression management research are easy to summarize. The 'theory' is too general, lacking in the prediction of genuinely novel and distinctive phenomena. It tends to provide a ready-made, *post hoc*, alternative account of existing findings, but rarely produces any great surprises. There is a danger that the field could become a long list of demonstrations that all behaviours can be affected by self-presentational concerns without showing that this is their necessary condition or adding much to their explanation. One can also add that it has a too simple and almost empty view of the private self. To suppose that the motivation of the private self is to achieve desired ends, gain approval, maximize rewards compared to costs, and so on, seems banal and circular if no more precise analysis is attempted. Finally, social identity cannot be reduced to the public self, i.e. the individual self as perceived by others; there is also the shared, collective, group self to consider.

On the other hand, there is much of value in the demonstration that self-identity varies from situation to situation, that the self is constructed in social settings and that attitudes and behaviour are constrained and modified by the identity, social evaluative and normative implications of social contexts. The perspective provides a welcome antidote to the unrelenting explication of social behaviour in terms of intra-individual cognitive processes and information processing activities by reintroducing the social normative context of behaviour as a determining process.

The next step is to develop a social contextual perspective on the private as well as the public self. Intra-personal psychological processes are not merely constrained by the social context but actively function in interplay with it. Social influence is not merely compliance, but also gets to the psychological core of the self (Sherif, 1936). The need is to shift the focus of research to the theoretical elucidation of the relations between the nature of the self, social influence and the precise character of social settings. If impression management research takes this step, we shall move to a more social, complex and richer view of the self and its relationship to the social world.

## Power and social structure

There is clear evidence of a correlation between the capacity to exert influence and one's position in a hierarchical social structure. This is not the place to discuss research on social structure. Suffice it to say that there are sound theoretical reasons to suppose that there will be both a causal and a correlational relationship between power and one's position in the social structure. Leaders tend to be popular,

high in status and occupy central positions in communication net-
works. The general relationship between social status in society and
influence has also been verified (Moscovici, 1985).

Such a correlation would not be expected if the hierarchy were
psychologically rejected: the group may be rejected, the rewards
devalued, the information disputed. At this point influence becomes
bound up with social change. Tajfel and Turner (1986) have argued
that intergroup relations tend to be transformed into insecure relations of intergroup conflict and ethnocentrism when the dominant
and subordinate social groups experience their relations as illegitimate and unstable and barriers to social mobility enhance ingroup
identification. Under such conditions, influence would emanate from
ingroups. The erstwhile social hierarchy would be unlikely to determine relations of influence. In Moscovici's phrase, the dominant
group would resort to force where it had lost its influence and, as Ng
(1980) points out, the success of the active minority in converting the
population would presage its own resort to force to counter the
power of the originally dominant group. These issues have as yet
been little explored in social psychology. A promising beginning can
be found in Paicheler's (1976, 1977, 1979) studies of the 'Zeitgeist'
effect and in her distinction between progressive and reactionary
minorities (see Chapter 3).

Social psychologists have nevertheless approached the relation
between power and social structure in research on leadership roles
and obedience to authority.

## Leadership

Leaders are persons or social roles who exert more influence in a
group than others. They tend to be of high status, to occupy a central
position in the communication structure of the group and to display
more effective initiative than others in the group, i.e. they tend to
suggest, direct, instruct and advise courses of action that the group
actually follows. They play the most important role in directing
the group's activities, maintaining its traditions and customs and
ensuring that it reaches its goals.

Early leadership research (see Hollander, 1985) established that
no consistent set of personality traits distinguishes leaders from
others. There is no distinctive type of personality that leaders tend to
have or that predicts who will become leaders. The kinds of traits a

leader needs will vary from group to group and from problem to problem. In general, personality traits have been found not to be good predictors of individual behaviour in specific situations (see Ajzen, 1988). People's behaviour tends not to be consistent across varying situations, as the trait concept implies, but is a function of the specific person in the specific situation. So the trait concept may not be an adequate way of conceptualizing any psychological qualities that leaders do bring to a particular situation. Some traits have been found to correlate very modestly with leadership across situations (Stogdill, 1974). These findings, however, are too weak to imply that some people are 'natural' leaders, while others are not.

The alternative conception is that leaders are people who serve a function for the group and that people become leaders if they have the right attributes for the right group at the right time. For example, Merei's (1949) research shows that it is the group that determines who will be accepted as a leader. The leader cannot impose him- or herself on the group. Sherif (1967) observed that as intergroup relations became more hostile and the needs of the group changed accordingly, so the relative position of an individual in the leadership hierarchy altered to reflect the new contribution that member could make. What kinds of functions do leaders serve? Two main ones have been identified (Bales, 1950; Slater, 1955): the task specialist who 'initiates structure' in relation to the task and the socio-emotional specialist who displays 'consideration' towards group members and is relationship-oriented. The task leader takes the central role in enabling the group to deal with its tasks and reach its goals. The socio-emotional specialist maintains good interpersonal relationships in the group, to keep the group functioning as a solidary, cohesive social unit.

Bales suggests that these functions are inversely related and therefore two different leaders are often required for effective functioning. Other researchers (Stogdill, 1974) have found initiating structure and consideration to be independent dimensions of leader activity. Still others break these functions and role activities down into more dimensions (Bowers and Seashore, 1966). The person who will become leader, therefore, and be a good leader, will be the one who looks after the feelings of subordinates and/or organizes to get the job done (Sorrentino and Field, 1986), when the group is in need of these functions being served.

More than personality, the issue is whether the leader can produce the behaviours and the style of behaviour that the group needs in specific circumstances. A classic study of the influence of leadership style on the social atmosphere of the group was performed by Lewin *et al.* (1939), who investigated the effects of 'autocratic', 'democratic' and '*laissez-faire*' styles on group productivity and morale (see Sayles, 1966, for a review). They found that both autocratic and democratic styles were effective in terms of the productivity of the groups, but that the latter was superior in terms of morale, motivation and satisfaction of members.

The autocratic and democratic style embody the task and socio-emotional specialist roles, but are represented as opposites. The ideal leader may be the person who can be both or either when the situation demands, but under what circumstances is it better to act more autocratically, more democratically or to have access to both styles?

Theories that seek to specify leadership effectiveness in terms of the match between leadership style and the situation are known as *contingency* theories: which style is more effective is seen as contingent on the situation. The best known example is Fiedler's (1964, 1978) theory. Fiedler measures leadership style in terms of the leader's 'Least Preferred Co-worker' score (high LPC leaders being relationship-oriented) and classifies situations in terms of being more or less favourable to the leader in terms of leader–member relations, task structure and leader's power. Basically, he hypothesizes that low LPC leaders do better than high LPC ones in highly favourable and highly unfavourable situations, and high LPC leaders do better than low LPC ones in situations of intermediate favourableness to the leader. There are correlational data broadly consistent with the predicted relationships (Strube and Garcia, 1981) and some supportive experimental evidence (Chemers *et al.*, 1975).

There is also an argument about the actual degree of correlational support. There would seem to be a large degree of variability in the observed relationships. Considering the complexities of group functioning in real life and the crudeness of the theoretical categories employed to distinguish between leaders and situations, such variability is probably not surprising. More problematic is the issue of what the LPC score means and its relationship to the actual behaviour of leaders, i.e. what they actually do in the varying situations. Fiedler suggests that the leadership style represented by LPC reflects a fixed personality trait, but traits do not predict consistent behaviour across situations. Later he implies that leaders may differ not in their access to these styles but in the relative importance they attach to them and that they may be able to use either style in appropriate situations. If this is so, then it becomes much less clear what high- or low-LPC leaders are actually doing to be effective: it seems likely that the way they behave will be a function of a complex interaction between their motives, abilities and the specifics of the situation.

To some degree, different issues are being confused. What kinds of behaviours does a person need to enact in which situation in which group to be effective as a leader? Are there differences between people in the degree to which they are able to produce the specific behaviours required by specific groups in specific situations? Are these differences between people stable and how should we conceptualize the 'kinds' of people who are better or less able to produce some of them than others? Are some kinds of people better able to vary appropriately their behaviour/style to produce effective leadership across differing groups and changing circumstances? We probably have reasonable if crude answers to the first two questions, but less satisfactory ones to the last two. Given certain minimum qualifications, probably anyone can act as an effective leader in the right group at the right time. There is no type of personality with a mystical, special 'divine right' to lead. Yet people whom we think of as excelling at leadership are probably people who are generally more skilled at being able to vary their actions to suit the group and the moment as a function of real insight into changing group dynamics, not persons who cannot change or help the group to change with the times because they are imprisoned in some rigid, fixed leadership style. It is surely an elementary requirement of leadership that the leader should be able to see what is needed at any given moment and adapt his or her own behaviour accordingly. Leadership behaviours are a function of complex processes of interaction between varying person attributes and a changing situation. How are we to conceptualize the person attributes that predict effective leadership across a variety of situations without falling into the trap of reducing them to rigid, consistent traits? The idea of people with consistent leadership styles is a version of the too simple trait approach and has the same problems.

One solution is to look at how leaders emerge and gain influence in the context of basic theories of the influence process. Hollander (1958; Hollander and Julian, 1970), for example, has studied how leaders gain the power to deviate from current practices and change the group in the context of the dependence theory of conformity. He argues that people must deviate to lead and that, to avoid rejection in the process, they must build up 'idiosyncrasy credit' with the group through a certain amount of prior conformity. Other ways in which they can build up credit include demonstrated competence, perceived identification with group and obtaining legitimate power. Moscovici (1976) looks at the effect of minorities in producing social change in the context of his social conflict model of the influence process as a whole. Similarly, Turner (Turner et al., 1987) approaches the concept of leadership in terms of a basic analysis of the psychological group and norm formation (see Chapter 6). In general, the data (e.g. Bray et al., 1982) are consistent in indicating that groups must believe in people before they will follow them – leaders must prove themselves to be people worth following, who can be trusted, who are not enemies, idiots, incompetents, but people who are skilled, who identify with 'us' and who have the group's interests at heart (Kirkhart, 1963).

## Obedience to authority

In his research on obedience to legitimate authority, Milgram (1974) conducted what has become one of the best known series of experiments in social psychology. The research used the same basic paradigm for 18 separate experiments. In all but one experiment the participants were males, they were always non-students, they ranged from 20 to 50 years of age and were drawn from different occupations and classes. The studies were usually conducted in the prestigious setting of the Interaction Laboratory of Yale University.

The basic procedure was as follows. A person (recruited by advertisement or telephone) comes to the laboratory and is told to carry out a series of acts that come increasingly into conflict with his conscience. The issue is how far the person will go in complying with the experimenter's instructions before refusing to carry out the actions required of him. The experimenter is the legitimate authority in this situation; the compliance of the subject up to the point of refusing to carry out the experimenter's orders is the measure of obedience.

When the subject arrives he finds another person also present. They are to take part in a study of memory and learning. One of them is designated (apparently by chance) as a 'teacher' (the genuine subject) and the other as a 'learner' (who is in fact a confederate of the experimenter playing an arranged role). The study is ostensibly concerned with the effects of punishment on learning. The learner is led to another room, put in a chair, his arms strapped to the chair and an electrode attached to his wrist. He is told that he is to learn a list of word pairs and that whenever he makes a mistake he will receive electric shocks of increasing intensity. After watching the learner being strapped into place, the teacher is taken to the main experimental room and seated in front of an impressive-looking shock generator. Its main feature is a line of 30 switches ranging from 15 to 450 volts in 15-volt increments. The switches are also labelled from 'slight shock' to 'danger – severe shock'; the two most severe switches, after severe shock, are marked 'XXX'. The teacher is told that he is to administer the learning test to the learner. If the learner responds correctly on a trial (by remembering the right word for a given stimulus word), the teacher is to proceed to the next item. If the learner makes a mistake (i.e. he does not recall the correct word), the teacher is to give him an electric shock. The shocks are to start at the lowest level of 15 volts and increase in level every time the learner makes a mistake, moving to 30, 45, 60 volts, and so on, until the highest level is reached.

The learner/victim, being a confederate, actually receives no shocks at all, but acts out a prearranged role of making errors in a certain sequence and suffering the effects of being shocked. The situation is very real and gripping to the teacher, producing intense conflict. At 75 volts, the learner 'grunts', at 120 volts he complains out loud, at 150 volts he demands to be released from the experiment. As the shocks increase in intensity, his protests grow more vehement and emotional. His response at 250 volts is described by Milgram as an 'agonized scream'. Whenever the subject asks advice from the experimenter about continuing in face of the victim's protests or indicates that he no longer wishes to continue, the experimenter responds with an ordered sequence of 'prods' to bring the subject back into line: 'please continue', 'the experiment requires that you continue', 'it is absolutely essential that you continue', culminating in the strident untruth 'you have no other choice, you *must* go on'.

The question is at what point will the subject, an ordinary citizen, act to stop the obvious and growing distress of his fellow participant, an innocent victim, by defying the authority of the experimenter. One might think that many subjects would refuse to take part in the study right at the beginning and walk out of the laboratory. In fact, nobody ever did – evidence that at least at the outset the experimenter's aims and instructions were perceived as legitimate. Milgram also asked three groups of people, including 39 psychiatrists, to predict their own likely reaction to the situation. Every one of the 110 respondents assumed that at some point they would refuse to continue (the mean *maximum* shock level they believed they would administer was around level 9 out of 30, as 'moderate' became 'strong shock').

In experiment 1, the 'remote' victim could not be seen or heard and made no verbal complaint. He pounded loudly on the walls in protest at 300 and 315 volts. Thereafter no more was heard and no further responses of the subject appeared on the signal box. Even so, 26 out of 40 subjects (65 per cent) obeyed the orders of the experimenter to the very end, punishing a worryingly silent victim right up to the 450 shock level (which was labelled 'XXX' and came five steps *after* the first level marked 'danger – severe shock'). The mean maximum level administered was 27 out of 30. Three studies progressively lessened the remoteness of the victim, adding the victim's vocal protests, his presence in the same room as the teacher, and finally requiring the teacher to force the victim's hand onto the shock plate to administer the punishment the victim refused to accept voluntarily. The results were that 62.5, 40 and 30 per cent of subjects still punished the learner to the maximum extent (respective mean levels being 24.53, 20.8 and 17.88). The salience and closeness of the victim plainly reduced obedience, but the striking result is still the degree of obedience, the power of legitimate authority to compel what in isolation seems unjustifiable and immoral cruelty.

In experiment 5, the study was moved out of the Interaction Laboratory and into a more modest, less impressive setting in the basement of the same building. The victim not only made verbal protests as in experiment 2, but also mentioned that he had a heart problem. Obedience did not decrease (26 out of 40 continued to the end). The removal of the physical presence of the experimenter in experiment 7, however, did decrease obedience dramatically (only 9 out of 40 carried on to the end). Other interesting findings were that female subjects performed comparably to men and that changing the institutional context of the study from Yale University to an office building in a nearby industrial city and removing any visible tie to the university lowered the obedience of the local subjects, but not significantly so (47.5 per cent were maximally obedient). When the learner demanded to be shocked, but the experimenter forbade the shocks, all subjects obeyed the experimenter. Similarly, when the authority was an 'ordinary man' rather than a Yale scientist, obedience dropped dramatically, with only 4 out of 20 subjects going to the maximal level. The subjects even began to defend the victim if the shocks were administered illegitimately by another supposed subject (experiment 13a). Other experimental variations convincingly demonstrated that 'the decisive factor [in the obedience] is the response to authority, rather than the response to the particular order to administer shocks. Orders originating outside of authority lose all force' (Milgram, 1974, p. 104).

Two final studies showed that the example of two peers who defied the experimenter and refused to carry out his orders led 36 out of 40 subjects to rebel before the final shock level, whereas the presence of an accessory who did the 'dirty work' of administering the shocks increased the obedience of subjects in carrying out related tasks (92.5 per cent obeyed). The obedience or disobedience of subjects was related to the influence and authority of the experimenter and others in the situation, the definition of the situation and the salience of the victim.

Why did the subject continue to obey the experimenter? Milgram points to several factors. First, there are 'binding factors' that lock the subject into the situation, e.g. politeness, his desire to keep his initial promise to help the experimenter, the awkwardness of withdrawal. Then there are a number of adjustments that the subject makes in his thinking to maintain his relationship with the experimenter and reduce the strain of the conflict. He becomes absorbed in the narrow technical aspects of the task and loses sight of or denies its broader consequences. He immerses himself in the procedures, puts great care into doing a good job, but appears blind to the moral implications of his actions. In a sense, the subject tries to deny his own human role in what is going on, acting as if he were only a part of the unthinking technical apparatus. The purposes and morality of what he is doing are defined as the responsibility of the experimenter.

The most common mental adjustment in the obedient subject is for him to see himself as not responsible for his own actions. He sees himself as an agent of external authority, locked into a subordinate position in a social structure, responsible to others in authority but not for himself. The consequence of submission to authority, Milgram argues, is the disappearance of a sense of responsibility. A typical subject will state after the study 'I wouldn't have done it by myself. I was just doing what I was told' – as if he had no choice.

Milgram describes this mental condition as the 'agentic state', in which a person sees him- or herself as the agent of another person, carrying out that person's wishes (the opposite of autonomy). Milgram believes that it represents the shift in attitude that allows human beings to function in organized, hierarchical social systems, ceding control at the local level to central authority. For the group to function as a unified whole, humans are able to give up individual responsibility and defer to regulation by a person of higher status. The shift to the agentic state, the ceding of control to the representative of established institutions, norms and reference groups, implies that legitimate authority substitutes for the person's own self-regulation.

Other factors at work are tendencies on the part of subjects to see the study as expressing not the will of other humans but an impersonal process with its own momentum and to justify one's actions by blaming and derogating the victim. Nothing can be done, what is happening is inevitable, the result of an impersonal, natural process, and, in any case, the victim deserves what's coming to him, it's his fault, not mine – in this way guilt is denied and immorality rationalized.

The agentic state is reminiscent of LeBon's (1896) theory of de-individuation, which implied loss of personal responsibility and regression to the anti-social impulses and desires of the racial (collective) unconscious. For Milgram, immoral, anti-social acts are sanctioned by legitimate authority. For Baumeister (1982), de-individuation effects derive from the weakening of the social (public) self and an accentuation of private identity. It appears that the group can induce public identity and conformity to others' norms (impression management), an accentuation of private identity (see F. H. Allport, 1924), objective self-awareness and adherence to personal standards (Duval and Wicklund, 1972), loss of personal responsibility and transfer of self-regulation to authority leading to 'legitimate', if personally immoral, behaviour, and de-individuation leading to freedom from moral constraints in the service of an inherited, collective unconscious mind. There is a general recognition of the importance of the self-process to understanding the influence of the group on the person, but it cannot be claimed that we have a coherent picture of this influence (Hogg and Abrams, 1988). Is de-individuation loss of personal or public identity, the substitution of

another's identity, or a change in one's own identity? We need to specify the nature of the social situation, the relationship of the person to the group and the aspect of the self being modified in order to clarify matters. In the next chapter, we shall introduce a new distinction between personal and social identity that may help to resolve some of these issues.

## Conclusion

Once one distinguishes between power and influence, compliance and authority emerge as fascinating topics in their own right, ones that are surprisingly little researched in any direct or systematic fashion. Impression management theory has made an important indirect contribution to our understanding of compliance processes and the concepts of legitimate power and the agentic state are important theoretical directions for work on authority.

Is the dependence theory really satisfactory even as an explanation of compliance? In many respects, the dependence formulation appears to be a metatheory that substitutes for predictive understanding instead of adding much to our knowledge of how the public self functions. Once we acknowledge the need to specify subjectively valued outcomes in advance of the compliance which they supposedly motivate, then we need theories of how the private self functions in social settings. We must understand how the individual's private motives, goals and values vary with the social context and social influence. It is, therefore, just as true theoretically that power depends on influence (and the social values internalized by a person and made salient in particular contexts) as vice versa. Dependence is not self-explanatory and neither, therefore, is power. The conclusion to be drawn is that there is much to be gained from seeking to integrate systematic theories of influence with a more open-minded and detailed examination of notions of public and social identity.

## Suggestions for further reading

Collins, B. and Raven, B. H. (1969). Group structure: Attraction, coalitions, communication, and power. In G. Lindzey and E. Aronson (eds), *Handbook of social psychology*, Vol. 4. Reading, Mass.: Addison-

Wesley. A thorough review of influence and power from a dependence perspective.

Hollander, E. P. (1985). Leadership and power. In G. Lindzey and E. Aronson (eds), *The handbook of social psychology*, Vol. 2, 3rd edn. New York: Random House. A good overview of leadership research.

Milgram, S. (1974). *Obedience to authority*. London: Tavistock. Fascinating, readable and highly recommended.

Ng, S. K. (1980). *The social psychology of power*. London: Academic Press. A thoughtful, scholarly monograph that ranges widely.

Tetlock, P. E. and Manstead, A. S. R. (1985). Impression management versus intrapsychic explanations in social psychology: A useful dichotomy? *Psychological Review*, 92, 59–77. A good review of impression management research that attempts to push the field forward theoretically.

# 6 / THE DUAL-PROCESS MODEL, SELF-CATEGORIZATION AND SOCIAL INFLUENCE

In concluding I shall attempt to integrate our understanding of influence. I shall provide a critique of the dual-process model that currently dominates the field and argue for a self-categorization theory that retains the insights of the dual-process model but is more consistent with the research data and has more explanatory power. The ideas are proffered tentatively as hypotheses fully capable of being empirically tested and already summarizing a mass of research data.

## The dual-process model of normative and informational influence

The social psychology of influence comprises five main research areas: social conformity, group polarization, minority influence, power (obedience, compliance and impression management) and persuasion (influence-induced attitude change). The single most important theme that emerges from a survey of these areas is the widespread acceptance of a distinction between normative and informational processes of influence. The dual-process model of normative and informational influence is, in its varying forms, the dominant theory in the field.

The model was first explicitly stated in the conformity area by Deutsch and Gerard (1955). It was anticipated in Festinger's (1950, 1954) theory of the social reality and group locomotion functions of uniformity pressures and in Asch's (1952, 1956) insistence that influence was unlikely to be a unitary process and could not be reduced to slavish submission to social pressure. Others in the conformity area have made similar distinctions (see Jones and Gerard, 1967, for a summary, and Kaplan, 1987, for a recent discussion). I shall use Deutsch and Gerard's terminology because it describes well the general model, not to emphasize their specific version.

Normative influence is conformity to the positive expectations of self and others in order to gain approval and avoid rejection. This is conformity as a power process. Informational influence is conformity to others' behaviour as information about reality in order to cognize and act correctly, appropriately, to be right, or in Festinger's terms to achieve subjective validity. In a sense, this is 'true' influence; one conforms because one has been genuinely persuaded of the validity of others' views. The former process is the specifically group form of influence, related to social interdependence and surveillance by group members, and leading to public compliance. The latter process is the specifically cognitive kind of influence related to knowing reality correctly and leading to private attitude change.

The distinction between the two processes has not only persisted over time, but, if anything, has grown sharper. There is at least one exception to this general trend, in the early work of Moscovici, but the basic point is easy to argue. In the polarization area, the most researched ideas have grouped themselves into a debate between social comparison theories emphasizing positive self-presentation (normative influence) and theories of persuasive argumentation and the exchange of information (informational influence). Since the mid-1970s, some theorists have been calling for an integration of the two forms of influence.

In minority influence, Moscovici (e.g. 1976) began by criticizing dependence theory for supposing that influence reflected asocial states of uncertainty and informational power independent of social relationships and norms. He argued firmly that conformity in, for example, the Asch paradigm was socially based influence (not power), reflecting a consistent style of behaviour on the part of the experimental majority (the societal minority). Since 1980, however, he, Mugny and others have been arguing for a dual-process model in which majority influence is seen as conformity in the sense of compliance, a power process of submission to social pressure, and minority influence is seen as conversion, a cognitively mediated, informational process of private attitude change. They have introduced the concepts of 'comparison' and 'validation' – almost identical to those used by polarization researchers – to explain majority compliance and minority conversion.

Research on impression management embodies the dichotomy in dividing the public from the private self and assuming that public behaviour is actively modified as a function of one's dependence on others (i.e. power relations). Its central idea is that one's behaviour is governed by the social (public) identity implications of one's actions in the social context. Public identity, the public self, is how one is perceived by others. The public presentation of self is very much like normative influence but viewed from the perspective of an active managing conformer. When we seek to maximize rewards by managing others' impressions of self, we are 'conforming' to the positive expectations of others. The basic precondition of both normative influence and impression management is that one is under surveillance by others. The former is, in fact, influence based on the public presentation of self. It is the kind of conformity motivated by the desire to achieve a valued public identity.

In recent persuasion research, the focus is on the cognitive analysis of persuasion (see Eagly and Chaiken, 1984, for a review). One influential theory is Petty and Cacioppo's (1986) Elaboration Likelihood Model. They make a distinction between 'central' and 'peripheral' routes to attitude change. In essence, long-lasting, genuine, true, rational attitude change is a matter of processing cognitively the information contained in strong (valid) messages. This central route depends on the motivation and ability to elaborate cognitively the information presented. In the absence of the central route, one falls back on the peripheral route, i.e. the short-term, superficial acceptance of some message not on the basis of its content but as a function of social and affective cues such as the attractiveness of the source. The impact of one's social relationship to the source and the social context is the peripheral route. Persuasion through information processing is central. The Elaboration Likelihood Model is reminiscent of Festinger's physical and social reality testing model of subjective validity.

The point is not that all these theorists are saying the same thing; indeed, they are not. There are, for example, important differences between Moscovici's conversion process and Petty and Cacioppo's central route, or Burnstein and Vinokur's persuasive argumentation. They all emphasize the role of cognitive activity in persuasion, seeing the cognitive elaboration of messages as mediating attitude change, but for Moscovici the basis of all influence is not the reduction of uncertainty, a cognitive need, but social conflict and the resolution of conflict, i.e. the harmonization of social relationships. Nevertheless, despite the differences, there is the same fundamental theme at the core of each theory of a dichotomy between socially motivated, normative processes of influence affecting the public self and cognitively motivated, informational processes affecting the private self.

Why has everybody made this distinction? One reason has been the need to distinguish between power and influence, not in the sense of power as the basis of influence, but as alternatives, as coercive, naked, forcible compulsion versus persuasion. We know that sometimes people are controlled – they modify their behaviour not from inner conviction but tactically as a function of others' power over them – and that sometimes changes in behaviour reflect changes in the private self. The legitimate distinction betwen private acceptance and compliance gives the dual-process model much of its plausibility and usefulness.

Another reason is the need to distinguish between the different kinds of issues, motivations and tasks that are found in group discussions. Discussion sometimes focuses on 'intellective', factual issues and sometimes on 'judgemental' issues relating to preferences and values (Kaplan, 1987; Kaplan and Miller, 1987). Sometimes, relevant norms are so well-established, internalized and shared that the only issue is the factual demonstration of a correct solution; at other times, there may be argument about the relevance and applicability of norms or concern to shape new ones.

Another reason for the distinction is more problematic. The power/influence distinction has become mixed up with an important but different distinction between the individual and society, between the psychological (perceptual, cognitive) processes of the individual and the social relationships, group memberships and norms of society. Power is explained in terms of *social* relationships and influence in terms of *individual* cognitive activity or information processing. Group relationships are seen as power relations, relations of dependence, and social identity is equated with the public self, as if the social component of the self were purely external and constraining and the private self asocial. In contrast, cognitive activity, information processing, tends to be seen as individual, asocial, private and non-normative. This picture is arguable, not because there is anything wrong with the power/influence distinction (or the facts versus preferences one), or because there are not some social relationships that are relations of power and compliance, or because the public–private distinction is not valid and important. It is arguable because the social self includes private as well as public elements and because influence and cognitive activity have a social–normative dimension. The normative component is not peripheral but central. The difficulty with the dual-process model are the implications that social norms have no effect on private attitude change and that informational influence is non-normative. It suggests that the role of social relationships and reference group norms is solely to constrain and compel, as if society were alien and external to the individual and had no effect on the private self. It implies that influence is cognitive and asocial, society constraining and its norms adhered to blindly.

In contrast, it can be argued that informational influence is socially mediated and normative, that norms about preferences and values are informative about appropriate, correct beliefs in the same way and reflect the same processes as norms about facts and demonstrably correct solutions, and that individual and society are not in antagonism but are interdependent at the level of self and cognition as well as overt behaviour.

## Subjective validity and reality testing

To develop the argument, let us focus on informational influence and the problem of subjective validity. Informational influence is mediated by information perceived to provide evidence about reality, i.e. (subjectively) valid information. All theorists agree that what matters for influence is not just information, but *valid* information. The notion of true influence being mediated by valid information is apparent in the ideas of responses 'providing evidence about reality' (Deutsch and Gerard), 'persuasive arguments' (Burnstein and Vinokur), the 'validation' process (Moscovici and Mugny) and the central route as the processing of 'strong' messages (Petty and Cacioppo).

How do we determine the validity of some opinion? As Festinger (1950) pointed out, we test it against reality. There are two kinds of reality testing and hence two bases of subjective validity. People can employ *physical reality tests*: they can employ objective, physical, non-social means to test a belief directly against reality. For example, they can hit a sheet of glass with a hammer to test the belief that it will break. In other words, the *physical* mode of testing reality is to act on it directly, employing one's own perceptual, cognitive or behavioural capacities without recourse to the opinions of others.

Alternatively, they can use *social reality tests*: where objective, non-social means of testing some opinion are unavailable, people can compare their views with others and seek the agreement of reference group members. Social reality testing is a matter of social comparison and consensual validation. If the right people (similar, relevant others) agree with our point of view, then we are confident of its correctness, and, by extension, any message that embodies an in-group consensus tends to be perceived as valid. The agreed, shared, consensual attitude of a reference group that a certain way of thinking or acting is correct, appropriate, proper (and therefore desirable) constitutes a social norm. Consensual validation is therefore *normative validation* and social reality testing is the process of finding normative support for subjective validity.

In Festinger's theory, physical reality testing does not involve social influence at all. The individual tests reality directly and does not need social comparison. In the absence of direct tests of reality, reference group norms establish the validity of opinions. Informational influence is movement to others' opinions perceived as valid because they embody and represent reference group norms. Thus informational influence and social comparison (social reality testing) go hand in hand. Indeed, the latter is the basis of the former. For Festinger, then, *informational influence is normative influence* (but not compliance; compliance is the special kind of counter-normative influence exerted by a membership group that is not a reference group, Festinger, 1953). The agreement of others is a social norm and it is social comparison with this norm that validates or invalidates one's behaviour and induces resistance or susceptibility to influence.

As the field has progressed, the idea of social reality testing has been invoked less frequently. Social processes of influence have been interpreted as normative in the sense of going along with group pressure (compliance), not as having to do with subjective validity. Since Festinger's (1950) theory, the trend has been to divide and even oppose informational influence and social comparison. Festinger himself began this process. In 1954, his theory changed to imply that the achievement of agreement within reference groups is merely a consequence of a cognitive need to appraise abilities and opinions more accurately by comparing with similar people. The agreement of others, the social norm, no longer directly validates the response, but functions as the backdrop for the individual's own efforts to achieve stable and accurate appraisals of his or her position.

In polarization research, persuasive arguments theory states that informational influence has nothing to do with social comparison, that the latter is not *necessary* for influence. The model of social comparison advocated in the polarization area is that of 'abilities' rather than 'opinions'. It has to do with rank-order rather than accuracy evaluation, i.e. comparing to be positively evaluated and to look better than others rather than to validate one's opinions and be right (see Chapter 3). Just as persuasive arguments theory divorces social comparison from informational influence, so too value theory develops the link between social comparison and normative influence (shifting to attract a positive evaluation from self and others) to explain polarization. Moscovici (1980) argues that validation of the minority position leading to conversion is made possible by *freedom from social comparison* with the minority and that comparison with the majority impedes acceptance of its point of view and results only in compliance. In impression management theory, the normative implications of social contexts modify the public self but not privately accepted attitudes. Finally, the Elaboration Likelihood Model suggests that social comparison with reference group others is part of the peripheral route to persuasion and does not affect the validity of messages and the central route. Peripheral factors have no way of directly modifying the perceived validity of the issues being processed (see Petty and Cacioppo, 1986, p. 126, fig. 1). In sum, the validity of opinions, arguments, messages, points of view (which we summarize as 'information') is not related to, and is even hindered by, social comparison with others.

## A physical reality testing model of influence

Theorists have come very close to saying that validity is an objective property of arguments and that persuasion is just a matter of processing 'good' information. In persuasive arguments theory, the Elaboration Likelihood Model and the validation process, for example, there is the idea of 'persuasive', 'strong', 'good' – as if inherently valid – arguments that exist in the culture and persuade anybody exposed to them, as if arguments were valid in a social vacuum. Vinokur and Burnstein (1974) speak of the 'inherent logic and plausibility' of arguments that ensure that their correctness is easily recognized. Moscovici (1980) implies that being stimulated to think about the arguments of the minority will tend to be sufficient to accept them. Petty and Cacioppo (1986) are explicit that only the cognitive processing of 'strong' arguments persuades. They refer to this as 'objective' processing and operationalize validity as a rated property of messages. They state clearly that they do not know what makes an argument persuasive – it is simply defined as 'strong' or 'weak' on the basis of its subjective effects (rated persuasiveness and capacity to stimulate favourable or unfavourable thoughts) – the possible social and cultural bases of such subjective evaluations are simply ignored (Petty and Cacioppo, 1986, pp. 132–4).

I do not want to overstate this or put words into theorists' mouths. Nobody has said explicitly that persuasion, agreeing, accepting, yielding, is the same as processing information. They have made it clear that it is only the processing of good, valid, strong, sound, etc., information that leads to acceptance. But in neglecting the social basis of validity, there is an implication that validity is an objective, intrinsic property of information.

The trend has been to interpret all validity testing as if it were a kind of physical reality testing – even where the judgements are about issues, attitudes and beliefs far removed from the simple perceptual or physical tasks that Festinger had in mind. The implication is that one can determine the validity of information through individual perceptual, cognitive or behavioural activities that directly assess that information in the same way that one tests a simple physical belief against the objective world. Merely by reading, thinking about, processing some message I can know whether it is valid or not in the same way that I can test a physical belief by trying it out practically. Implicitly, a physical reality testing model of informational (subjective) validity has been adopted to the exclusion of the social model. Validity is found directly in the processing of the message (in detecting self-evident 'facts and correct answers', Kaplan and Miller, 1987), not through social comparison with others.

## Is a physical reality testing model of validity adequate?

There are several reservations to be expressed about a physical reality testing model of valid information. There are, first, common-sense objections. The validity of information is not actually an 'informational' property at all, i.e. it does not exist in the substantive content of a message (what a message actually says or how it says it). It is a property of the perceiver, a social value judgement that I have accepted the information as providing evidence about reality. It is, if one likes, an 'attributional' property, a judgement that information is to be attributed externally to objective reality (and so is objectively appropriate and valid) rather than to the subjective biases, idiosyncrasies or partisan prejudices of the source. I can say that a person's argument is powerful, coherent, relevant, original, valid, competent, correct, etc. I am saying that I judge the argument as providing evidence about reality, as being objectively true. I have not said anything about what the person actually said in terms of the substantive content of the message. There is no coherent theoretical concept of how the validity of arguments might be operationalized other than in terms of people's ratings or social conventions and rules.

Next, there are the metatheoretical objections raised by Tajfel (1969a, 1972) and Moscovici (1976). It is doubtful that physical reality testing actually exists in isolation from social reality testing. The physically isolated person judging some stimulus, for example, is not asocial, but always acts as a member of a social group, a society and a culture. The meaning of sensory data is interpreted in terms of the normative categories, theories, assumptions, standards and procedures of one's culture (see Chapter 4). Nor is social reality testing secondary or optional. Uncertainty leading to social comparison does not arise only when physical tests produce ambiguous results. It is a direct product of disagreement with relevant others in the context of a shared reality. Similarly, the reduction of uncertainty is a matter of social consensual support, as the many studies reviewed in Chapter 2 show, not information in the abstract. Physical tests do not directly produce or reduce uncertainty. The influence of experts is not due to the fact that they possess demonstrably correct information. Their information is perceived as valid because they are socially designated as 'experts', the legitimate representatives of normative cultural institutions and values (Moscovici, 1976). When studies purport to show the effects of 'objective feedback' (i.e. physically valid information) on conformity to the group (e.g. that an individual who is successful on a task conforms less) we find, on closer inspection, that the 'objective' information is socially validated. For example, the experimenter, a legitimate authority, provides the feedback or endorses the criteria by which success is defined and measured. In sum, physical reality testing does not exist in isolation, social reality testing is not secondary, and reference group norms rather than information in the abstract provide subjective validity.

Thirdly, the divorce between informational influence and social comparison implied by a physical reality model has led to theoretical difficulties. It has not worked in terms of explaining plausibly and heuristically what is going on. For example, we have seen in the conformity field that Festinger's idea that social reality testing is secondary has not been supported. Nobody, I suggest, has identified a purely 'informational' influence independent of the target's social relationship to the source and the established norms and values a person brings to the situation. Certainly, the power of 'facts' cannot be described in this way. The same applies to the power of 'experts' and of 'rational demonstration'. Facts and experts are socially designated as such and, like rational demonstration, presuppose cultural consensus about rules, procedures, technologies, categories and 'taken-for-granted' knowledge.

In polarization research, the attempt to explain polarization solely in terms of the 'informational' properties of arguments has come to rest upon an *ad hoc* assumption that majorities are more novel than minorities (or other assumptions that also seem *ad hoc* and re-descriptive). In minority influence, the idea of conversion free from comparison fails to explain the validation effects of the majority and the enhanced influence that results from social identification with the minority (which should encourage social comparison with it). Iden-tification with an ingroup minority implies that it is a reference group for comparison, yet the conversion effect of the minority is not abolished by such identification. There are also the theoretical difficulties of explaining why (a) disagreement with a minority does not represent comparison, (b) such disagreement leads to attempts to understand rather than reject and derogate the minority position, and (c) understanding should lead to acceptance.

### Individual reality testing and social validation as interdependent phases of social cognition

Physical testing, it appears, incorporates a disguised form of social reality testing. Social reality may be the sole basis of subjective validity. To anticipate misunderstanding, however, this statement should not be interpreted in too simple-minded a fashion. The point is not just to reject the idea of physical testing and replace it by social testing. It is not being argued that direct individual activity (perceptual, cognitive, behavioural) to test reality cannot achieve subjective validity, but that such activity *only does so in so far as the individual perceives, believes or expects that the activities of similar others would have produced the same results*, i.e. that they are not personally idiosyncratic, unique, deviant.

Rather than thinking of two alternative bases of validity, the physical versus the social, we should think of one basis with two interdependent phases, the phase of direct individual testing of reality and the phase of consensual validation by similar others. Agreement and consensus that are not based on the independent cognitive activity of individuals are worthless as evidence about reality, but, equally, an individual whose cognitive activity produces results that nobody else agrees with will not have confidence in their validity. The validity that arises from an individual or 'physical' test presupposes the shared norms, values, procedures, categories and meanings of society. The individual must be sure that the right others in the same situation would see, think and do the same thing, and such an assurance is usually provided by the fact that he or she is applying familiar, well-established conventions. The validity that arises from agreement rests, in turn, on the integrity and the autonomy of the individual (cf. Gerard *et al.*, 1968; Wilder, 1977).

In sum, the normative/informational dichotomy tends to favour a *physical* over a *social* reality testing model of validity and to restrict the social self to public identity. I suggest that the private self is also social and group-based and that informational validity is social-normative. Power and influence are not distinguished by being normative or non-normative, but by one's relationship to the norms in question. The distinction between physical and social reality testing has served to embody the contrast between direct individual testing and consensual validation. We need to see these as inter-dependent phases of one process of achieving valid social cognition, not as alternatives. Informational validity, therefore, cannot be opposed to normative influence. It *is* normative, a matter of social comparison with and the agreement of reference group others. The validity of information is always determined by its (direct or indirect) relationship to reference group norms.

## Subjective validity and similarity relations

I have argued that individual testing of information establishes subjective validity in so far as the individual employs pre-established norms and values and assumes that others would produce the same responses. What is the social-normative basis of subjective validity? Can we simply return to Festinger's (1950) idea and say that information with which we believe similar others to agree is valid? To some extent we can, but only if that hypothesis is modified in important respects.

First, as stated already, we must reject the idea of individual versus social reality testing as alternatives. We need to see the activity of the individual in producing perceptual and cognitive data and the search for agreement within the group to establish the validity of such data as complementary, interdependent phases of one human process of achieving valid social cognition. We do not make social tests when we cannot make physical ones; we are always acting as social group members when we make physical tests and subjective validity always has its basis in the perceived or assumed agreement of others. This is not to deny that sometimes we will disagree with our group and seek to persuade them of the validity of our personal views.

Secondly, we need to understand why researchers have moved away from the social reality model. The original hypothesis was not fully satisfactory. For example, if the agreement of similar people is informative and persuasive, how can we explain the influence of experts? Are they not different from self by definition in having more, or better, or more credible information at their disposal? Are we not persuaded by experts precisely *because* they are different from us? In the polarization area, why do groups not converge on the average position? Surely the average position is the consensual position, the one that best sums up the similarity of the reference group? In minority influence, are minorities not different from us by definition, too? If the consensual norm of one's group tends to be subjectively valid, how can a deviant minority challenging the dominant ingroup consensus produce influence and change? Researchers have moved away from Festinger's original hypothesis because of the need to answer these questions.

These issues have to do with the failure of a simple idea of similarity relations between people, and between self and others, to make sense of the research data. In fact, ideas of 'similarity', 'self' and 'agreement' were taken as unproblematic givens, unspecified and self-evident, but they are not. They need a more sophisticated interpretation. This is the contribution of self-categorization theory. It offers a modern, complex treatment of self, similarity and the group. If we adopt the perspective of this theory, we shall be able to see that the 'disconfirmations' of the similarity idea are, in reality, confirmations. What is being advocated, then, is not a return to, but an updating of, the social reality hypothesis within the context of a new theory of the self and similarity relations.

## Self-categorization theory

Self-categorization theory (Turner, 1982, 1985; Turner *et al.*, 1987) provides an analysis of the self and the relations between self, social norms and social context. It is like impression management theory in its emphasis on the social identity and normative implications of actions and on the variation of identity with this social context, but it differs in its ideas that social identity extends into the private self and that social norms define and shape the activity of the private self and vice versa.

It is also a general theory of group behaviour. The central hypothesis is that group behaviour can be understood as individuals acting in terms of a shared identity than as different individual persons (i.e. more in terms of their personal identities). It seeks to explain variations in how people define and categorize themselves and the effects of such variations. It supposes that influence phenomena are one effect of people categorizing themselves in terms of shared social identity (other effects being social cohesion, cooperation, etc.).

The main ideas are as follows. One aspect of the self is the cognitive aspect, the system of concepts of self a person uses to define him- or herself. Self-concepts can be thought of as self-categories or self-categorizations: cognitive groupings of the self as identical, similar, equivalent to some class of stimuli in contrast to some other class. Self-categorizations are assumed to vary in their level of inclusiveness or abstraction. People may categorize themselves as individual persons, defined by their differences from other individuals, or as social groups, in terms of some ingroup membership compared to some outgroup membership. Ingroup–outgroup memberships represent self-categorization at the level of social identity, a more inclusive level than the personal self. People can also employ even more superordinate (e.g. 'humanity') or subordinate (the 'real me') levels.

Self-categories vary in content as well as level, and in the meaning of that content as a function of specific contexts. Which self-category is salient at any particular time is a function of people being ready to use a specific category (its accessibility relative to other categories) and its fit with the stimulus data (Oakes, 1987). There are two interrelated aspects of fit, namely *comparative fit*, defined by the principle of *meta-contrast*, and *normative fit*, defined by the congruence of the stereotypical content of the category with the actual behaviour that is being represented.

The meta-contrast principle is that a group of stimuli is more likely to be categorized as a single entity to the degree that the differences within that group (on relevant dimensions) are smaller than the differences between that group and other stimuli. So, for example, we call a certain group of things 'chairs' because, the principle states, the differences between chairs are smaller than the differences between 'chairs' and 'tables'. Categories form in such a way as to ensure that the differences between categories are larger than the differences within categories. The *meta-contrast ratio* – the average perceived inter-category difference over the average perceived intra-category difference – provides a simple quantitative measure of the degree to which any collection of stimuli within a given frame of reference will tend to be categorized as a perceptual unit (or, in the case of people, of the degree to which a collection of individuals will be perceived as a social group).

The meta-contrast principle as described is a convenient simplification. A full explanation of how we categorize people must also take into account the social meaning of the similarities and differences between them (i.e. category content, which is related to normative fit) and the relationship of social categories to the values, needs and goals of the perceiver (their relative accessibility). For example, if some social categorization such as men/women is already available to perceivers, then it is likely to become cognitively salient to the degree both that it is *relatively accessible* (the perceivers may be feminists or male chauvinists who are highly motivated and ready to think in terms of men and women) and fits *comparatively* (the people being represented may be men and women arguing with each other so that there are greater differences *between than within* the sexes in the attitudes they express) and *normatively* (the men may be taking an anti-feminist and the women a pro-feminist stand on the relevant issue).

The effect of the salience of an ingroup–outgroup membership is to enhance the perceived similarities within and the differences between groups (McGarty and Penny, 1988; Tajfel, 1969b). As social identity becomes salient, individual self-perception becomes *deper-*

*sonalized*, i.e. people tend to perceive themselves more in terms of the shared stereotypes that define their social category membership (the attributes that define their common social identity) and less in terms of their personal differences and individuality.

Oakes *et al.* (in press) conducted two studies that illustrate the importance of fit. Their experiment 1 manipulated the comparative fit between sex categories and the observed behaviour of male and female confederates. Eighty 16- to 17-year-old male and female school pupils were assigned to one of four conditions to watch a tape-and-slide presentation of a six-person discussion group. The stimulus group discussed whether two fictional persons should get married and the nature of the discussion varied across the four conditions. In the 'deviance' conditions, one person disagreed with the other five members of the stimulus group (who agreed among themselves); in the 'conflict' conditions, three people disagreed with the three others (the members of each subgroup agreeing among themselves). The other variable (superimposed to produce a 2 × 2 factorial design) was the sex composition of the group: one man and five women ('solo' conditions) versus three men and three women ('collective' conditions).

The crucial point about the design was that in the solo-deviance and collective-conflict conditions, there was a correlation between the sex categorization and the expressed attitudes of the stimulus group: one man disagreed with five women or three men disagreed with three women. There was no such correlation in the solo-conflict and collective-deviance conditions, where two women and a man argued with three women or one man argued with two men and three women, respectively. In the former conditions, the sex categorization 'fits' the observed data – the perceived differences within the sexes are smaller than the perceived differences between the sexes. In the uncorrelated conditions, the sex categorization does not fit the data – the differences within the sexes are as large as the differences between the sexes. Self-categorization theory hypothesizes that subjects will categorize confederates into males and females more in the former than in the latter conditions. The subjects rated one target male person who was held constant across all four stimulus group conditions. Partly as predicted, subjects attributed the target person's attitudes to his being a typical man, and sex-stereotyped him as a male and less as a female, significantly more in the collective-conflict than in the uncorrelated conditions, but not more in the solo-deviance condition where his similarities to other men were not explicit. It appeared that in this study, where normative fit was low, only fully explicit comparative fit made the target's social identity as a man salient.

Oakes *et al.* (in press) experiment 2 manipulated both comparative and normative fit. Ninety science students were assigned to six conditions in a 3 × 2 experimental design. They watched a tape-and-slide presentation of three 'arts' and three 'science' students discussing attitudes to university life. In the 'consensus' conditions, there was complete agreement in the stimulus group. In the 'conflict' conditions, the three arts students took one view and the three science students took an opposite view. In the 'deviance' conditions, one arts student disagreed with the other five students (who agreed among themselves). The argument was about whether university was important for social life or academic work. The subjects' stereotypes are that arts students favour the importance of social life, whereas science students favour the importance of academic work. In the 'consistent' conditions, the target stimulus individual – one arts student who was held constant across the three agreement conditions (she was part of the arts subgroup or the deviant, depending on condition) – took the stereotypical arts line of favouring social life over work. In the 'inconsistent' conditions, she took the stereotypical science line of favouring academic work over social life. The subjects rated the target individual and the stimulus group as a whole on a variety of measures.

The different patterns of agreement varied the *comparative fit* between the arts/science social categorization and the observed behaviour of the stimulus group. The consistent/inconsistent variable manipulated its *normative fit* with the content of people's attitudes. The results provided good support for the predictions derived from self-categorization theory, the most important one being that the arts/science categorization would be most salient under conditions of both comparative and normative fit, i.e. in the consistent-conflict condition where three arts students disagree in a stereotypical direction with three science students.

The main findings were that the target person's attitudes were explained more in terms of her arts *social category membership* ('she is an arts student') in the consistent-conflict condition, her *personality* in the inconsistent-deviance condition, and *externally* in the consensus conditions. Interestingly, attribution to social category membership in the consistent-conflict condition functioned as an internal attribution to the individual (rather than to external social pressure) as much as did personality. Correspondingly, she was categorized as more similar to the other arts students and different from the science students and was expected to like the former more and the science students less in the consistent-conflict condition. Again, the salience of a social categorization leads to explanations of people's conduct in terms of their social identity and a perceptual accentuation of that identity.

There is also evidence that the salience of an ingroup–outgroup categorization leads to the social stereotyping of the *self* (e.g. Dion *et al.*, 1978). Hogg and Turner (1987b) have shown directly that the salience of a shared social identity increases self-definition and self-stereotyping in terms of the relevant social category and produces group behaviour. A total of 70 male and 60 female university students were assigned to intra-sex or inter-sex conditions. In the former, one individual discussed an issue with one person of the same sex. In the latter, two males discussed an issue with two females. These subjects were not watching a stimulus group but actively and spontaneously participating in discussion. Nevertheless, the issues had been carefully selected and the discussions ingeniously stage-managed to ensure that there was disagreement about the issue within and between the sexes in the intra- and inter-sex conditions, respectively. Because there are differences of opinion *within* the sexes in the intra-sex condition, but *between* (and not within) the sexes in the inter-sex condition, the sex-categorization should be more salient in the latter condition.

It was found that both the males and females categorized themselves as more typical of their own sex, and stereotyped themselves more after than before social interaction in terms of the traits they ascribed to their own sex in that situation, in the inter-sex than the intra-sex condition. Interestingly, the evaluative implications of self-stereotyping varied between the sexes: males attributed both positive and negative traits to themselves more strongly, while females were more 'ethnocentric', attributing positive traits to themselves more strongly but negative traits less strongly where sex was salient. The salience of social identity also lowered females' self-esteem and led them to dislike and discriminate against males, but raised self-esteem in males and increased their liking of and fairness to females.

Ullah (1987) tested the hypothesis of self-categorization theory that self-definition in terms of a shared social category membership is associated with psychological group formation in a study of second-generation 'Irish' youths living in England. Respondents choosing 'Irish' as a self-definition showed more group formation than those choosing 'half-English, half-Irish', who in turn showed more than those choosing 'English'. Group formation was expressed in attraction to the Irish people and distinctive Irish culture, participation in traditional Irish cultural activities, perceived difference from English people and a negative orientation to being English.

The meta-contrast principle is assumed to be a general principle of categorization. It is explicit that categorizing is an active, dynamic process, intrinsically comparative, variable, contextual and relative to a frame of reference (see Oakes and Turner, 1990; Turner and Oakes, 1989). The level of inclusiveness of a self-categorization, for example, tends to increase with the extent of the frame of reference, i.e. the more people included within the comparative situation (Haslam, 1988). Which specific self-category best fits the comparative relations between self and others, the level at which it fits, and the member which best represents the category as a whole all vary with changes in the comparative context. Who the self is, the similarity perceived between self and others (i.e. the degree of identification with others) and the degree to which others' responses are perceived as similar (the degree to which they are consensual, agree) are not static givens, but a function of how self and others are categorized in differing social contexts. They are variable outcomes of an active self-categorizing process (Haslam, 1988; Oakes and Turner, 1990; Turner and Oakes, 1989).

## Self-categorization and influence

To show how depersonalization (self-perception and action in terms of a shared social identity) can provide a unifying explanation of the major group phenomena is a large task, as these embody massive amounts of research data with their own theoretical traditions and issues. It must suffice to state that self-categorization theory explains group cohesion as an effect of the mutually perceived similarity between self and ingroup others produced by the formation and salience of shared social category memberships. Social cohesion is seen fundamentally to be a product of identity rather than vice versa (e.g. Turner et al., 1983). Similarly, it is assumed that social cooperation (in, for example, mixed-motive games) is a product of the transformation of individuals into a psychological group, a 'we-group', because this transforms competitive personal self-interests into collective self-interest defined by shared self-identity. Support for this analysis is provided by a series of studies on social dilemmas conducted by Brewer and Kramer, showing that the salience of a superordinate social identification can raise the level of cooperation (Brewer and Kramer, 1986; Kramer and Brewer, 1984, 1986; see also Caporael et al., 1989; Orbell et al., 1988).

The link between self-categorization and influence is provided by the issue of subjective validity. The theory argues that similar people in the same situation not only tend to act in the same way but expect to act in the same way. In so far as we categorize ourselves as similar to others in the same situation (in relevant respects), it is natural and logical to think that we should tend to respond in the same way. In so far as we do, we should experience subjective validity. The perceived, expected or believed agreement of similar others in the same situation implies that our behaviour is a function of the objective world rather than our personal biases, prejudices and idiosyncrasies.

A possible qualification to this point is suggested by Goethals and Darley (1977). They agree with Festinger (1954) that comparison with similar others provides information about abilities and preferences, but suggest that comparison with dissimilar rather than similar others is more informative with respect to the validity of a belief that can be true or false. They argue that if others are similar to oneself in terms of the needs, values and interests likely to bias one's own appraisal of reality, then their agreement can be plausibly discounted as a function of those same biasing attributes. If dissimilar others agree with one's opinion, on the other hand, so that the agreement cannot be explained in terms of personal attributes, it becomes more plausible that one's opinion reflects external reality. This analysis is consistent with self-categorization theory if one still accepts the validating role of others who are similar in respect of attributes likely to produce a correct, competent, accurate judgement. One is likely to be most sure of one's beliefs if the people who agree are similar in terms of the faculties and competencies (including sometimes values) perceived to be necessary for correct judgement, but differ from self in respect of any characteristics likely to bias one's judgement. A naive subject in the Asch paradigm, for example, is hardly likely to identify with others perceived to be blind or indeed known to be confederates, but he or she will refer to others who seem to have normal competent eyesight. The importance of the independence and integrity of group members (cf. Wilder, 1977) referred to earlier is a special case of this argument: any agreement is worthless if it is based on some shared 'incompetence', such as a desire to go along with and please the group rather than the free, autonomous judgement of competent individuals.

Strictly speaking, ingroup consensual (social-normative) responses are a function of a 'person × situation' interaction – in fact, an 'us × situation' interaction – and tend to be attributed to that interaction. They imply that things are right 'for us', but the 'we' tends to be silent, i.e. ingroup members tend to forget that what they perceive as valid is from their own relative position. From the perspective of ingroup members, shared ingroup norms tend to be perceived as objectively appropriate in general.

Self-categorization theory sees subjective validity and uncertainty as a function of agreement and disagreement about the same stimulus in the context of a shared social identity. The expectation of agreement is a function of shared social identity in a shared context and hence mutual influence to produce agreement is not the only reaction to disagreement and uncertainty. Other reactions are to recategorize the self or differentiate the situation. People's need to reach agreement will increase as a multiplicative function of the degree to which (a) they categorize themselves as similar to each other in situationally relevant respects, (b) they perceive themselves as sharing the same stimulus situation, (c) they are uncertain about the appropriate response (there is perceived or believed disagreement), and (d) a correct response is important to the group. It also follows that the degree of agreement within the group is a variable (and not a matter of all-or-none unanimity) and that the more persuasive members of the group will be those who best represent the ingroup consensus.

How can these ideas be applied to conformity and the other research areas we have reviewed? In general, one would expect a person to be more uncertain and open to influence the more the person categorizes him- or herself as similar to a group, i.e. identifies with it, sees him- or herself as sharing the same stimulus situation; the more the group is distinctive, consistent and consensual (leading to the attribution of its response to objective reality); and the less consensual the person's own position. Evidence is good for these notions. Most conformity generalizations can be happily and distinctively reinterpreted within this framework (see Turner et al., 1987). The research reviewed in Chapter 2, for example, shows the importance of reference group identification, majority unanimity and social support, a shared stimulus situation (i.e. public versus private responding) and uncertainty in conformity to the group.

Studies show that people are more influenced by ingroups to which they categorize themselves as belonging than by outgroups, that responses consistent with and exemplary of ingroup norms are more persuasive than counter-normative responses, and that ingroup norms do not merely produce compliance (e.g. Abrams *et al.*, 1990; Clark and Maass, 1988a,b; Hogg and Turner, 1987a; Mackie, 1986, 1987; Mackie and Cooper, 1984; Martin, 1988a,b,c; Turner *et al.*, 1988, 1989; van Knippenberg and Wilke, 1988). Other studies show that where social identity is salient people tend to conform to the norms which define their ingroup identity (Reicher, 1984a,b; Spears *et al.*, 1990; Turner, 1982; Wilder and Shapiro, 1984).

Hogg and Turner (1987a, experiments 3 and 4) summarize two studies that attempted to demonstrate directly the role of self-categorization in a modified Asch conformity paradigm (see also Abrams *et al.*, 1990; van Knippenberg and Wilke, 1988). In experiment 3, the subjects in each session were assigned to seven private booths and made anonymous individual judgements about the degree of social approval associated with a series of personality traits. The popular response for each trait, the one subjects were most likely to give, had been previously ascertained. Before judging a trait, a subject heard the responses of the other six persons in the session. Each subject believed that he or she was responding last, but, in fact, the feedback from the other subjects was faked and all subjects responded last. The six fake responses on each trial were designed so that they always fell into two implicit subgroups of approval or disapproval on the 9-point rating scale, e.g. the responses might have been 3, 4 and 5, and 7, 8 and 9, where '9' is extreme disapproval. One of the fake responses was always the popular one that the subject might be expected to give in isolation.

In the 'uncategorized' conditions, neither the subjects nor the fake 'others' were categorized into groups: the subgroupings on each trial remained implicit. In the 'categorized' conditions, the subjects and 'others' were categorized explicitly into two groups and the social categorization always correlated with the response subgroupings: ingroup members always gave the three responses which included the popular response. This 'correct' response was always the ingroup response closest to the outgroup, e.g. if the outgroup responses were 1, 2 and 3, then the correct response might have been 5 and the remaining ingroup responses 6 and 7.

The measure of conformity was the degree to which subjects shifted on average away from the correct response and the outgroup in the direction of the other ingroup members. There were no informational or other differences between conditions apart from the categorization variable. In fact, it is not obvious why normative or informational influence processes should operate at all in this paradigm. The subjects were anonymous, the others were not unanimous and social support was available for any one of six responses. The subjects were not particularly uncertain and were free to endorse the correct response provided by an implicit or explicit ingroup member. Nevertheless, the subjects shifted significantly more towards the ingroup norm in the categorized than uncategorized conditions. Furthermore, it made no difference whether the subjects were categorized into groups on an explicitly random basis or on the basis of previously similar judgements.

In experiment 4, the main finding was that the direction in which subjects shifted was indeed determined by the side to which they categorized themselves as belonging. For example, if the subgroupings on a trial were 3, 4 and 5, and 7, 8 and 9, with 5 as the correct response (assumed to be the subject's own), then it was predicted that the subject would identify with the approval group and shift away from 5 towards approval. If in other conditions on the same trial the responses were shifted as a whole towards approval, so that the correct response now belonged to the disapproval group (e.g. 1, 2 and 3 versus 5, 6 and 9), then it was predicted that the subject would identify with the disapproval group and shift away from 5 towards disapproval. This is exactly what was found. Shifting all six responses in one direction and holding all else constant would nevertheless produce a shift in the opposite direction, because what determined shift was the side of the intergroup boundary on which the subjects found themselves. In this study, the implicit groupings were so powerful that explicit social categorizations had no additional effect.

## Experts, prototypical norms and minorities

### Experts

What about expert influence? In self-categorization theory, the expert/leader is the individual who best represents the group consensus. Some individuals both are and are perceived as more competent, successful, confident and able than others. The theory uses the concept of 'prototypicality' derived from research on categorization (Rosch, 1978) to explain how there can be differences between category members in the degree to which they represent categorical identity. Thus there can be individual differences between members in the degree to which they exemplify the group as a whole (compared to other groups), and a person can be perceived as *different from one's individual self in better expressing one's shared social identity*. The idea of levels of self-identity clarifies that an expert may be different from one's personal self at the same time as being (and indeed just because they are) more similar to our shared social categorical self. This point needs to be understood in conjunction with Moscovici's (see Chapter 4) analysis of experts as people who represent internalized social values and social institutions with which one identifies. One takes advice from a medical doctor, for example, because he or she has been socially designated as an acceptable representative of modern, scientific medicine, an institution defined by social values one shares (such as the belief in science and its normative procedures). Some simple examples of the basic idea that another person can better define one's own group than one's (personal) self are provided in the next section.

## Prototypical norms

The idea that there are differences between individuals in the degree to which they represent ingroup norms and that norms are attributes of social identity can explain group polarization. Let us suppose that people converge on the consensual position of the group and that the consensual position is what group members have in common. Then the most influential person will be the one who best represents what the group has in common. The relatively traditional assertion is being made that people tend to conform to the consensual position of the group, the position perceived as representing the shared views of group members. However, it is argued that the consensual position is *not* defined by the mean position as is usually assumed (although the consensual and mean positions may sometimes coincide). It is defined instead as the most *prototypical* position, the position that best represents the group as a whole.

The prototypicality of ingroup members can be easily defined by means of the meta-contrast principle. The more an individual differs from outgroup members and the less he or she differs from ingroup members, the better he or she represents the ingroup. For example, in the British Conservative Party, members must differ in politics from members of the British Labour Party, but they must not be so right-wing that they begin to differ significantly from other Conservatives. For any comparative dimension, the mean perceived difference between an ingroup member (the target) and outgroup members, divided by the mean perceived difference between the target and other ingroup members, provides an index of their representativeness of the ingroup (in this comparative context). The person with the highest prototypicality ratio (the ingroup member whose average difference from outgroup members divided by his or her average difference from ingroup members produces the highest number) holds the most consensual position.

Sometimes, the most prototypical position (which we shall summarize as the prototype) and the mean pre-test position of ingroup members will coincide, sometimes the prototype will be less extreme than the mean, and sometimes the prototype will be more extreme than the mean. Whether social conformity (in the sense of convergence on the mean), group polarization or depolarization (the group moving in the opposite direction to the mean) occurs depends on whether the prototype is perceived as coinciding with, more extreme than or less extreme than the pre-test mean. It is assumed that the process underlying all three phenomena is the same – conformity to the prototype – and that what differs between them is only the perceived position of the norm relative to the pre-test mean.

It is the relationship between the distribution of ingroup responses and the comparative context within which the ingroup defines itself that determines the degree to which the ingroup prototype coincides with or differs from the ingroup mean. As the comparative context changes, so, too, does the relative prototypicality of ingroup members.

For example, in the following instance where ingroup members (I) occupy the middle ground on an issue in comparison with others (outgroup members: O), it is obvious that ingroup member E is most prototypical of the ingroup and that D and F are as prototypical as each other. It can be seen without doing any calculations that E is least different from other ingroup members and most different from outgroup members:

| Group membership: | O | O | O | I | I | I | O | O | O |
|---|---|---|---|---|---|---|---|---|---|
| Individuals: | A | B | C | D | E | F | G | H | I |
| Scale positions: | −4 | −3 | −2 | −1 | 0 | +1 | +2 | +3 | +4 |

If we shift the comparative context to the right of the scale (displacing the ingroup to the left) as follows, we find that D has now gained substantially in relative prototypicality over F and more extreme positions have become more normative than moderate positions:

| Group membership: | I | I | I | O | O | O | O | O | O |
|---|---|---|---|---|---|---|---|---|---|
| Individuals: | D | E | F | G | H | I | J | K | L |
| Scale positions: | $-1$ | 0 | $+1$ | $+2$ | $+3$ | $+4$ | $+5$ | $+6$ | $+7$ |

The prototypicality ratios for each ingroup member are obtained by dividing their mean absolute difference from outgroup members on the scale by their mean absolute difference from the other ingroup members. Thus $D = 3 + 4 + 5 + 6 + 7 + 8/6 = 5.5$ (average distance from outgroup members) over $1 + 2/2 = 1.5$ (average distance from other ingroup members) $= 5.5/1.5 = 3.67$. Similarly, $F = 3.5/1.5 = 2.33$. The extremist D now begins to approximate E in relative prototypicality ($D = 3.67$ versus $E = 4.5/1 = 4.5$) compared to the middle ground example (where $D = 2$ and $E = 3$).

Conversely, if we shift the frame of reference to the left (and displace the ingroup to the right), we find that what was the moderate position of F at $+1$ has now become an extreme and more prototypical ingroup position:

| Group membership: | O | O | O | O | O | O | I | I | I |
|---|---|---|---|---|---|---|---|---|---|
| Individuals: | U | V | W | X | Y | Z | D | E | F |
| Scale positions: | $-7$ | $-6$ | $-5$ | $-4$ | $-3$ | $-2$ | $-1$ | 0 | $+1$ |

As a concrete example of these kinds of shifts, imagine a social democratic party wedded to welfare capitalism. Where such a political party compares its policies to those of the extreme Right and the extreme Left and sees itself as occupying the middle ground, it will tend to see itself as 'centrist' or 'moderate', defining itself in terms of the views of its average member. Now suppose that it enters into a political alliance with a right-wing conservative party and that this alliance is so successful that it becomes the new political frame of reference. In this instance, its most prototypical member will no longer be at its exact centre, but will tend to be on the left of the party. In comparison with the conservative party, the social democrats will tend to see and define themselves as left-wing (but not too much so). Similarly, if it enters into an alliance and compares itself with a left-wing socialist party, it will tend to see itself as more right-wing in consequence.

The pre-test mean of any ingroup will tend to be most prototypical of that group compared to others to the degree that the mean is at the middle of the reference dimension defined by the comparative context (see the middle ground example above). This will also be true where the comparative context is defined solely by ingroup positions, i.e. where ingroup members do not make intergroup comparisons but focus only on intragroup differences. In this situation, the ingroup mean and scale midpoint will tend to be the same by definition.

As ingroup responses tend to shift (by a change in the group and/or the social context) towards the extreme of any comparative context (the other extreme being defined by the outgroup), then more extreme responses will tend to gain in relative prototypicality over more moderate ones. Their average intergroup differences will increase and average intragroup differences decrease relative to those of moderates. It becomes more likely that the most prototypical response will be more extreme than the mean in the same direction. As ingroup responses move to an extreme, it becomes more likely that extremists will start to bunch up at the scale endpoint (assuming that there are limits to how extreme one can become) and so such members will decrease their mean intragroup differences as well as increase their mean intergroup differences.

One question that arises is where in ordinary group polarization research are the outgroups that we have used to define the comparative context. The answer is that they are there, but hidden. They are implicit in the response scale employed to measure subjects' attitudes. The response scale is a symbolic representation of the shared frame of reference that is subjectively salient in the experimental situation. It is a relative ordering of the different responses of different people that can be made and are known to be made to an issue. For example, an 'attitudes to Charles de Gaulle' scale (Moscovici and Zavalloni, 1969) does not describe different aspects of de Gaulle; rather, it orders the different responses of people to the same social object (from pro to anti) – it is a dimension of social comparison, not a stimulus dimension.

The reason that we can meaningfully employ such a scale and the reason it has the possible values it does is because we know that there are in reality people who are pro and people who are anti. The same is just as true in some more *ad hoc* decision. When we decide on a scale to be more or less risky, or in a jury to be harsh or lenient, we are aware that other people might and do make different decisions. If this were not so, there would be no need for a decision, no need for the whole or even part of the scale. The scale as employed is implicitly a reflection of social reality. The outgroup, comprising those who take a different/opposed view, does not disappear from reality and our awareness of reality simply because it is not physically present in the laboratory.

When we respond on a scale in an ordinary polarization study and indicate what we think, we are also indicating what we do *not* think. We are identifying ourselves with others who take the same stand, saying who we are and who we are not. Who we are not, the outgroup, are people who in this situation respond differently from ourselves. This means that it is possible to use the ingroup's responses on a scale as a more or less direct operationalization of the intra- and intergroup differences perceived by subjects in the situation.

At this point, it should become clear why the conditions under which the ingroup prototype differs from or coincides with the pre-test mean parallel the major empirical finding embodied in the definition of group polarization: that it is the prevailing tendency of the group that best predicts the direction and magnitude of extremitization. The pre-test mean will directly tend to predict the direction and magnitude of the difference between the prototype and mean, because it summarizes the relationship between the ingroup and the social frame of reference.

It has been shown that the prototype varies as a function of the comparative context within which the group defines itself. Because social identity is defined comparatively and hence varies with the comparative context, ingroup norms are also defined comparatively and vary with the social context. Polarization is simply convergence within a special kind of intergroup context. Polarization beyond the mean is not movement *away* from what the group has in common, but *towards* it, because social categorical identity is defined by the prototypical and not the mean position. People are moving towards what defines them as a category as a whole in contrast to other categories.

Studies show empirically that ingroup prototypes do tend to be more extreme than the pre-test mean in the same direction (i.e. as some group becomes more pro on a scale, the more likely it is that its prototype will be even more pro than its initial mean position), that polarization is related to the degree to which groups move towards these extremitized prototypes, and that ingroup members do judge their consensual position as being more extreme than their pre-test mean under appropriate conditions (Mackie, 1986; McGarty *et al.*, 1990). People also tend to polarize more when they are categorized as a group, or when group membership is salient, than when they are defined as individuals (Spears *et al.*, 1990; Turner *et al.*, 1989). Other studies suggest that by manipulating the frame of reference implicit in a situation and redefining the prototypical position of the group, one can both change the direction of polarization and transform convergence into polarization in the autokinetic paradigm (Abrams *et al.*, 1990; Hogg and Turner, 1989; Hogg *et al.*, 1990).

## Minorities

Self-categorization theory does not imply that people always conform. One can recategorize oneself, the group and/or the situation. Alternatively, one can seek to influence the group by recreating a group consensus around one's own position, i.e. by engaging in minority influence. The distinctive point about the self-categorization theory of minority influence, contrary to Moscovici's conflict model, is the hypothesis that to exert influence the minority must be perceived and must project itself as part of the ingroup rather than the outgroup, as a pro-normative and consensual subgroup. If minority conflict polarizes an intragroup disagreement into an intergroup conflict, then direct influence should decrease. I suggest that this is what is happening in the minority influence studies that find less direct than indirect minority influence. The direct influence of minorities is not enhanced but is actually reduced by social conflict.

There is much evidence within minority influence research congruent with this notion. Direct minority influence is increased by a flexible rather than a rigid, conflictual style of negotiation on the part of the minority (a style which maintains social closeness), by majority–minority cohesion and shared group membership (the minority is still basically 'on our side') and by a pro-normative stance (consensual, congruent with the higher-order norms of the majority, not indicating individual deviance). Minority conversion depends upon the minority being a distinctive, consistent, consensual subgroup, not 'individualized', 'psychologized', or categorized as outgroup members, and presenting a coherent, alternative norm that is congruent with the higher-order norms and values of the ingroup.

Once again, the idea of levels of self-identity helps us to understand how a subgroup dissenting at one level can nevertheless be part of the ingroup at a higher level. Where intragroup comparisons are made, the disagreement of the minority may lead them to be perceived as different from self, outgroup members, deviants, and hence reduce their influence. Within a wider context, however, where intergroup comparisons are made, the same minority may now be seen as part of 'us' rather than 'them', basically on our side, standing for basic values that 'we' all share (Davidson, 1987), without any change in its point of view. For a minority to achieve direct influence, it has to present a new, distinctive vision that does not lead it to be categorized as an outgroup. It may well be the difficulty of this task that explains why minorities tend to have less direct than indirect influence. Their indirect influence, in turn, may reflect a shift from an intragroup to an intergroup context that redefines them as ingroup members in a wider situation, e.g. in the context of considering more fundamental values.

The idea that individual testing and social validation are interdependent aspects of social cognition indicates that self-categorization theory is not a simple conformity or majority influence model. No individual can be 'forced' to see reality in a certain way. The individual is always free to see things differently from the group, but if that point of view cannot be made consensual for at least some ingroup, then the individual will experience uncertainty.

## A unified theory

The self-categorization theory unifies our understanding of influence in several respects. Normalization, conformity and innovation are processes of influence related to the formation, maintenance or change of ingroup norms. Polarization and convergence on the central tendency both represent movement to the ingroup norm in varying comparative contexts. Shift to the ingroup norm is neither 'normative' nor 'informational' in the old sense. The distinction between normative and informational influence is replaced by the idea that the basic influence process is one where the normative position of people categorized as similar to self tends to be subjectively accepted as valid. The validity of information is (psychologically) established by ingroup norms. People shift towards persuasive material, but what is persuasive is not a matter of information that can be abstracted from the social context but of the degree to which material has been validated through its participation in an ingroup consensus. Arguments have informational validity and others' positions are socially valued to the degree that they represent the shared responses of the ingroup as a whole, which in turn is a matter of social comparison and self-categorization in a social context. Social value and informational processes are brought together in an integrated explanation.

This is a way of thinking about informational influence that is very different from the theory of informational dependence. Here psychological group formation is the basis of influence and not simply its outcome. The dependence theory supposes that stimulus ambiguity produces uncertainty and informational dependence on others, and that the latter is the basis of influence and leads to the formation of social norms and group structure. We find, however, that group formation is a precondition of influence. The social categorization of others as identical to self, as an appropriate reference group for social comparison, produces shared expectations of agreement. It is the disconfirmation of these expectations that creates uncertainty and openness to influence.

It is still important to keep the power/influence distinction. Its explanation in terms of 'norms' versus 'information', however, is misleading. Instead, it can be related to the difference between 'self' and 'others'. The social categorization of others as different from self, i.e. outgroup members, implies that one would not expect to be influenced by them, agree with them or feel uncertain when confronted by their different views. Such people can only resort to power to enforce their control. Power refers to the processes of social control over self exercised by people socially categorized as different from self. Putting it simply, power represents counter-normative and influence pro-normative influence. We also need to distinguish between authority (legitimate power) and compliance proper within this analysis. In the case of authority, we are referring to social norms within the ingroup which designate certain members as people by whom one ought to be influenced, even where this may not be, for various reasons, accompanied by full or immediate internalization of their point of view.

The concluding message is that the interdependence of individual and group is reflected in the interdependence of psychological and social processes, individual cognition and social influence. Influence has a social-cognitive basis and information processing has a social-normative aspect. The latter is affected by social relationships between self and others within varying social contexts, embodied in one's social identity and group memberships.

## Suggestions for further reading

Abrams, D. and Hogg, M. A. (1990). Social identification, self-categorization and social influence. In W. Stroebe and M. Hewstone (eds), *European review of social psychology*, Vol. 1. Chichester: John Wiley. A survey of recent influence research from the perspective of self-categorization theory.

Oakes, P. J. and Turner, J. C. (1990). Is limited information processing capacity the cause of social stereotyping? In W. Stroebe and M. Hewstone (eds), *European review of social psychology*, Vol. 1. Chichester: John Wiley. A discussion of stereotyping, not influence, but one that develops the idea of self-categories as variable and context-dependent, because they are comparative.

Turner, J. C. and Oakes, P. J. (1989). Self-categorization theory and social influence. In P. B. Paulus (ed.), *The psychology of group influence*, 2nd edn. Hillsdale, N.J.: Lawrence Erlbaum Associates. A more detailed discussion of self-categorization and influence, which also looks at the relationship between personal and social identity and the origins and implications of the theory.

Turner, J. C., Hogg, M. A., Oakes, P. J., Reicher, S. D. and Wetherell, M. S. (1987). *Rediscovering the social group: A self-categorization theory.* Oxford: Basil Blackwell. The major statement of self-categorization theory, including analyses of group formation, the salience of social categories, social cooperation and crowd behaviour, as well as influence.

# REFERENCES

Abrams, D. and Hogg, M. A. (1990). Social identification, self-categorization and social influence. In W. Stroebe and M. Hewstone (eds), *European Review of Social Psychology*, Vol. 1. 195–228. Chichester: John Wiley.

Abrams, D., Wetherell, M. S., Cochrane, S., Hogg, M. A. and Turner, J. C. (1990). Knowing what to think by knowing who you are: Self-categorization and the nature of norm formation, conformity and group polarization. *British Journal of Social Psychology*, **29**, 97–119.

Aebischer, V., Hewstone, M. and Henderson, M. (1984). Minority influence and musical preference: Innovation by conversion not coercion. *European Journal of Social Psychology*, **14**, 23–33.

Ajzen, I. (1988). *Attitudes, personality, and behavior*. Milton Keynes: Open University Press.

Alexander, C. N., Zucker, L. G. and Brody, C. L. (1970). Experimental expectations and autokinetic experiences: Consistency theories and judgmental convergence. *Sociometry*, **33**, 108–122.

Allen, V. L. (1965). Situational factors in conformity. In L. Berkowitz (ed.), *Advances in experimental social psychology*, Vol. 2, pp. 133–75. New York: Academic Press.

Allen, V. L. (1975). Social support for nonconformity. In L. Berkowitz (ed.), *Advances in experimental social psychology*, Vol. 8, pp. 2–43. New York: Academic Press.

Allen, V. L. and Wilder, D. A. (1977). Social comparison, self-evaluation, and conformity to the group. In J. M. Suls and R. L. Miller (eds), *Social comparison processes*. Washington: Hemisphere, 187–208.

Allen, V. L. and Wilder, D. A. (1978). Perceived persuasiveness as a function of response style: Multi-issue consistency over time. *European Journal of Social Psychology*, 8, 289–96.

Allport, F. H. (1924). *Social psychology*. New York: Houghton, Mifflin.

Allport, G. W. (1985). The historical background of social psychology. In G. Lindzey and E. Aronson (eds), *The handbook of social psychology*, Vol. 1, 3rd ed. New York: Random House, 1–46.

Anderson, N. H. and Graesser, C. G. (1976). An information integration analysis of attitude change in group discussion. *Journal of Personality and Social Psychology*, 34, 210–22.

Arbuthnot, J. and Wayner, M. (1982). Minority influence: Effects of size, conversion, and sex. *Journal of Psychology*, 111, 285–95.

Arkin, R. M., Appelman, A. J. and Burger, J. M. (1980). Social anxiety, self-presentation, and the self-serving bias in causal attribution. *Journal of Personality and Social Psychology*, 38, 23–35.

Asch, S. E. (1951). Effects of group pressure upon the modification and distortion of judgements. In H. Guetzkow (ed.), *Groups, leadership and men*. Pittsburg, Penn.: Carnegie Press, 177–90.

Asch, S. E. (1952). *Social psychology.* Englewood Cliffs, N.J.: Prentice-Hall.

Asch, S. E. (1956). Studies of independence and conformity: A minority of one against a unanimous majority. *Psychological Monographs: General and Applied*, 70, 1–70 (whole No. 416).

Back, K. W. (1951). Influence through social communication. *Journal of Abnormal and Social Psychology*, 46, 9–23.

Baer, R., Hinkle, S., Smith, K. and Fenton, M. (1980). Reactance as a function of actual versus projected autonomy. *Journal of Personality and Social Psychology*, 38, 416–22.

Bales, R. F. (1950). *Interaction process analysis.* Chicago, Ill.: University of Chicago Press.

Baron, R. S. and Roper, G. (1976). Reaffirmation of social comparison views of choice shifts: Averaging and extremitization in an autokinetic situation. *Journal of Personality and Social Psychology*, 35, 521–30.

Baron, R. S., Dion, K. L., Baron, P. H. and Miller, N. (1971). Group consensus and cultural values as determinants of risk-taking. *Journal of Personality and Social Psychology*, 20, 446–55.

Baron, R. S., Monson, T. C. and Baron, P. H. (1973). Conformity pressure as a determinant of risk-taking: Replication and extension. *Journal of Personality and Social Psychology*, 28, 406–413.

Baron, R. S., Sanders, G. S. and Baron, P. H. (1975). *Social comparison reconceptualized: Implications for choice shifts, averaging effects and social facilitation.* Unpublished paper, University of Iowa.

Baumeister, R. F. (1982). A self-presentational view of social phenomena. *Psychological Bulletin*, 91, 3–26.

Baumeister, R. F. and Jones, E. E. (1978). When self-presentation is constrained by the target's knowledge: Consistency and compensation. *Journal of Personality and Social Psychology*, 36, 608–618.

Baumeister, R. F., Cooper, J. and Skib, B. A. (1979). Inferior performance as a selective response to expectancy: Taking a dive to make a point. *Journal of Personality and Social Psychology*, 37, 424–32.

Bennett, E. B. (1955). Discussion, decision commitment, and consensus in 'group decision'. *Human Relations*, 8, 251–74.

Bickman, L. (1971). The effects of another bystander's ability to help on bystander intervention in an emergency. *Journal of Experimental Social Psychology*, 7, 367–79.

Bishop, G. D. and Myers, D. G. (1974). Informational influence in group discussion. *Organizational Behavior and Human Performance*, 12, 92–104.

Blascovich, J. and Ginsburg, G. P. (1974). Emergent norms and choice shifts involving risk. *Sociometry*, 37, 205–218.

Blascovich, J., Ginsburg, G. P. and Veach, T. L. (1975). A pluralistic explanation of choice shifts on the risk dimension. *Journal of Personality and Social Psychology*, 31, 422–9.

Bochner, S. and Insko, C. A. (1966). Communicator discrepancy, source credibility, and opinion change. *Journal of Personality and Social Psychology*, 4, 614–21.

Borden, R. J. (1975). Witnessed aggression: Influence of an observer's sex and values on aggressive responding. *Journal of Personality and Social Psychology*, 31, 567–73.

Bovard, E. W. (1948). Social norms and the individual. *Journal of Abnormal and Social Psychology*, 43, 62–9.

Bowers, D. G. and Seashore, S. E. (1966). Predicting organizational effectiveness with a four-factor theory of leadership. *Administrative Science Quarterly*, 11, 238–63.

Boyanowsky, E. O. and Allen, V. L. (1973). Ingroup norms and self-identity as determinants of discriminatory behaviour. *Journal of Personality and Social Psychology*, 25, 408–418.

Braver, S., Linder, D., Corwin, T. and Cialdini, R. B. (1977). Some conditions that affect admissions of attitude change. *Journal of Personality and Social Psychology*, 13, 565–76.

Bray, R. M., Johnson, D. and Chilstrom, J. T. (1982). Social influence by group members with minority opinions: A comparison of Hollander and Moscovici. *Journal of Personality and Social Psychology*, 43, 78–88.

Brehm, J. W. (1966). *A theory of psychological reactance*. New York: Academic Press.

Brewer, M. B. and Kramer, R. M. (1986). Choice behavior in social dilemmas: Effects of social identity, group size and decision framing. *Journal of Personality and Social Psychology*, 50, 543–9.

Brown, H. (1985). *People, groups and society*. Milton Keynes: Open University Press.

Brown, R. (1965). *Social psychology*. New York: Free Press.

Bryan, J. and Test, M. (1967). Models and helping: Naturalistic studies in aiding behavior. *Journal of Personality and Social Psychology*, 6, 400–407.

Burnstein, E. (1982). Persuasion as argument processing. In H. Brandstatter, J. H. Davis and G. Stocker-Kreichgauer (eds), *Group decision-making*. London: Academic Press, 103–24.

Burnstein, E. and Vinokur, A. (1973). Testing two classes of theories about group induced shifts in individual choices. *Journal of Personality and Social Psychology*, 9, 123–37.

Burnstein, E. and Vinokur, A. (1975). What a person thinks upon learning he has chosen differently from others: Nice evidence for the persuasive-arguments explanation of choice shifts. *Journal of Experimental Social Psychology*, 11, 412–26.

Burnstein, E. and Vinokur. A. (1977). Persuasive argumentation and social comparison as determinants of attitude polarization. *Journal of Experimental Social Psychology*, 13, 315–32.

Burnstein, E., Vinokur, A. and Trope, Y. (1973). Interpersonal comparison versus persuasive argumentation: A more direct test of alternative explanations for group-induced shifts in individual choice. *Journal of Experimental Social Psychology*, 9, 236–45.

Caporael, L. R., Dawes, R. M., Orbell, J. M. and van de Kragt, A. J. C. (1989). Selfishness examined: Cooperation in the absence of egoistic incentives. *Behavioral and Brain Sciences*, 12, 683–99.

Cartwright, D. and Zander, A. (1968). *Group dynamics*. London: Tavistock.

Cecil, E. A., Chertkoff, J. M. and Cummings, L. A. (1970). Risk-taking in groups as a function of group pressure. *Journal of Social Psychology*, 81, 273–4.

Chaiken, S. and Stangor, C. (1987). Attitudes and attitude change. *Annual Review of Psychology*, 38, 575–630.

Chemers, M. M., Rice, R. W., Sundstorm, E. and Butler, W. M. (1975). Leader esteem for the least preferred co-worker score, training and effectiveness: An experimental investigation. *Journal of Personality and Social Psychology*, 31, 401–409.

Cialdini, R. B., Levy, A., Herman, C. P. and Evenbeck, S. (1973). Attitudinal politics: The strategy of moderation. *Journal of Personality and Social Psychology*, 25, 100–108.

Cialdini, R. B., Petty, R. E. and Cacioppo, J. T. (1981). Attitude and attitude change. *Annual Review of Psychology*, 32, 357–404.

Clark, R. D., III and Crockett, W. H. (1971). Subjects' initial positions, exposure to varying opinions and the risky-shift. *Psychonomic Science*, 23, 277–9.

Clark, R. D., III and Maass, A. (1988a). Social categorization in minority influence: The case of homosexuality. *European Journal of Social Psychology*, 18, 347–64.

Clark, R. D., III and Maass, A. (1988b). The role of social categorization and perceived source credibility in minority influence. *European Journal of Social Psychology*, 18, 381–94.

Coch, L. and French, J. R. P. (1948). Overcoming resistance to change. *Human Relations*, 11, 512–32.

Codol, J.-P. (1975). On the so-called 'superior conformity of the self' behavior: Twenty experimental investigations. *European Journal of Social Psychology*, 5, 457–501.

Collins, B. and Raven, B. H. (1969). Group structure: Attraction, coalitions, communication, and power. In G. Lindzey and E. Aronson (eds), *Handbook of social psychology*, Vol. 4. Reading, Mass.: Addison-Wesley, 102–204.

Cooper, J. and Croyle, R. T. (1984). Attitudes and attitude change. *Annual Review of Psychology*, 35, 395–426.

Cooper, J. and Jones, E. E. (1969). Opinion divergence as a strategy to avoid being miscast. *Journal of Personality and Social Psychology*, 13, 23–30.

Cotton, J. L. (1981). A review of research on Schachter's theory of emotion and the misattribution of arousal. *European Journal of Social Psychology*, 11, 365–97.

Cotton, J. L. and Baron, R. S. (1980). Anonymity, persuasive arguments and choice shifts. *Social Psychology Quarterly*, 43, 391–404.

Cottrell, N. B. and Epley, S. W. (1977). Affiliation, social comparison, and socially mediated stress reduction. In J. M. Suls and R. L. Miller (eds), *Social comparison processes*. Washington: Hemisphere, 43–68.

Crutchfield, R. S. (1955). Conformity and character. *American Psychologist*, 10, 191–8.

Darley, J. M. and Latané, B. (1968). Bystander intervention in emergencies: Diffusion of responsibility. *Journal of Personality and Social Psychology*, 8, 377–83.

Davidson, B. (1987). Moscovici's theory of majority and minority influence: A necessary distinction or false dichotomy? Unpublished Honours Thesis, Macquarie University, Sydney.

Davidson, B. (1988). *Social identity and minority influence*. Paper presented to 24th International Congress of Psychology, Sydney.

Deutsch, M. and Gerard, H. B. (1955). A study of normative and informational social influences upon individual judgment. *Journal of Abnormal and Social Psychology*, 51, 629–36.

Dion, K. L., Earn, B. N. and Yee, P. H. N. (1978). The experience of being a victim of prejudice: An experimental approach. *International Journal of Psychology*, 13, 197–294.

Doise, W. (1969). Intergroup relations and polarization of individual and collective judgments. *Journal of Personality and Social Psychology*, 12, 136–43.

Doise, W. (1971). An apparent exception to the extremitization of collective judgments. *European Journal of Social Psychology*, 1, 511–18.

Doms, M. and Van Avermaet, E. (1980). Majority influence, minority influence and conversion behavior: A replication. *Journal of Experimental Social Psychology*, 16, 283–92.

Downing, J. (1958). Cohesiveness, perception and values. *Human Relations*, 11, 157–66.

Duval, S. and Wicklund, R. A. (1972). *A theory of objective self-awareness.* New York: Academic Press.

Eagly, A. H. and Chaiken, S. (1984). Cognitive theories of persuasion. In L. Berkowitz (ed.), *Advances in experimental social psychology*, Vol. 17. New York: Academic Press, 267–359.

Ebbesen, E. B. and Bowers, J. J. (1974). Proportion of risky to conservative arguments in a group discussion and choice shift. *Journal of Personality and Social Psychology*, 29, 316–27.

Eiser, J. R. and van der Pligt, J. (1984). Attitudes in a social context. In H. Tajfel (ed.), *The social dimension: European developments in social psychology*, Vol. 2. Cambridge: Cambridge University Press/Paris: Editions de la Maison des Sciences de l'Homme, 363–78.

Festinger, L. (1950). Informal social communication. *Psychological Review*, 57, 271–82.

Festinger, L. (1953). An analysis of compliant behavior. In M. Sherif and M. O. Wilson (eds), *Group relations at the crossroads*. New York: Harper, 232–56.

Festinger, L. (1954). A theory of social comparison processes. *Human Relations*, 7, 117–40.

Festinger, L. and Carlsmith, J. M. (1959). Cognitive consequences of forced compliance. *Journal of Abnormal and Social Psychology*, 58, 203–210.

Festinger, L. and Thibaut, J. (1951). Interpersonal communications in small groups. *Journal of Abnormal and Social Psychology*, 46, 92–100.

Festinger, L., Schachter, S. and Back, K. (1950). *Social pressures in informal groups.* New York: Harper and Row.

Festinger, L., Gerard, H. B., Hymovitch, B., Kelley, H. H. and Raven, B. (1952). The influence process in the presence of extreme deviants. *Human Relations*, 5, 327–46.

Fiedler, F. E. (1964). A contingency model of leadership effectiveness. In L. Berkowitz (ed.), *Advances in experimental social psychology*, Vol. 1. New York: Academic Press, 149–90.

Fiedler, F. E. (1978). The contingency model and the dynamics of the leadership process. In L. Berkowitz (ed.), *Advances in experimental social psychology*, Vol. 11, New York: Academic Press, 59–112.

Fiske, S. T. and Taylor, S. E. (1984). *Social cognition.* Reading, Mass.: Addison-Wesley.

Fraser, C. and Foster, D. (1984). Social groups, nonsense groups and group polarization. In H. Tajfel (ed.), *The social dimension: European developments in social psychology*, Vol. 2. Cambridge: Cambridge University Press/Paris: Editions de la Maison des Sciences de l'Homme, 473–97.

Fraser, C., Gouge, C. and Billig, M. (1971). Risky shifts, cautious shifts and group polarization. *European Journal of Social Psychology*, 1, 7–29.

French, J. R. P. and Raven, B. H. (1959). The bases of social power. In D. Cartwright (ed.), *Studies in social power*. Ann Arbor, Mich.: Institute of Social Research, 150–67.

Freud, S. (1921). *Group psychology and the analysis of the ego*. London: Hogarth Press.

Gaes, G. G., Kalle, R. J. and Tedeschi, J. T. (1978). Impression management in the forced compliance situation: Two studies using the bogus pipeline. *Journal of Experimental Social Psychology*, 14, 493–510.

Gerard, H. B. (1953). The effect of different dimensions of disagreement on the communication process is small groups. *Human Relations*, 6, 249–71.

Gerard, H. B. (1954). The anchorage of opinions in small face-to-face-groups. *Human Relations*, 7, 313–26.

Gerard, H. B. (1963). Emotional uncertainty and social comparison. *Journal of Abnormal Social Psychology*, 66, 568–73.

Gerard, H. B. and Rabbie, J. M. (1961). Fear and social comparison. *Journal of Abnormal Social Psychology*, 62, 586–92.

Gerard, H. B., Wilhelmy, R. A. and Connolley, E. S. (1968). Conformity and group size. *Journal of Personality and Social Psychology*, 8, 79–82.

Goethals, G. R. and Darley, J. M. (1977). Social comparison theory: An attributional approach. In J. M. Suls and R. L. Miller (eds), *Social comparison processes*. Washington: Hemisphere, 259–78.

Goethals, G. R. and Darley, J. M. (1987). Social comparison theory: Self-evaluation and group life. In B. Mullen and G. R. Goethals (eds), *Theories of group behavior*. New York: Springer-Verlag, 21–47.

Goethals, G. R. and Zanna, M. P. (1979). The role of social comparison in choice shifts. *Journal of Personality and Social Psychology*, 37, 1469–76.

Gottlieb, J. and Carver, C. (1980). Anticipation of future interaction and the bystander effect. *Journal of Experimental Social Psychology*, 16, 253–60.

Gouge, C. and Fraser, C. (1972). A further demonstration of group polarization. *European Journal of Social Psychology*, 2, 95–7.

Greenwald, A. G. and Pratkanis, A. R. (1984). The self. In R. S. Wyer and T. K. Srull (eds), *Handbook of social cognition*, Vol. 3, Hillsdale, N.J.: Lawrence Erlbaum Associates, 129–78.

Haslam, S. A. (1988). *The social comparative context of stereotyping*. Paper presented to the Australian Bicentennial Meeting of Social Psychologists, Leura, NSW, Australia.

Hass, R. G. (1975). Persuasion or moderation? Two experiments on anticipatory belief change. *Journal of Personality and Social Psychology*, 31, 1155–62.

Hogg, M. A. (1987). Social identity and group cohesiveness. In J. C. Turner, M. A. Hogg, P. J. Oakes, S. D. Reicher and M. S. Wetherell, *Rediscovering the social group: A self-categorization theory*. Oxford: Basil Blackwell, 89–116.

Hogg, M. A. and Abrams, D. (1988). *Social identifications: A social psychology of intergroup relations and group processes.* London: Routledge and Kegan Paul.

Hogg, M. A. and Turner, J. C. (1987a). Social identity and conformity: A theory of referent informational influence. In W. Doise and S. Moscovici (eds), *Current issues in European social psychology,* Vol. 2, pp. 139–82. Cambridge: Cambridge University Press.

Hogg, M. A. and Turner, J. C. (1987b). Intergroup behavior, self-stereotyping and the salience of social categories. *British Journal of Social Psychology,* 26, 325–40.

Hogg, M. A. and Turner, J. C. (1989). *Group polarization in the autokinetic paradigm.* Melbourne/Sydney: University of Melbourne/Macquarie University.

Hogg, M. A., Turner, J. C. and Davidson, B. (1990). Polarized norms and social frames of reference: A test of the self-categorization theory of group polarization. *Basic and Applied Social Psychology,* 11, 77–100.

Hollander, E. P. (1958). Conformity, status, and idiosyncrasy credit. *Psychological Review,* 65, 117–27.

Hollander, E. P. (1985). Leadership and power. In G. Linndzey and E. Aronson (eds), *The handbook of social psychology,* Vol. 2, 3rd ed. New York: Random House, 485–537.

Hollander, E. P. and Julian, J. W. (1970). Studies in leader legitimacy, influence, and innovation. In L. Berkowitz (ed.), *Advances in experimental social psychology,* Vol. 5. New York: Academic Press, 33–69.

Isenberg, D. J. (1986). Group polarization: A critical review and meta-analysis. *Journal of Personality and Social Psychology,* 50, 1141–51.

Israel, J. (1963). Experimental change of attitude using the Asch-effect. *Acta Sociologica,* 7, 95–104.

Jackson, J. M. and Saltzstein, H. D. (1958). The effect of person–group relationships on conformity pressures. *Journal of Abnormal and Social Psychology,* 57, 17–24.

Jacobs, R. and Campbell, D. T. (1961). The perpetuation of an arbitrary tradition through several generations of a laboratory micro-culture. *Journal of Abnormal and Social Psychology,* 62, 649–58.

Jellison, J. and Arkin, R. (1977). Social comparison of abilities: A self-presentation approach to decision-making in groups. In J. M. Suls and R. L. Miller (eds), *Social comparison processes.* Washington: Hemisphere, 235–57.

Jellison, J. and Riskind, J. (1970). A social comparison of abilities interpretation of risk-taking behavior. *Journal of Personality and Social Psychology,* 15, 375–90.

Jones, E. E. and Gerard, H. B. (1967). *Foundations of social psychology.* New York: John Wiley.

Jones, E. E., Wells, H. H. and Torrey, R. (1958). Some effects of feedback from the experimenter on conformity behavior. *Journal of Abnormal and Social Psychology*, 57, 207–213.

Kaplan, M. F. (1977). Discussion polarization effects in a modified jury decision paradigm: Informational influences. *Sociometry*, 40, 262–71.

Kaplan, M. F. (1987). The influence process in group decision making. In C. Hendrick (ed.), *Group processes*. London: Sage, 189–212.

Kaplan, M. F. and Miller, C. E. (1977). Judgments and group discussion: Effect of presentation and memory factors on polarization. *Sociometry*, 40, 337–43.

Kaplan, M. F. and Miller, C. E. (1987). Group decision making and normative versus informational influence: Effects of type of issue and assigned decision rule. *Journal of Personality and Social Psychology*, 53, 306–313.

Kelley, H. H. (1952). The two functions of reference groups. In G. E. Swanson, T. M. Newcomb and E. L. Hartley (eds), *Readings in social psychology*. New York: Holt, revised ed., 410–14.

Kelley, H. H. (1967). Attribution theory in social psychology. In D. Levine (ed.), *Nebraska Symposium on Motivation*, Vol. 15, pp. 192–238. Lincoln, Nebraska: University of Nebraska Press.

Kelley, H. H. and Lamb, T. W. (1957). Certainty of judgment and resistance to social influence. *Journal of Abnormal and Social Psychology*, 55, 137–9.

Kelly, H. H. and Shapiro, M. M. (1954). An experiment on conformity to group norms where conformity is detrimental to group achievement. *American Sociological Review*, 19, 667–77.

Kelman, H. C. (1958). Compliance, identification, and internalization: Three processes of attitude change. *Journal of Conflict Resolution*, 2, 51–60.

Kelman, H. C. (1961). Processes of opinion change. *Public Opinion Quarterly*, 25, 57–78.

Kiesler, C. A. and Kiesler, S. B. (1969). *Conformity*. Reading, Mass.: Addison-Wesley.

Kiesler, C. A. and Pallak, M. S. (1975). Minority influence: The effect of majority reactionaries and defectors, and minority and majority compromisers, upon majority opinion and attraction. *European Journal of Social Psychology*, 5, 237–56.

Kirkhart, R. O. (1963). Minority group identification and group leadership. *Journal of Social Psychology*, 59, 111–17.

Kramer, R. M. and Brewer, M. B. (1984). Effects of group identity on resource use in a simulated commons dilemma. *Journal of Personality and Social Psychology*, 46, 1044–57.

Kramer, R. M. and Brewer, M. B. (1986). Social group identity and the emergence of cooperation in resource conservation dilemmas. In H. Wilke, D. Messick and C. Rutte (eds), *Psychology of decisions and conflict, Vol. 3: Experimental social dilemmas.* Frankfurt: Verlag Peter Lang, 205–30.

Lamm, H. and Myers, D. G. (1978). Group-induced polarization of attitudes and behaviour. In L. Berkowitz (ed.), *Advances in experimental social psychology,* Vol. 11. New York: Academic Press, 145–95.

Latané, B. (1981). The psychology of social impact. *American Psychologist,* 36, 343–56.

Latané, B. and Darley, J. M. (1970). *The unresponsive bystander: Why doesn't he help?* New York: Appleton-Century-Crofts.

Latané, B. and Nida, S. (1980). Social impact theory and group influence: A social engineering perspective. In P. B. Paulus (ed.), *Psychology of group influence.* Hillsdale, N. J.: Lawrence Erlbaum Associates, 3–34.

Latané, B. and Rodin, J. (1969). A lady in distress: Inhibiting effects of friends and strangers on bystander intervention. *Journal of Experimental Social Psychology,* 5, 189–202.

Latané, B. and Wolf, S. (1981). The social impact of majorities and minorities. *Psychological Review,* 88, 438–53.

LeBon, G. (1896). *The crowd: A study of the popular mind.* London: Unwin.

Levine, J. M. (1989). Reaction to opinion deviance in small groups. In P. B. Paulus (ed.), *The psychology of group influence,* 2nd ed. Hillsdale, NJ: Lawrence Erlbaum Associates, 187–231.

Levinger, G. and Schneider, D. J. (1969). Test of the 'risk is a value' hypothesis. *Journal of Personality and Social Psychology,* 11, 165–70.

Lewin, K. (1947). Group decision and social change. In T. M. Newcomb and E. L. Hartley (eds), *Readings in social psychology.* New York: Holt, Rinehart and Winston, 330–44.

Lewin, K., Lippitt, R. and White, R. (1939). Patterns of aggressive behavior in experimentally created 'social climates'. *Journal of Social Psychology,* 10, 271–99.

Linde, T. F. and Patterson, C. H. (1964). Influence of orthopedic disability on conforming behavior. *Journal of Abnormal and Social Psychology,* 68, 115–18.

Lott, A. J. and Lott, B. E. (1961). Group cohesiveness, communication level and conformity. *Journal of Abnormal and Social Psychology,* 62, 408–412.

MacNeil, M. and Sherif, M. (1976). Norm change over subject generations as a function of arbitrariness of prescribed norms. *Journal of Personality and Social Psychology,* 34, 762–73.

McGarty, C. and Penny, R. E. C. (1988). Categorization, accentuation and social judgement. *British Journal of Social Psychology,* 22, 147–57.

McGarty, C., Turner, J. C., Hogg, M. A., Davidson, B. and Wetherell, M. S. (1990). *Group polarization as conformity to the prototypical group member.* Macquarie University, Sydney.

Maass, A. and Clark, R. D., III (1983). Internalization versus compliance:

Differential processes underlying minority influence and conformity. *European Journal of Social Psychology*, 13, 197–215.

Maass, A. and Clark, R. D., III (1984). Hidden impact of minorities: Fifteen years of minority influence research. *Psychological Bulletin*, 95, 428–50.

Maass, A. and Clark, R. D., III (1986). Conversion theory and simultaneous majority/minority influence: Can reactance offer an alternative explanation. *European Journal of Social Psychology*, 16, 305–309.

Maass, A., Clark, R. D., III and Haberkorn, G. (1982). The effects of differential ascribed category membership and norms on minority influence. *European Journal of Social Psychology*, 12, 89–104.

Mackie, D. (1986). Social identification effects in group polarization. *Journal of Personality and Social Psychology*, 50, 720–28.

Mackie, D. (1987). Systematic and nonsystematic processing of majority and minority persuasive communications. *Journal of Personality and Social Psychology*, 53, 41–52.

Mackie, D. and Cooper, J. (1984). Attitude polarization: The effects of group membership. *Journal of Personality and Social Psychology*, 46, 575–85.

Manstead, A. S. R. and Wagner, H. L. (1981). Arousal, cognition and emotion: An appraisal of two-factor theory. *Current Psychological Reviews*, I, 35–54.

Marshall, G. D. and Zimbardo, P. G. (1979). Affective consequences of inadequately explained physiological arousal. *Journal of Personality and Social Psychology*, 37, 970–88.

Martin, R. (1988a). Ingroup and outgroup minorities: Differential impact upon public and private responses. *European Journal of Social Psychology*, 18, 39–52.

Martin, R. (1988b). Minority influence and social categorization: A replication. *European Journal of Social Psychology*, 18, 369–73.

Martin, R. (1988c). Minority influence and 'trivial social categorization'. *European Journal of Social Psychology*, 18, 465–70.

Maslach, C. (1979). Negative emotional biasing of unexplained arousal. *Journal of Personality and Social Psychology*, 37, 953–69.

Merei, F. (1949). Group leadership and institutionalization. *Human Relations*, 2, 23–39.

Milgram, S. (1974). *Obedience to authority*. London: Tavistock.

Moore, H. T. (1921). The comparative influence of majority and expert opinion. *American Journal of Psychology*, 32, 16–20.

Morse, S. J., Gruzen, J. and Reis, H. T. (1976). The nature of equity-restoration: Some approval-seeking considerations. *Journal of Experimental Social Psychology*, 12, 1–8.

Moscovici, S. (1976). *Social influence and social change*. London: Academic Press.

Moscovici, S. (1980). Towards a theory of conversion behavior. In L.

Berkowitz (ed.), *Advances in experimental social psychology*, Vol. 13, pp. 209–239. New York: Academic Press.

Moscovici, S. (1985). Social influence and conformity. In G. Lindzey and E. Aronson (eds), *The handbook of social psychology*, Vol. 2, 3rd edn. New York: Random House, 347–412.

Moscovici, S. and Faucheux, C. (1972). Social influence, conformity bias and the study of active minorities. In L. Berkowitz (ed.), *Advances in experimental social psychology*, Vol. 6, London: Academic Press, 149–202.

Moscovici, S. and Lage, E. (1976). Studies in social influence: III. Majority and minority influence in a group. *European Journal of Social Psychology*, 6, 149–74.

Moscovici, S. and Lage, E. (1978). Studies in social influence IV: Minority influence in a context of original judgements. *European Journal of Social Psychology*, 8, 349–65.

Moscovici, S. and Lecuyer, R. (1972). Studies in group decisions I: Social space, patterns of communication and group consensus. *European Journal of Social Psychology*, 2, 221–44.

Moscovici, S. and Mugny, G. (1983). Minority influence. In P. B. Paulus (ed.), *Basic group processes*. New York: Springer-Verlag, 41–64.

Moscovici, S. and Neve, P. (1973). Studies in social influence: II. Instrumental and symbolic influence. *European Journal of Social Psychology*, 3, 461–71.

Moscovici, S. and Personnaz, B. (1980). Studies in social influence: V. Minority influence and conversion behavior in a perceptual task. *Journal of Experimental Social Psychology*, 16, 270–82.

Moscovici, S. and Personnaz, B. (1986). Studies on latent influence by the spectrometer method I: The impact of psychologization in the case of conversion by a minority or a majority. *European Journal of Social Psychology*, 16, 345–60.

Moscovici, S. and Zavalloni, M. (1969). The group as a polarizer of attitudes. *Journal of Personality and Social Psychology*, 12, 125–35.

Moscovici, S., Lage, E. and Naffrechoux, M. (1969). Influence of a consistent minority on the responses of a majority in a color perception task. *Sociometry*, 32, 365–80.

Mugny, G. (1975a). Negotiations, image of the other and the process of minority influence. *European Journal of Social Psychology*, 5, 209–228.

Mugny, G. (1982). *The power of minorities*. London: Academic Press.

Mugny, G. (1984a). The influence of minorities: Ten years later. In H. Tajfel (ed.), *The social dimension: European developments in social psychology*, Vol. 2. Cambridge: Cambridge University Press/Paris: Editions de la Maison des Sciences de l'Homme, 498–517.

Mugny, G. (1984b). Compliance, conversion and the Asch paradigm. *European Journal of Social Psychology*, 14, 353–68.

Mugny, G. (1985). Direct and indirect influence in the Asch paradigm: Effect of 'valid' or 'denied' information. *European Journal of Social Psychology*, **15**, 457–61.

Mugny, G. and Papastamou, S. (1980). When rigidity does not fail: Individualization and psychologization as resistances to the diffusion of minority innovations. *European Journal of Social Psychology*, **10**, 43–62.

Mugny, G. and Papastamou, S. (1982). Minority influence and psychosocial identity. *European Journal of Social Psychology*, **12**, 379–94.

Mugny, G. and Perez, J. A. (1987). *The constructivist contribution of minorities to attitude change*. Paper presented to ONR Conference on The Psychology of Social Groups, London.

Mugny, G., Kaiser, C. and Papastamou, S. (1983). Influence minoritaire, identification et relations entre groupes: Etude expérimentale autour d'une votation. *Cahiers de Psychologie Sociale*, **19**, 1–30.

Mugny, G., Kaiser, C., Papastamou, S. and Perez, J. A. (1984). Intergroup relations, identification and social influence. *British Journal of Social Psychology*, **23**, 317–22.

Mullen, B. (1983). Operationalizing the effect of the group on the individual: A self-attention perspective. *Journal of Experimental Social Psychology*, **19**, 295–322.

Mullen, B. (1985). Strength and immediacy of sources: A meta-analytic evaluation of the forgotten elements of social impact theory. *Journal of Personality and Social Psychology*, **48**, 1458–66.

Mullen, B. (1986). Effects of strength and immediacy in group contexts: A reply to Jackson. *Journal of Personality and Social Psychology*, **50**, 514–16.

Myers, D. G. (1982). Polarizing effects of social interaction. In H. Brandstatter, J. H. Davis and G. Stocker-Kreichgauer (eds), *Group decision-making*. London: Academic Press, 125–161.

Myers, D. G. and Bishop, G. D. (1970). Discussion effects on racial attitudes. *Science*, **169**, 778–89.

Myers, D. G. and Bishop, G. D. (1971). Enhancement of dominant attitudes in a group discussion. *Journal of Personality and Social Psychology*, **20**, 386–91.

Myers, D. G. and Lamm, H. (1976). The group polarization phenomenon. *Psychological Bulletin*, **83**, 602–627.

Myers, D. G., Bach, P. J. and Schreiber, F. B. (1974). Normative and informational effects of group interaction. *Sociometry*, **37**, 275–86.

Nemeth, C. J. (1986). Differential contributions of majority and minority influence. *Psychological Review*, **93**, 1–10.

Nemeth, C. J. and Brilmayer, A. G. (1987). Negotiation versus influence. *European Journal of Social Psychology*, **17**, 45–56.

Nemeth, C. J. and Chiles, C. (1988). Modelling courage: The role of dissent in fostering independence. *European Journal of Social Psychology*, 18, 275–80.

Nemeth, C. J. and Kwan. J. (1985). Originality of word associations as a function of majority vs. minority influence. *Social Psychology Quarterly*, 48, 277–82.

Nemeth, C. J. and Mayseless, O. (1987). *Enhancing recall: The contributions of conflict, minorities and consistency.* Berkeley, Calif.: University of California.

Nemeth, C. J. and Wachtler, J. (1973). Consistency and modification of judgment. *Journal of Experimental Social Psychology*, 9, 65–79.

Nemeth, C. J. and Wachtler, J. (1974). Creating the perceptions of consistency and confidence: A necessary condition for minority influence. *Sociometry*, 37, 529–40.

Nemeth, C. J. and Wachtler, J. (1983). Creative problem solving as a result of majority vs. minority influence. *European Journal of Social Psychology*, 13, 45–55.

Nemeth, C. J., Swedlund, M. and Kanki, B. (1974). Patterning of the minority's responses and their influence on the majority. *European Journal of Social Psychology*, 4, 53–64.

Nemeth, C. J., Wachtler, J. and Endicott, J. (1977). Increasing the size of the minority: Some gains and some losses. *European Journal of Social Psychology*, 7, 15–27.

Newcomb, T. M. (1943). *Personality and social change.* New York: Holt, Rinehart and Winston.

Newcomb. T. M., Koenig, L. E., Flacks, R. and Warwick, D. P. (1967). *Persistence and change: Bennington College and its students after twenty-five years.* New York: John Wiley.

Ng, S. H. (1980). *The social psychology of power.* London: Academic Press.

Oakes, P. J. (1987). The salience of social categories. In J. C. Turner, M. A. Hogg, P. J. Oakes, S. D. Reicher and M. S. Wetherell. *Rediscovering the social group: A self-categorization theory.* Oxford: Basil Blackwell, 117–41.

Oakes, P. J., Turner, J. C. and Haslam, S. A. (in press). Perceiving people as group members: The role of fit in the salience of social categorizations. *British Journal of Social Psychology.*

Oakes, P. J. and Turner, J. C. (1990). Is limited information processing capacity the cause of social stereotyping? In W. Stroebe and M. Hewstone (eds). *European review of social psychology*, Vol. 1. Chichester: John Wiley, 111–35.

Orbell, J. M., van de Kragt, A. J. C. and Dawes, R. M. (1988). Explaining discussion-induced cooperation. *Journal of Personality and Social Psychology*, 54, 811–19.

Paicheler, G. (1976). Norms and attitude change: I. Polarization and styles of behavior. *European Journal of Social Psychology*, 6, 405–27.

Paicheler, G. (1977). Norms and attitude change: II. The phenomenon of bipolarization. *European Journal of Social Psychology*, 7, 5–14.

Paicheler, G. (1979). Polarization of attitudes in homogeneous and heterogeneous groups. *European Journal of Social Psychology*, 9, 85–96.

Papastamou, S. (1983). Strategies of minority and majority influence. In W. Doise and S. Moscovici (eds), *Current issues in European social psychology*, Vol. 1, pp. 33–84. Cambridge: Cambridge University Press.

Papastamou, S. (1986). Psychologization and processes of minority and majority influence. *European Journal of Social Psychology*, 16, 165–80.

Pelz, E. B. (1958). Some factors in group decision. In E. E. Maccoby, T. M. Newcomb and E. L. Hartley (eds), *Readings in social psychology*, 3rd edn. New York: Holt, Rinehart and Winston, 212–19.

Perez, J. A. and Mugny, G. (1987). Paradoxical effects of categorization in minority influence: When being an outgroup is an advantage. *European Journal of Social Psychology*, 17, 157–69.

Personnaz, B. (1981). Study in social influence using the spectrometer method: Dynamics of the phenomena of conversion and covertness in perceptual responses. *European Journal of Social Psychology*, 11, 431–8.

Petty, R. E. and Cacioppo, J. T. (1986). The elaboration likelihood model in persuasion. In L. Berkowitz (ed.), *Advances in experimental social psychology*, Vol. 19, pp. 123–205. New York: Academic Press.

Pruitt, D. G. (1971a). Choice shifts in group discussion: An introductory review. *Journal of Personality and Social Psychology*, 20, 339–60.

Pruitt, D. G. (1971b). Conclusions: Toward an understanding of choice shifts in group discussion. *Journal of Personality and Social Psychology*, 20, 495–510.

Rabbie, J. M. (1963). Differential preference for companionship under threat. *Journal of Abnormal Social Psychology*, 67, 643–8.

Raven, B. H. (1965). Social influence and power. In I. D. Steiner and M. Fishbein (eds), *Current studies in social psychology*. New York: Holt, Rinehart and Winston, 371–82.

Reicher, S. D. (1984a). The St. Pauls riot: An explanation of the limits of crowd action in terms of a social identity model. *European Journal of Social Psychology*, 14, 1–21.

Reicher, S. D. (1984b). Social influence in the crowd: Attitudinal and behavioural effects of de-individuation in conditions of high and low group salience. *British Journal of Social Psychology*, 23, 341–50.

Reid, F. J. M. (1983). Polarizing effects of intergroup comparison. *European Journal of Social Psychology*, 13, 103–106.

Reid, F. J. M. and Sumiga, L. (1984). Attitudinal politics in intergroup behaviour: Interpersonal and intergroup determinants of attitude change. *British Journal of Social Psychology*, 23, 335–40.

Reis, H. and Gruzen, J. (1976). On mediating equity, equality, and self-interest: The role of self-presentation in social exchange. *Journal of Experimental Social Psychology*, 12, 487–503.

Reisenzein, R. (1983). The Schachter theory of emotion: Two decades later. *Psychological Bulletin*, 94, 239–64.

Ricateau, P. (1971). Processus de catégorisation d'autrui et les mécanismes d'influence sociale. *Bulletin de Psychologie*, 24, 909–919.

Roberts, J. C. and Castore, C. H. (1972). The effect of conformity, information and confidence upon subjects' willingness to take risks following a group discussion. *Organizational Behaviour and Human Performance*, 8, 384–94.

Rohrer, J. H., Baron, S. H., Hoffman, E. L. and Swander, D. V. (1954). The stability of autokinetic judgments. *Journal of Abnormal and Social Psychology*, 49, 595–7.

Rosch, E. (1978). Principles of categorization. In E. Rosch and B. B. Lloyd (eds), *Cognition and categorization*, pp. 27–48. Hillsdale, N.J.: Lawrence Erlbaum Associates.

St. Jean, R. and Percival, E. (1974). The role of argumentation and comparison processes in choice shifts: Another assessment. *Canadian Journal of Behavioural Science*, 6, 297–308.

Sanders, G. S. and Baron, R. S. (1977). Is social comparison irrelevant for producing choice shifts? *Journal of Experimental Social Psychology*, 13, 303–314.

Satow, K. (1975). Social approval and helping. *Journal of Experimental Social Psychology*, 11, 501–509.

Sayles, S. M. (1966). Supervisory style and productivity: Review and theory. *Personnel Psychology*, 19, 275–86.

Schachter, S. (1951). Deviation, rejection and communication. *Journal of Abnormal and Social Psychology*, 46, 190–207.

Schachter, S. (1959). *The psychology of affiliation*. Stanford, Calif.: Stanford University Press.

Schachter, S. and Singer, J. E. (1962). Cognitive, social and physiological determinants of emotional state. *Psychological Review*, 69, 379–99.

Schlenker, B. R. (1975). Self-presentation: Managing the impression of consistency when reality interferes with self-enhancement. *Journal of Personality and Social Psychology*, 32, 1030–37.

Schlenker, B. R. (1980). *Impression management: The self-concept, social identity, and interpersonal relations*. Monterey, Calif.: Brooks/Cole.

Schlenker, B. R., Forsyth, D. R., Leary, M. R. and Miller, R. S. (1980). Self-presentational analysis of the effects of incentives on attitude change following counterattitudinal behavior. *Journal of Personality and Social Psychology*, 39, 553–77.

Schneider, D. J. (1969). Tactical self-presentation after success and failure. *Journal of Personality and Social Psychology*, 13, 262–8.

Shaw, M. E. (1976). *Group dynamics: The psychology of small group behavior.* New Delhi: Tata McGraw-Hill.

Sherif, M. (1936). *The psychology of social norms.* New York: Harper and Brothers (Harper Torchbook edition, 1966).

Sherif, M. (1967). *Group conflict and cooperation: Their social psychology.* London: Routledge and Kegan Paul.

Sherif, M. and Sherif, C. W. (1956). *An outline of social psychology.* New York: Harper.

Sherif, M. and Sherif, C. W. (1969). *Social psychology.* New York: Harper and Row.

Singleton, R. Jr. (1979). Another look at the conformity explanation of group-induced shifts in choice. *Human Relations,* 32, 37–56.

Skinner, M. and Stephenson, G. M. (1981). The effects of intergroup comparison on the polarization of opinions. *Current Psychological Research,* 1, 49–61.

Slater, P. E. (1955). Role differentiation in small groups. *American Sociological Review,* 20, 296–311.

Sorentino, R. M. and Field, N. (1986). Emergent leadership over time: The functional value of positive motivation. *Journal of Personality and Social Psychology,* 50, 1091–9.

Sorrentino, R. M., King, G. and Leo, G. (1980). The influence of the minority on perception: A note on a possible alternative explanation. *Journal of Experimental Social Psychology,* 16, 293–301.

Spears, R., Lea, M. and Lee, S. (1990). De-individuation and group polarization in computer-mediated communication. *British Journal of Social Psychology,* 29, 121–34.

Stogdill, R. M. (1974). *Handbook of leadership.* New York: Free Press.

Stoner, J. A. F. (1961). *A comparison of individual and group decisions involving risk.* Unpublished Master's thesis, School of Industrial Management, Massachusetts Institute of Technology.

Strube, M. J. and Garcia, J. E. (1981). A meta-analytic investigation of Fiedler's contingency model of leadership effectiveness. *Psychological Bulletin,* 90, 307–321.

Suls, J. M. and Miller, R. L. (1977). *Social comparison processes.* Washington: Hemisphere.

Tajfel, H. (1969a). Social and cultural factors in perception. In G. Lindzey and E. Aronson (eds), *Handbook of social psychology,* Vol. 3. Reading, Mass.: Addison-Wesley, 315–94.

Tajfel, H. (1969b). Cognitive aspects of prejudice. *Journal of Social Issues,* 25, 79–97.

Tajfel, H. (1972). La catégorisation sociale. In S. Moscovici (ed.), *Introduction à la psychologie sociale,* pp. 272–302. Paris: Larousse.

Tajfel, H. and Turner, J. C. (1986). The social identity theory of intergroup behavior. In S. Worchel and W. G. Austin (eds), *Psychology of intergroup relations,* 2nd edn, pp. 7–24. Chicago: Nelson-Hall.

Tanford, S. and Penrod, S. (1984). Social influence model: A formal integration of research on majority and minority influence processes. *Psychological Bulletin*, 95, 189–225.

Tedeschi, J. T., Schlenker, B. R. and Bonoma, T. V. (1971). Cognitive dissonance: Private ratiocination or public spectacle? *American Psychologist*, 26, 685–95.

Teger, A. I. and Pruitt, D. G. (1967). Components of risk-taking. *Journal of Experimental Social Psychology*, 3, 189–205.

Tetlock, P. E. (1980). Explaining teacher explanations of pupil performance: A self-presentation interpretation. *Social Psychology Quarterly*, 43, 283–90.

Tetlock, P. E. and Manstead, A. S. R. (1985). Impression management versus intrapsychic explanations in social psychology: A useful dichotomy? *Psychological Review*, 92, 59–77.

Thibaut, J. W. and Kelley, H. H. (1959). *The social psychology of groups*. New York: John Wiley.

Thibaut, J. W. and Strickland, L. H. (1956). Psychological set and social conformity. *Journal of Personality*, 25, 115–29.

Turner, J. C. (1982). Towards a cognitive redefinition of the social group. In H. Tajfel (ed.), *Social identity and intergroup relations*, pp. 15–40. Cambridge: Cambridge University Press/Paris: Editions de la Maison des Sciences de l'Homme.

Turner, J. C. (1985). Social categorization and the self-concept: A social cognitive theory of group behavior. In E. J. Lawler (ed.), *Advances in group processes*, Vol. 2, pp. 77–122. Greenwich, Conn.: JAI Press.

Turner, J. C. and Oakes, P. J. (1986). The significance of the social identity concept for social psychology with reference to individualism, interactionism and social influence. *British Journal of Social Psychology*, 25, 237–52.

Turner, J. C. and Oakes, P. J. (1989). Self-categorization theory and social influence. In P. B. Paulus (ed.), *The psychology of group influence*, 2nd edn. Hillsdale, NJ: Lawrence Erlbaum Associates, 233–75.

Turner, J. C., Hogg, M. A., Oakes, P. J., Reicher, S. D. and Wetherell, M. S. (1987). *Rediscovering the social group: A self-categorization theory*. Oxford: Basil Blackwell.

Turner, J. C., Sachdev, I. and Hogg, M. A. (1983). Social categorization, interpersonal attraction and group formation. *British Journal of Social Psychology*, 22, 227–39.

Turner, J. C., Wetherell, M. S. and Hogg, M. A. (1988). *Referent informational influence and group polarization. Experiment 1*. Unpublished paper, Macquarie University, Sydney.

Turner, J. C., Wetherell, M. S. and Hogg, M. A. (1989). Referent informational influence and group polarization. *British Journal of Social Psychology*, 28, 135–47.

Ullah, P. (1987). Self-definition and psychological group formation in an ethnic minority. *British Journal of Social Psychology*, **26**, 17–23.

van Knippenberg, A. and Wilke, H. (1988). Social categorization and attitude change. *European Journal of Social Psychology*, **18**, 395–406.

Vidmar, N. (1974). Effects of group discussion on category width judgements. *Journal of Personality and Social Psychology*, **29**, 187–95.

Vinokur, A. and Burnstein, E. (1974). The effects of partially shared persuasive arguments on group-induced shifts: A problem solving approach. *Journal of Personality and Social Psychology*, **29**, 305–315.

Vinokur, A. and Burnstein, E. (1978a). Novel argumentation and attitude change: The case of polarization following group discussion. *European Journal of Social Psychology*, **8**, 335–48.

Vinokur, A. and Burnstein, E. (1978b). Depolarization of attitudes in groups. *Journal of Personality and Social Psychology*, **36**, 872–85.

Wachtler, J. (1976). The effect of conformity versus minority influence settings on the individual's ability to locate non-obvious solutions in a hidden figures task. *Dissertation Abstracts International*, **37**, 09-B, 4765–6.

Walker, E. L. and Heyns, R. W. (1962). *An anatomy for conformity*. Englewood Cliffs, NJ: Prentice-Hall.

Wetherell, M. S. (1983). *Social identification, social influence and group polarization*. Unpublished PhD Thesis, University of Bristol.

Wetherell, M. S. (1987). Social identity and group polarization. In J. C. Turner, M. A. Hogg, P. J. Oakes, S. D. Reicher and M. S. Wetherell, *Rediscovering the social group: A self-categorization theory*. Oxford: Basil Blackwell, 142–70.

Wheeler, L. and Zuckerman, M. (1977). Commentary. In J. M. Suls and R. L. Miller (eds), *Social comparison processes*. Washington: Hemisphere, 335–57.

Wiener, M. (1958). Certainty of judgment as a variable in conformity behavior. *Journal of Social Psychology*, **48**, 257–63.

Wiener, M., Carpenter, J. T. and Carpenter, B. (1957). Some determinants of conformity behavior. *Journal of Social Psychology*, **45**, 289–97.

Wilder, D. A. (1977). Perceptions of groups, size of opposition, and influence. *Journal of Experimental Social Psychology*, **13**, 253–68.

Wilder, D. A. and Shapiro, P. N. (1984). Role of outgroup cues in determining social identity. *Journal of Personality and Social Psychology*, **47**, 342–8.

Witte, E. H. (1987). Behaviour in group situations: An integrative model. *European Journal of Social Psychology*, **17**, 403–429.

Wolf, S. (1979). Behavioral style and group cohesiveness as sources of minority influence. *European Journal of Social Psychology*, **9**, 381–95.

Wolf, S. (1985). Manifest and latent influence of majorities and minorities. *Journal of Personality and Social Psychology*, **48**, 899–908.

Worchel, S. and Brehm, J. W. (1971). Direct and implied social restoration of freedom. *Journal of Personality and Social Psychology*, 18, 294–304.

Zaleska, M. (1978). *Climat des relations interpersonelles et polarization des attitudes dans les groupes.* Unpublished paper, Laboratoire de Psychologie Sociale de l'Universite, Paris VII.

Zimbardo, P. G. (1969). The human choice: Individuation, reason and order versus deindividuation, impulse and chaos. In W. J. Arnold and D. Levine (eds), *Nebraska Symposium on Motivation*, Vol. 17. Lincoln, Nebraska: University of Nebraska Press, 237–307.

# INDEX

he does not see the reduction of uncertainty as central to the influence process. His answer would seem to be that it is people who agree, who display certainty, confidence and commitment; it is people who are consistent. He points out that the idea that it is people with information who reduce uncertainty is circular. Informational dependence is a symptom rather than a cause of influence (Moscovici and Faucheux, 1972). Dependence on others for information reflects the fact that one has already been influenced to accept the social values underlying their position. An expert, for example, is defined by one's acceptance of the norms, values and rules embodied in the field they represent. One is not influenced by experts because they present valid information. One accepts their information as valid because they are defined as experts by social institutions whose values one has internalized.

In sum, the certain individual is not asocial, uncertainty is a product of conflictual social relationships, and what counts as information is defined by social norms and values. Uncertainty is not an asocial, cognitive property of the individual that exists prior to influence and as its basis; rather, the need for information is a product of influence.

*Power versus influence*

The dependence theory confuses power and influence: it makes power the basis of influence – those who are dependent conform to those who have power – and transforms influence into a unilateral process of submission to social pressure. In reality, power and influence are alternatives. One resorts to coercion when one cannot influence; and, if one can influence, one does not need power (Moscovici, 1976). It is questionable how far influence can be explained by power.

In the Asch paradigm, for example, is it really submission to social pressure? If so, why the cognitive conflict, why the uncertainty? The data actually show that what matters for conformity is the unanimity of the majority, its internal consistency, and not its power in the sense of the resources at its disposal, its capacity to reward or punish. A non-unanimous majority of 15 or 16 facing 2 naive subjects (a subject aided by one supporter) exerts less overt influence than a unanimous majority of 3 facing 1 subject. The former majority plainly has more power. The presence of just one other dissenter virtually eliminates conformity even where the supporter is also incorrect – so this is not a counter-conformity effect.

Likewise, if responses in the Asch paradigm are anonymous, conformity drops, but not by much – from 33 per cent of responses to about 5–10 per cent less (see Chapter 2). In Deutsch and Gerard's (1955) study, for example, removing surveillance by others in the context of an unambiguous stimulus eliminated the two sources of social dependence, but most of the usual conformity remained. Deutsch and Gerard suggest that subjects did not feel completely anonymous; the alternative view is that the observed influence only minimally reflects a power process.

In fact, Moscovici suggests, this is influence, not power. It does not reflect social dependence. The power of a unanimous majority to influence, supposedly based on dependence, is not 'power' at all; it is the influence of a consistent group, whose members are *in societal terms* a minority, a deviant subgroup. What is this power to influence based on, if not dependence? Moscovici's general answer is that we should think of influence as more in the nature of a collective negotiation between people to define a coherent and stable reality than an exchange of information. People are in a sense bargaining with each other and their 'rhetoric', the style of their behaviour, its consistency, autonomy, flexibility, fairness, etc., plays a major role in persuading others to adopt new positions. New positions are not adopted in some absolute sense as acts of powerless submission but as negotiating moves in a process of social co-ordination.

### Social conflict and the genetic model of influence

It is not the reduction of cognitive uncertainty but social conflict that is at the heart of the influence process. Influence in its three modalities of innovation, conformity and normalization reflects the production, resolution and avoidance of conflict. Influence is fundamentally about creating, coping with and negotiating social conflicts. Moscovici assumes that people do not like conflict and disagreement with others; it makes them uncertain and anxious. It is aversive and we seek to avoid it by normalizing and conforming, i.e. by reaching agreements through influence.

Herein lies the power of the minority. The minority can create conflict, refuse to compromise, create doubt and uncertainty, and produce a situation in which the only solution is for the majority

Persuasive arguments theory has separated informational influence from social comparison and social reality testing, and has defined informational validity in terms of message content and information processing. Conformity theory has addressed the idea that the ingroup norm, the consensual position, may not be the mean but rather the prototypical position of the group, defined by intergroup differences as well as intragroup similarities and existing prior to social interaction as a cognitive, social categorical property of the group.

## Suggestions for further reading

Burnstein, E. and Vinokur, A. (1977). Persuasive argumentation and social comparison as determinants of attitude polarization. *Journal of Experimental Social Psychology*, 13, 315–32. A cogent summary of the evidence for persuasive arguments theory.

Moscovici, S. and Zavalloni, M. (1969). The group as a polarizer of attitudes. *Journal of Personality and Social Psychology*, 12, 125–35. The insightful, key paper that redefined the risky shift as group polarization and helped (with others) to change the field.

Myers, D. G. (1982). Polarizing effects of social interaction. In H. Brandstatter, J. H. Davis and G. Stocker-Kreichgauer (eds), *Group decision-making*, London: Academic Press. A very readable description of Myers' influential programme of research.

Sanders, G. S. and Baron, R. S. (1977). Is social comparison irrelevant for producing choice shifts? *Journal of Experimental Social Psychology*, 13, 303–314. Two major social comparison theorists reply persuasively to Burnstein and Vinokur (1977).

Turner, J. C., Hogg, M. A., Oakes, P. J., Reicher, S. D. and Wetherell, M. S. (1987). *Rediscovering the social group: A self-categorization theory*. Oxford: Basil Blackwell. Chapters 4 and 7 present the self-categorization theory of group polarization and discuss the literature from that perspective.

# 4 / MINORITY INFLUENCE

The dominant perspective on influence until the 1970s was the dependence theory (Chapter 2). It explained conformity in terms of the normative and informational dependence of the individual on the group. In the 1970s, Moscovici and his colleagues (Moscovici, 1976; Moscovici and Faucheux, 1972) launched a sharp attack on this theory, which they called the 'functionalist' model of influence, and proposed an alternative conception. This chapter will outline Moscovici's critique and the alternative tradition of theory and research on minority influence that his ideas have produced.

## The critique of influence research

### The 'conformity bias'

There were several aspects to Moscovici's rejection of the functionalist model. He argued that influence research was characterized by a 'conformity bias', an assumption that all influence led to conformity or the opposite of conformity, i.e. deviance. Theories only explained and allowed for conformity, he maintained. They implied that conformity was the only process of influence.

Underlying the conformity bias is the functionalist model. This model sees the aim of influence as social control, the maintenance of the status quo. The task of influence is to adapt the individual to the social system, which is accepted as a given. The need is for social stability and equilibrium, with people adapting to pre-established social roles and norms. Social conformity to a social structure, which exists prior to social interaction and is not to be questioned, is an adaptive requirement of social life. Society, therefore, needs con-